Van Dyck, Rembrandt, AND THE Portrait Print

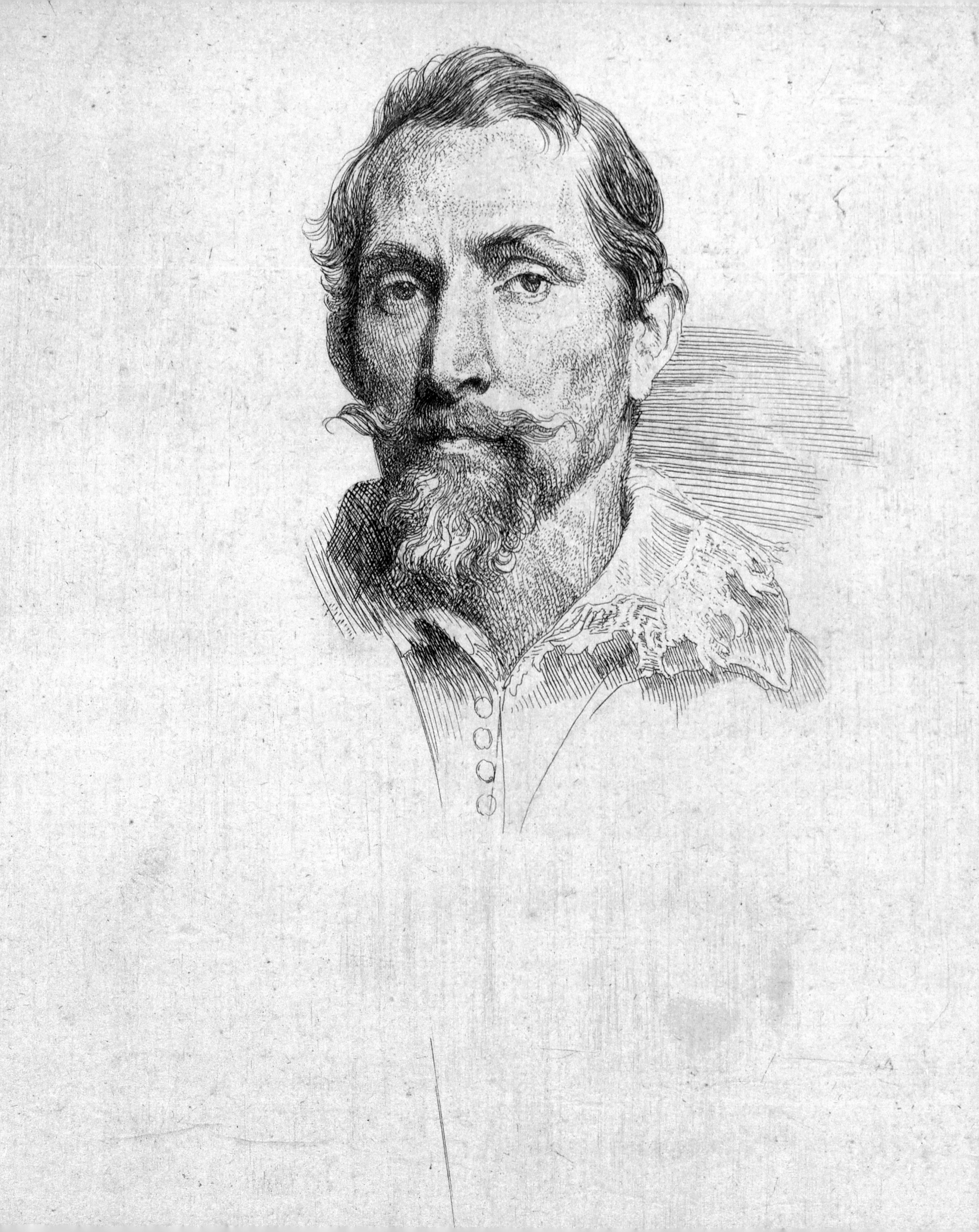

Van Dyck, Rembrandt, AND THE Portrait Print

Victoria Sancho Lobis

With an essay by Maureen Warren

THE ART INSTITUTE OF CHICAGO

DISTRIBUTED BY YALE UNIVERSITY PRESS, NEW HAVEN AND LONDON

Van Dyck, Rembrandt, and the Portrait Print was produced in conjunction with an exhibition of the same title organized by the Art Institute of Chicago, March 5–August 7, 2016.

© 2016 The Art Institute of Chicago

First edition
Printed in Canada
ISBN: 978-0-300-21882-4
Published by
The Art Institute of Chicago
111 South Michigan Avenue
Chicago, Illinois 60603-6404
www.artic.edu

Distributed by
Yale University Press
302 Temple Street
P.O. Box 209040
New Haven, Connecticut 06520-9040
www.yalebooks.com/art

Produced by
The Department of Publishing, the Art Institute of Chicago
Sarah E. Guernsey, Executive Director
Edited by Wilson McBee
Production by Joseph Mohan and Lauren Makholm
Photography research by Katie Levi
Unless otherwise noted, photography of works of art is by Chris Gallagher, Bob Hashimoto, and Robert Lifson, with postproduction by Jonathan Mathias and production coordination by P. D. Young, Department of Imaging, the Art Institute of Chicago.

Design and typesetting by Miko McGinty and Rita Jules, Miko McGinty Inc.

Separations by Professional Graphics, Rockford, Illinois
Printing and binding by Friesens Corporation, Altona, Manitoba, Canada

Library of Congress Cataloging-in-Publication Data

Names: Lobis, Victoria Sancho, 1976- author.
Title: Van Dyck, Rembrandt, and the portrait print / Victoria Sancho Lobis ; with an essay by Maureen Warren.
Description: First edition. | Chicago : Art Institute of Chicago, 2016.
Identifiers: LCCN 2015047946 | ISBN 9780300218824 (hardback)
Subjects: LCSH: Van Dyck, Anthony, 1599-1641—Criticism and interpretation. | Van Dyck, Anthony, 1599-1641—Influence. | Portrait prints. | BISAC: ART / Prints. | ART / Subjects & Themes / Portraits. | ART / History / Baroque & Rococo. | ART / Collections, Catalogs, Exhibitions / Group Shows.
Classification: LCC NE674.D95 L63 2016 | DDC 759.9493—dc23
LC record available at http://lccn.loc.gov/2015047946

Details:
Page 2: Anthony van Dyck. *Frans Snyders*, 1630/33. Cat. 53.
Page 8: Anthony van Dyck. *Joos de Momper*, 1630/33. Cat. 48.
Page 10: Anthony van Dyck. *Justus Sustermans*, 1630/33. Cat. 54.
Page 14: Hendrick Goltzius. *Philips Galle (1537–1612), Pupil of Coornhert from Haarlem, Engraver and Publisher in Antwerp from 1570; The Baptism of the Eunuch in Background Left*, 1582. Cat. 12.
Page 34: Rembrandt van Rijn. *Jan Lutma, Goldsmith*, 1656. Cat. 78.
Page 72: Johann Michael Püchler. *Joseph I (August), Holy Roman Emperor*, c. 1705. Cat. 113.
Page 86: Aegidius Sadeler. *Portrait of Bartolomeus Spranger with an Allegory of the Death of His Wife, Christina Müller*, 1600. Cat. 21.

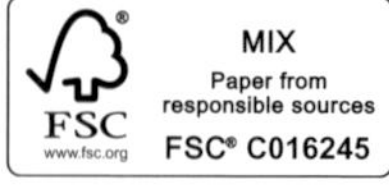

Contents

The exhibition catalogue for
Van Dyck, Rembrandt, and the Portrait Print
has been generously underwritten by
Alan Templeton and Prince Charitable Trusts.

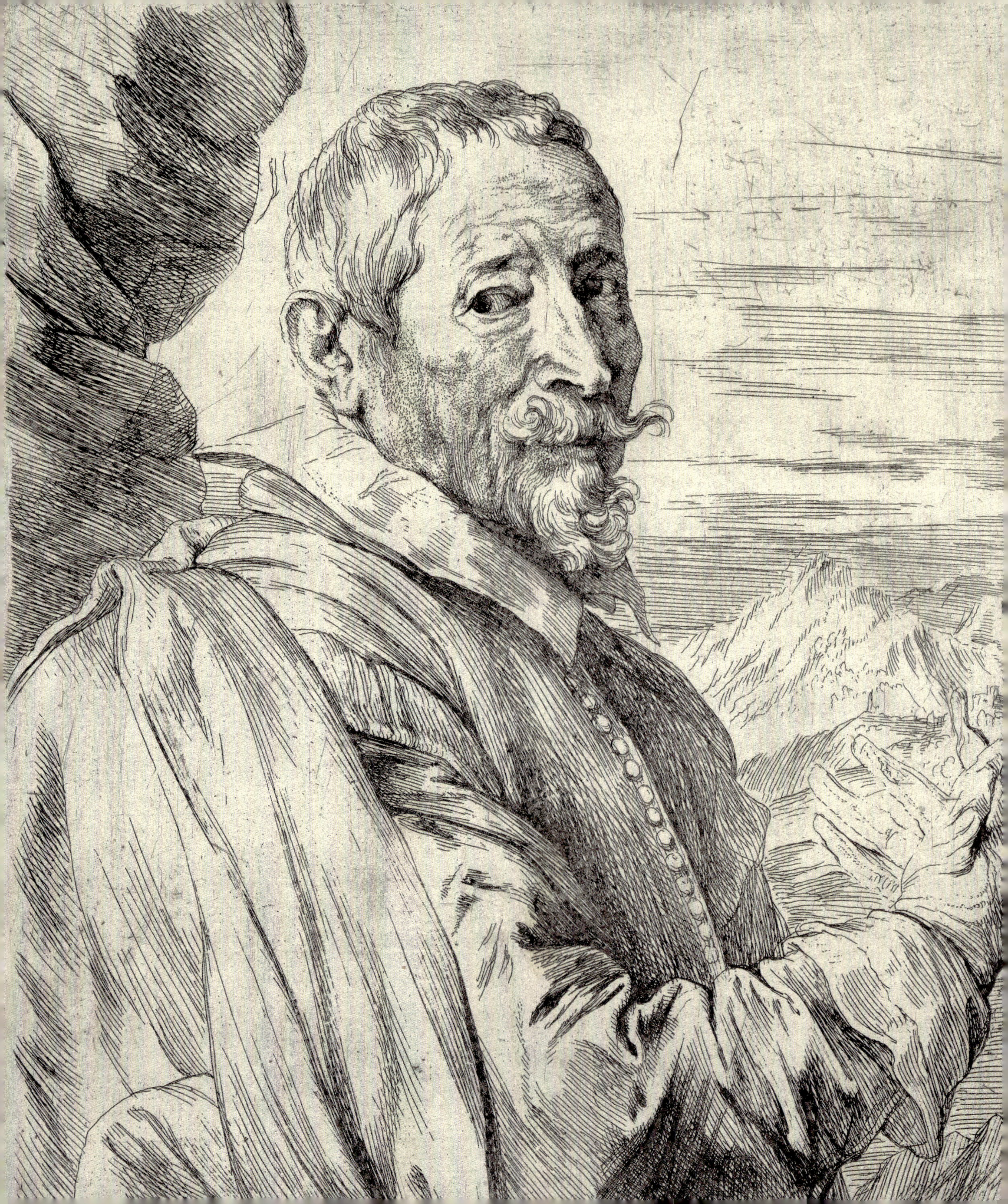

Foreword

In May of 1913, only months before he died, Art Institute of Chicago trustee Clarence Buckingham purchased an etching by Anthony van Dyck; this was the first state of the portrait of the seventeenth-century Flemish landscape painter Joos de Momper (see opposite page). As the invoice from dealer Albert Roullier indicates, the print came with the distinction of previous ownership by Henry Studdy Theobald, an English barrister who shared Buckingham's passion for the prints of Albrecht Dürer, Rembrandt van Rijn, and James McNeill Whistler, among others. A handwritten inventory of Buckingham's holdings (most likely at the time of Buckingham's death) includes three other portrait etchings by Van Dyck. After his death, Buckingham's sisters, Lucy Maud and Kate, became the custodians of his impressive collection, which they left on deposit at the Art Institute. Both sisters continued to acquire prints that they felt reflected their brother's refined taste and high standards of beauty. Lucy Maud died in 1920, and it was through Kate's efforts that by 1929 all twenty-one of the etchings that Van Dyck made himself were added to the group. After she died in 1937, the Clarence Buckingham Collection found a permanent home at the museum, together with a fund that has allowed successive generations of curators to continue developing the legacy of this visionary family of collectors and philanthropists.

In the May 1929 issue of the *Bulletin of the Art Institute of Chicago*—the museum's first celebration of Van Dyck's portrait etchings—a contributor remarked, "The imposing assembly of faces pleases the eye with the beauty of their drawing, and the mind with the subtlety and strength of their characterization." Now, more than eighty-five years later, we are delighted to explore these provocative works from a new perspective in *Van Dyck, Rembrandt, and the Portrait Print*. Van Dyck's etchings, which are no less pleasing today, spurred us to reassess our permanent collection through the lens of the portrait print—a genre that he revolutionized, as is so palpably felt in the examples created by his immediate successor, Rembrandt, as well as many other artists of the following

centuries. This project also presented the opportunity to publish works in our collection that had yet to receive the sustained attention they deserve.

Support for this catalogue has come from the Prince Charitable Trusts, whose collaboration with the Art Institute has long supported not only exhibitions and their interpretive components, but also two endowed positions: the Eleanor Wood Prince Curatorship, currently held by Martha Wolff in the Department of European Painting and Sculpture, and the Prince Trust Curatorship, occupied by Victoria Sancho Lobis in the Department of Prints and Drawings. Both are specialists in Dutch and Flemish art, and it is a great pleasure to underscore the museum's commitment to this field through this project and our ongoing relationship with the Prince Charitable Trusts. Special thanks are due to Benna Wilde for guiding this important partnership and to Patrick Wood-Prince for his continuing commitment and service to the Art Institute.

Additional funding for this publication has come from another valued member of the museum's community. Alan Templeton of Oakland, California, has been an enthusiastic visitor to the Art Institute for many years. His dedication to works on paper and his interest in portraiture have enriched this undertaking, and we are profoundly grateful for his generous support. Additionally, the Allan McNab Endowed Fund has provided sponsorship for a scholarly colloquium related to the exhibition.

Finally, I want to acknowledge the work of Victoria Sancho Lobis, exhibition curator and lead author of this catalogue, who has brought new energy to researching, interpreting, and developing the Art Institute's holdings in the field of Dutch and Flemish works on paper. While *Van Dyck, Rembrandt, and the Portrait Print* reminds us of the riches of our collection, it also points the way to further growth.

Douglas Druick
President and Eloise W. Martin Director
The Art Institute of Chicago

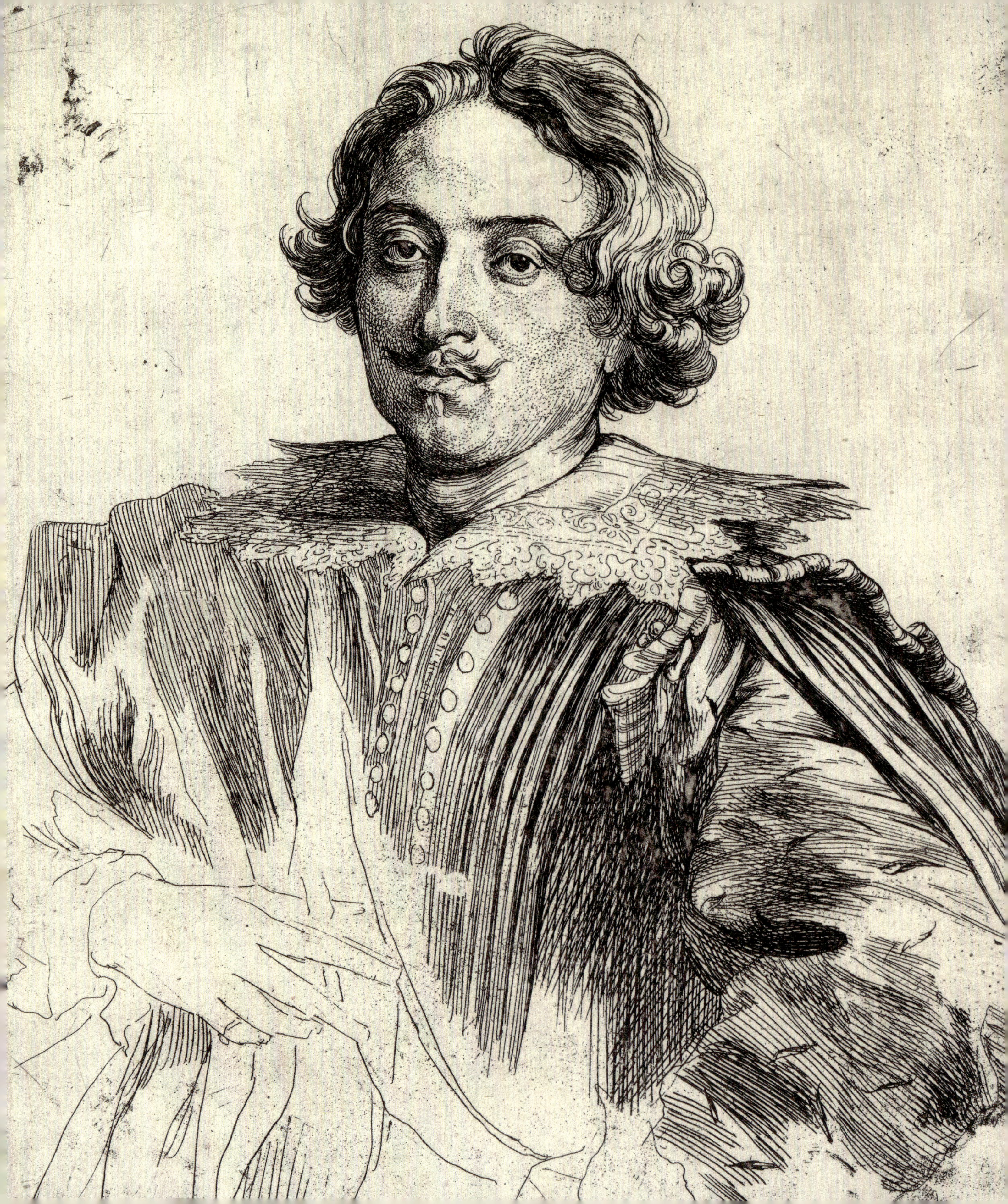

Acknowledgments

In 1915 Arthur Mayger Hind, Keeper of Prints and Drawings at the British Museum, published *Van Dyck: His Original Etchings and His Iconography*, still one of the most insightful assessments of Anthony van Dyck's work as a printmaker. In discussing the portrait etchings the artist made himself, Hind offered the following:

> Apart from [his] temptation to flattery, Van Dyck's etchings are faultless both as portraits or prints, and full of compelling inspiration. They are as modern in their style today as they were at the time of their production, and have remained the standard and commanded the emulation of all that is greatest among recent portrait etching.

As Hind so rightly summarized, Van Dyck managed to create portrait etchings that were at once modern and timeless, faultless and yet unfinished. The absence of documentary evidence to indicate his intentions and desires for what became such an expansive series only adds to its intriguing nature. I have long been drawn to these works not only for their beauty and mystery, but also for how, in their depiction of so many of Van Dyck's fellow artists, they represent a moving expression of friendship and a significant contribution to art history. When I came to the Art Institute in 2013, I was delighted to discover that the museum owned all the etchings that Van Dyck produced himself. Although we would like to represent this brilliant artist more thoroughly by adding drawings and paintings to our collection, this exhibition gives us a chance to celebrate what we do have from his hand and to examine the particular way in which these works contribute to our understanding of the portrait prints by other artists in our collection such as Albrecht Dürer, Hendrick Goltzius, Aegidius Sadeler, Willem Jacobsz. Delff, Rembrandt van Rijn, and Antoine Masson, among many others.

For the opportunity to explore Van Dyck's place in our permanent collection, I wish to thank Douglas Druick, President and Eloise W. Martin Director, who has not only embraced this project but also provided leadership for a renewed commitment to Dutch and Flemish art at the Art Institute. I am grateful for his mentorship, and I continue to be inspired by the high standards he holds, and indeed embodies, for all elements of curatorial work.

Benna Wilde, Program Director, Arts and Culture, at the Prince Charitable Trusts, encouraged me in the earliest days of conceiving this project, and I am deeply thankful for the funding provided by the Prince Charitable Trusts in support of this publication. Alan Templeton has also generously supported this catalogue; his interest in our collection, and in portraiture specifically, has provided much-appreciated encouragement and generated many thought-provoking conversations.

While interpretation of the museum's permanent collection is the guiding mission of this exhibition, the presentation of Art Institute works has been enhanced by a small group of loans from private collections. English prints from the collection of Nicholas Stogdon not only give a context for Van Dyck's etchings, but also add remarkable visual and historical interest. In addition to his generosity in lending these works, his knowledge of the history of print collecting has informed the exhibition as a whole. Shelley Reed kindly shared her series of drawings after Van Dyck, which rekindled my curiosity about Van Dyck's etchings when I saw them on view at the Museum of Fine Arts, Boston, many years ago. Meg and Mark Hausberg lent a curious Netherlandish satirical print, and another local collector generously lent a key portrait of Johan van Oldenbarnevelt. I am also indebted to my colleagues within the museum who have graciously shared the works of art in their care and made them accessible for public presentation: Christine Fabian, Gloria Groom, Jane Neet, Devon Lee Pyle-Vowles, and Martha Wolff, as well as former colleague Sylvain Bellenger.

When I was interviewing esteemed art historians a few years ago, Antony Griffiths, former Keeper of Prints and Drawings at the British Museum, mentioned the portrait print as a topic within the history of printmaking that he thought deserved more attention. Although I don't think that he had Van Dyck and Rembrandt in mind, I thank him for this prompt to think about portrait prints as an artistic genre. In my attempt to understand this category of portraiture, I studied the Art Institute's holdings and decided to include in the exhibition—and in the pages of this catalogue—an idiosyncratic survey of the genre from the sixteenth to the twentieth centuries. Adrian Eeles generously offered his opinions on my selections and guided me to expand the range of my choices; I am grateful for this advice and for sharing his passion for and deep knowledge of print connoisseurship. In my study of the Art Institute's impressions of Van Dyck's etchings, I consulted other collections in the United States and Europe. I wish to thank the staff of the following institutions for allowing me access to their collections: the British Museum, London; Victoria and Albert Museum, London; Rijksmuseum, Amsterdam; Philadelphia Museum of Art; and the Achenbach Foundation for Graphic Arts, Fine Arts Museums of San Francisco.

A number of friends and colleagues have generously shared their ideas and opinions over the course of this exhibition's development: Leo Ackerman, Jordan Bear, Esther Bell, James Bergquist, Rhea Sylvia Blok, Eddie Campbell, Joseph Clarke, Stephanie Dickey, Jesús Escobar, Lori Anne Ferrell, Rachel Freeman, Peter Fuhring, Jim Ganz, Charles Hack, Meg Hausberg, Karen and Robert Hoehn, John Ittmann, Ursula and Stanley Johnson, Jessica Keating, Deborah Krieger, Armin Kunz, Lowell Libson, Anne-Marie Logan, Louis Marchesano, Christopher Mendez, Diane Miliotes, Edward Minieka, Christopher Monkhouse, Clement Moore, Audrey Niffenegger, Mark Pascale, Tim Schmelcher, Joseph Semkiu, Eve Straussman-Pflanzer, Claudia Swan, Susan Tallman, Martha Tedeschi, Thomas Williams, Jessica Wolfe, and Steven Zick.

For their work in conceiving and realizing this catalogue, I thank my colleagues in the Art Institute's Department of Publishing, including Sarah Guernsey, Executive Director, Joseph Mohan, Associate Director of Production, and Lauren Makholm, Production Coordinator. Photography Editor Katie Levi handled photography rights and permissions. I want to extend special thanks to Assistant Editor Wilson McBee, who has ably, graciously, and patiently edited this publication. It has been a pleasure to work closely with him, not least because of his wise judgment and generous spirit of camaraderie. Gregory Nosan, Editorial Director, also made valuable improvements to the text. Acknowledgment is also due to Miko McGinty and Rita Jules of Miko McGinty Inc., who created the book's elegant design. Many new photographs were made for this project, and I thank the members of the Department of Imaging for their work as well.

One of the most important facets of this project was the occasion it created for the conservation and study of long-neglected works in the Art Institute's permanent collection. Antoinette Owen, Senior Conservator of Prints and Drawings, directed the paper conservation analysis and treatments. Many other members of our paper conservation lab became involved in the undertaking, and it has been a profound joy to work with so many of the talented and skilled members of our team, including Mary Broadway, Kristi Dahm, and Kimberly Nichols, as well as former colleague Liz Sorokin. Conservation of works in the department of European Painting and Sculpture was carried out by Suzanne Schnepp, whose guidance in the installation of the three-dimensional objects is also greatly appreciated.

Also in the Department of Prints and Drawings, Christine Conniff-O'Shea contributed her keen eye and sensitive approach to the presentation of works on paper. Collaborating with her to select the framing and matting of prints and drawings for exhibition is one of the great pleasures and privileges of my job. Collection and Exhibition Manager Emily Vokt Ziemba has seen this exhibition through from its beginnings and has provided important contributions to the publication, especially the checklist. The design of the exhibition has been realized by Junia Jorgji under the supervision of Sara Urizar; the installation has also benefited from the work of Cassie Tompkins in the Department of Graphic Design and Andrew Talley, the museum's gifted mount maker. Fawn Ring in the Department of Museum Education showed great creativity in developing public programs related to the exhibition.

Maureen Warren, former Andrew W. Mellon Curatorial Research Fellow at the Art Institute and current Curator of European and American Art at the Krannert Art Museum, the

University of Illinois at Urbana-Champaign, not only contributed an essay to this catalogue, but also executed preliminary research for many of the objects and wrote a number of the interpretative gallery texts. Over the course of the year that Maureen worked in the Department of Prints and Drawings, she played a vital role on our staff—cataloguing swaths of our permanent collection, preparing rotations for installation, researching objects for acquisition consideration, and generally providing good cheer. I consider myself lucky to have worked so closely with her, and I am delighted that this publication records our very happy collaboration. Kylie Escudero, undergraduate intern in Prints and Drawings, also contributed significant research related to watermarks and provenance. I want to thank her—and the other members of the summer 2015 intern cohort—for engaging with the topic of this exhibition so critically and enthusiastically. Department volunteer Frances Blair contributed additional provenance research.

A fellow traveler in the seventeenth century, Seth Lobis provided unwavering support for this project. I am grateful for his advice related to scientific and literary culture in the time of Van Dyck and for his thoughtful review of the manuscript. In addition to being the ideal reader, he is a most cherished companion and friend. For sacrifices great and small in aid of this work, I acknowledge him and other members of my family, most notably Claudia Lobis and Marta Zamora.

Finally, I wish to dedicate this publication to Suzanne Folds McCullagh, Anne Vogt Fuller and Marion Titus Searle Chair and Curator, Department of Prints and Drawings, who has encouraged me at every phase of this project. The opening of this exhibition coincides with Suzanne's final months at our museum. This modest publication can be only a small tribute to the profound impact she has had on our collection, on this institution, and on so many students and enthusiasts of works on paper. It has been a tremendous pleasure and an honor to work with her here, and I anticipate further collaborations in the years ahead. I expect that her well-deserved retirement will not keep her too far from our galleries, and I will continue to hold her image in mind as the model of elegant and wholehearted commitment to the field that we both love.

Victoria Sancho Lobis
Prince Trust Associate Curator
Department of Prints and Drawings

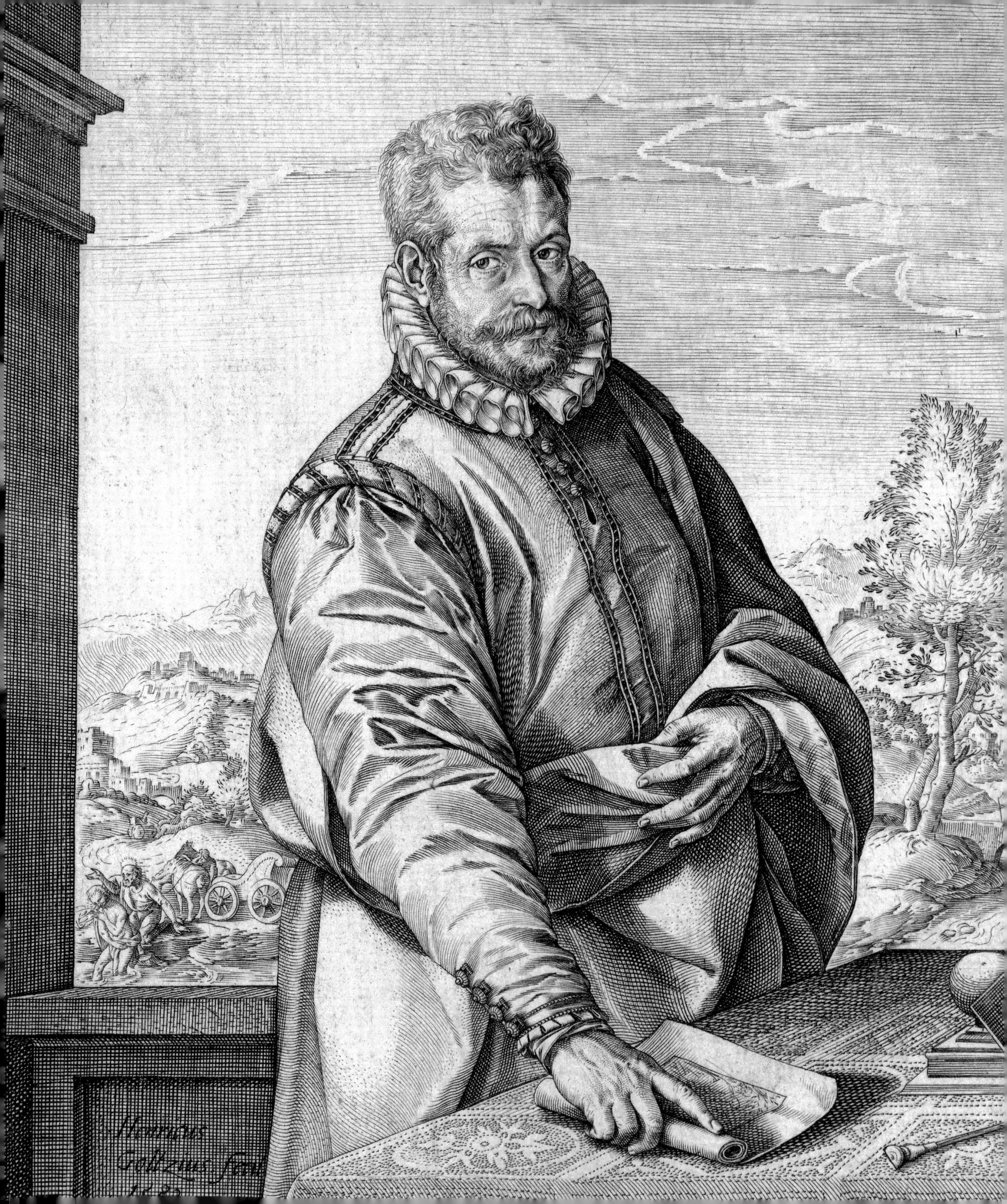

Introduction

THE RHETORIC OF THE PORTRAIT PRINT

Victoria Sancho Lobis

In 1810, when the budding writer, composer, and historian Alexandrine-Sophie de Bawr saw the trompe l'oeil portrait that Louis-Léopold Boilly created of her (fig. 1), what must she have thought? Boilly conceived the small-format, grayscale canvas in the form of a portrait print, going so far as to include the representation of a plate mark to identify it as an intaglio print with untrimmed margins. In choosing to depict a print, Boilly demonstrated his ability to paint illusionistically while also flattering his subject by suggesting that she was of interest to a broad audience. Not coincidentally, the new technique of lithography had been invented only a few years before, a development that prompted new questions about the role of painting in respect to other forms of representation.[1]

While a painting may be an object of greater luxury and may offer a more imposing physical presence, the reproducible nature of a portrait print implies that its subject has mass appeal. Bawr began her career around the time of Boilly's painting, but it was only later in life that she was sufficiently well known to warrant the creation of an actual portrait print.[2] Considered today, Boilly's canvas presents several interpretative questions: What are the material differences between a painting and a portrait print? How do these modes of portrai-ture convey meaning differently? In what ways do they serve the artists and their subjects distinctly? And perhaps most pressing for the subject at hand, how do we understand the special place that portrait prints occupy both in the history of art and in contemporary practice?

More than a century before Boilly's painting, the favorite mistress of King Charles II of England, Nell Gwyn, was featured in a mezzotint by Herman Hendrik Quiter (fig. 2); in both prints she is shown seated in the guise of a shepherdess. Gwyn's celebrity is demonstrated by numerous painted portraits and, perhaps more tellingly, several portrait prints.[3] The impression in the Art Institute's collection uses blue paper, a choice that makes both the print and its subject seem more exciting to the touch as well as to the eye.

More conventionally, portrait prints were used to depict internationally recognized figures such as monarchs, diplomats, and scholars. In Europe the genre can be traced to the late fifteenth century, with the notable example of Israhel van Meckenem's self-portrait, which is believed to be not only the oldest surviving self-portrait executed as a print, but also the first signed self-portrait in any medium.[4] Artists of the following decades continued to make portrait prints—of

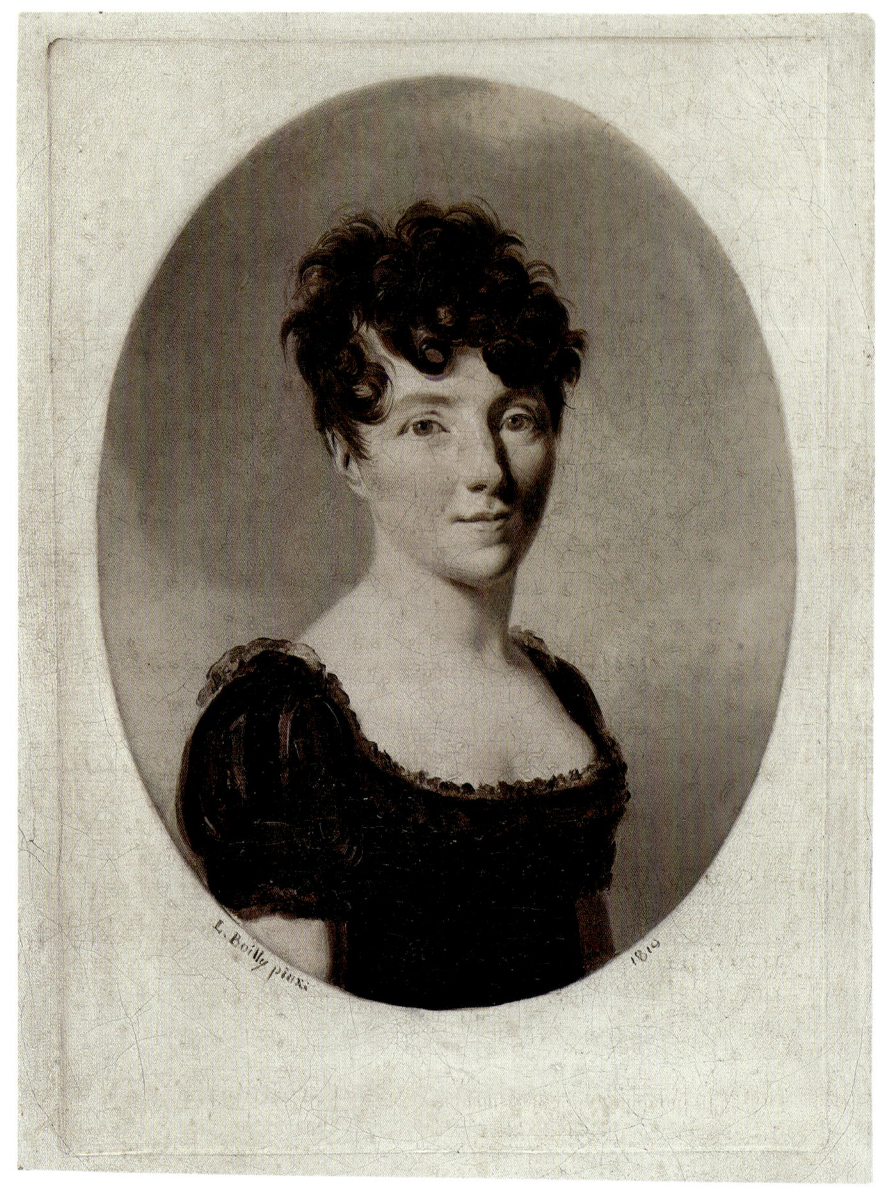

Fig. 1. Louis-Léopold Boilly (French, 1761–1845). *Alexandrine-Sophie de Bawr*, 1810.
Oil on canvas; 22 × 16 cm (8¹¹⁄₁₆ × 6⁵⁄₁₆ in.). Harvard Art Museums/
Fogg Museum, Bequest of Grenville L. Winthrop, by exchange, 2011.454.

themselves on occasion but more frequently of their patrons
and other illustrious individuals. Exceedingly proficient in the
art of printmaking, Albrecht Dürer created a number of significant examples, including those of humanists Philip Melanchthon (cat. 1), Erasmus of Rotterdam (fig. 3), and his close friend
Willibald Pirckheimer. The reputations of these men developed
from the circulation of their ideas about philosophy and theol-
ogy; their physical appearance was utterly secondary. While
Dürer described Melanchthon in specific terms, adapting the
popular Renaissance convention of the profile portrait, his
depiction of Erasmus devotes much less of its surface area to
the likeness itself. As others have observed, this work is among

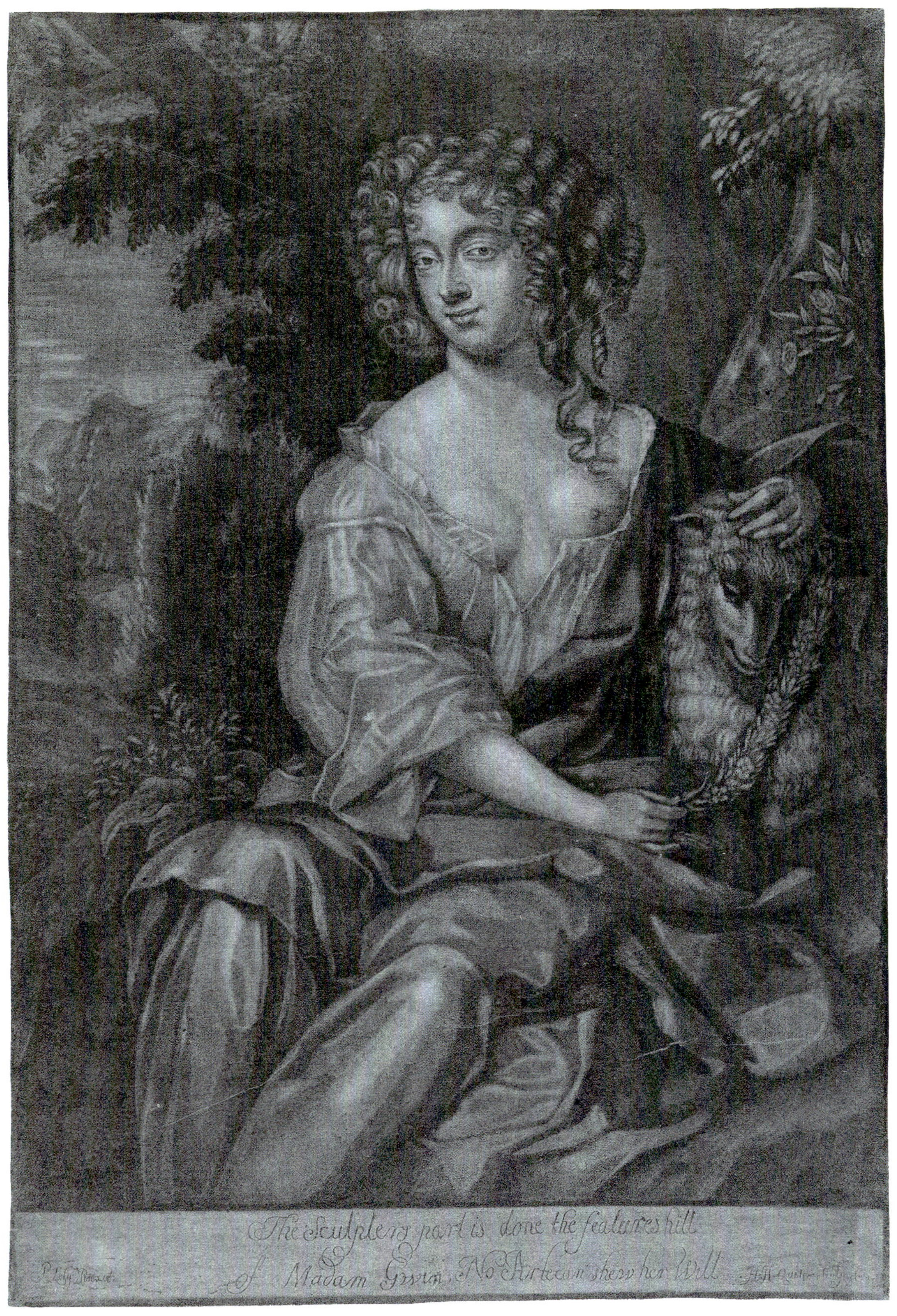

Fig. 2. Herman Hendrik Quiter. After Peter Lely. *Portrait of Nell Gwyn as a Shepherdess Garlanding a Lamb*, c. 1678. Cat. 105.

Dürer's largest engravings, larger even than the famous *Knight, Death, and Devil* and *Melancholia I*.[5] Intriguingly, the artist chose to dedicate an usual amount of space to text, setting it not on a plaque at the base of the composition but rather in the upper central passage. Indeed, between the text (the largest letters of which form Dürer's monogram), the central placement of the hands in the act of writing, and the arrangement of books at the lower edge, the portrait can be said to exalt the acts of writing, reading, and seeing printed content even more than it celebrates the legacy of its subject.[6] Similarly, Jacques de Gheyn's portrait of Carolus Clusius (cat. 19), Van Dyck's portrait of Antoon Triest (cat. 80), and Rembrandt van Rijn's portrait of Ephraim Bonus (cat. 74) share the promotion of the intellectual status of their subjects as their motivating premise.

Like the abundant sculpted images of emperors in ancient Rome, printed portraits helped not only to reinforce the legitimacy of political leaders but to inspire loyalty as well.[7] By circulating images of themselves, rulers extended their presence and thereby their authority. This notion is manifest in Crispijn de Passe the Elder's depiction of Elizabeth I (fig. 4) as well as in the portrait prints of Philip II of Spain (cat. 11), Holy Roman Emperor Matthias (cat. 24), and Charles I (cats. 30 and 92). De Passe's portrait canonizes a celebrated likeness of the recently deceased queen, depicting her many decades younger than she was at the time of her death. Prominently displayed are the monarch's orb and scepter, coat of arms, and sword of justice, which rests over the Bible, emphasizing her role as a divinely inspired ruler.[8] The work capitalizes on one of the advantages of portrait prints, the easy integration of text, which in this case identifies the subject, elaborates on her biography with a laudatory poem, and provides the date of the work.[9]

Since the time of Erasmus, friends often exchanged portraits—in printed as well as other media—to express their mutual regard. This was especially common among men of learning, as evidenced by a group of related portrait prints made at the turn of the seventeenth century by Netherlandish artists to celebrate their artistic peers.[10] One print from this group is Hendrick Goltzius's portrait of publisher Philips Galle (fig. 5). Shown standing gallantly before a deeply receding landscape, Galle holds a half-unrolled print. Close by on the carpet-covered table, a burin and other printmaking tools help clarify his professional identity. Latin verses composed by the humanist poet Janus Dousa the Elder occupy nearly a third of the plate and testify to the friendship between subject and artist: "Reader, if you have ever seen Galle before you will have no need whatsoever of my assurance, or that of another, to know that the features you see engraved in copper are a likeness of Galle. Oh skillful burin, oh nimble hand, hand of Goltzius blessed with Galle; face of Galle blessed with Goltzius."[11] As in Dürer's portrait of Erasmus, in which the text affirms the successes of both artist and subject, Dousa's poem reminds the viewer that the likeness is the product of Goltzius's skill.

Van Dyck, Rembrandt, and the Portrait Print considers these functions of the genre during what was arguably its high point, the seventeenth century. By examining Anthony van Dyck's contribution to this tradition before continuing forward to Rembrandt's printed portraits and those of artists from successive centuries, we hope to highlight the range of artistic expression that has been applied to the portrait print's dynamic means of asserting identity in political, intellectual, and cultural spheres.[12]

In the time of Van Dyck, portraits were commonly produced as paintings—Van Dyck's most important means of advancement—but also as prints, drawings, wax reliefs, painted miniatures, cast medallions, and busts and other types of sculptures. In painting, an artist could employ a full range of color and adjust the application of paint to create the illusion of varied textures, distinguishing skin from hair, fur from armor. The Art Institute's compelling yet unattributed *Portrait of a Man* (fig. 6) offers an example of how such choices can best be put to advantage. The dense application of white paint in the passage describing the lace collar sets off the sitter's face, whose tense expression and arresting gaze are further emphasized by the restrained background setting and simple treatment of the black costume.[13]

Though drawings often served as preparatory works for portraits in other media, two oval-format examples by Jan de Bray of an older couple (figs. 7a and b) demonstrate that drawings could function independently as well.[14] Here De Bray realized the facial features and clothing of his sitters through the controlled use of black and red chalks, resulting

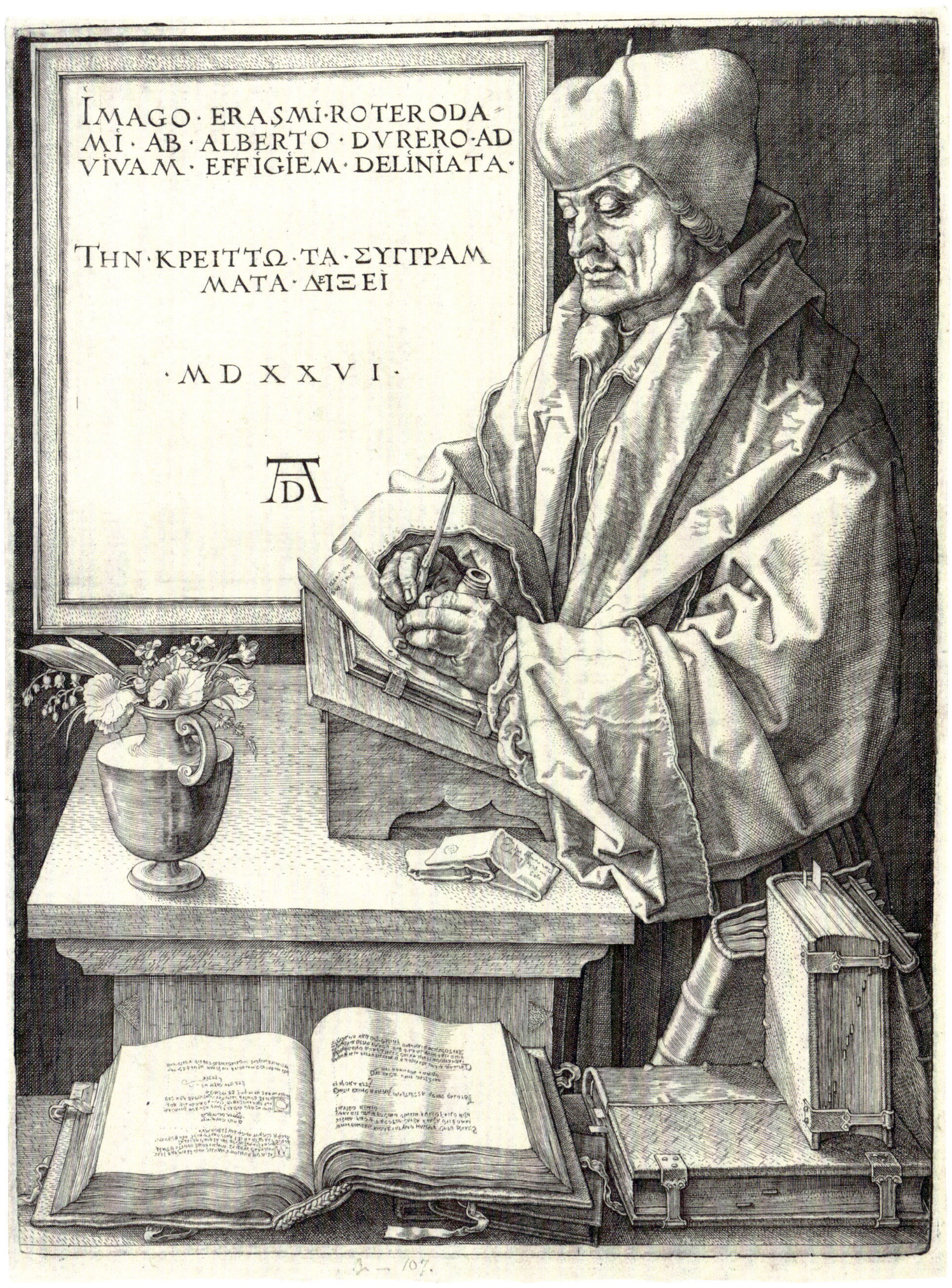

Fig. 3. Albrecht Dürer. *Erasmus of Rotterdam*, 1526. Cat. 2.

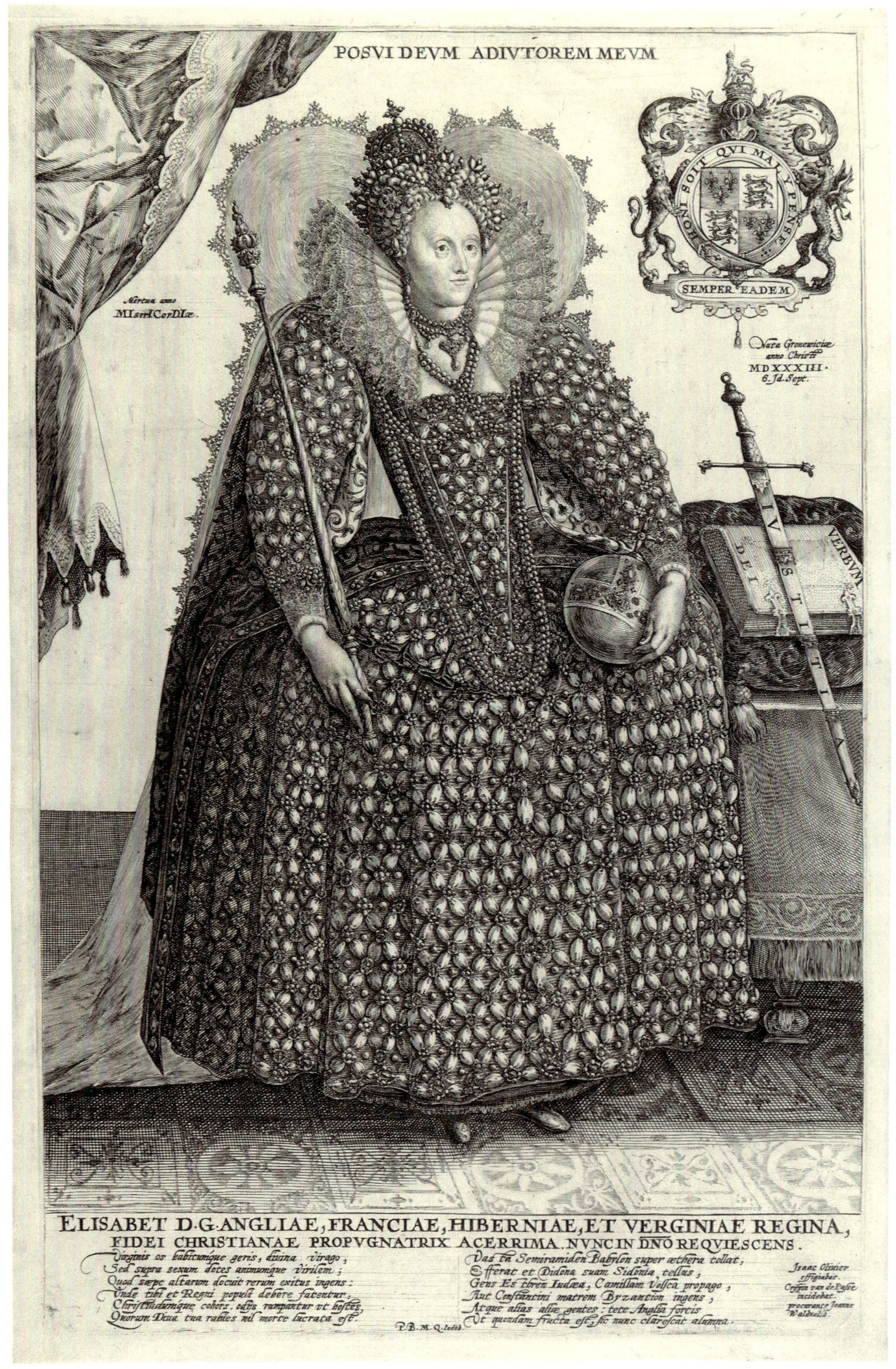

Fig. 4. Crispijn de Passe the Elder. After Isaac Oliver. *Queen Elizabeth I*, 1603/04. Collection of Nicholas Stogdon. Cat. 17.

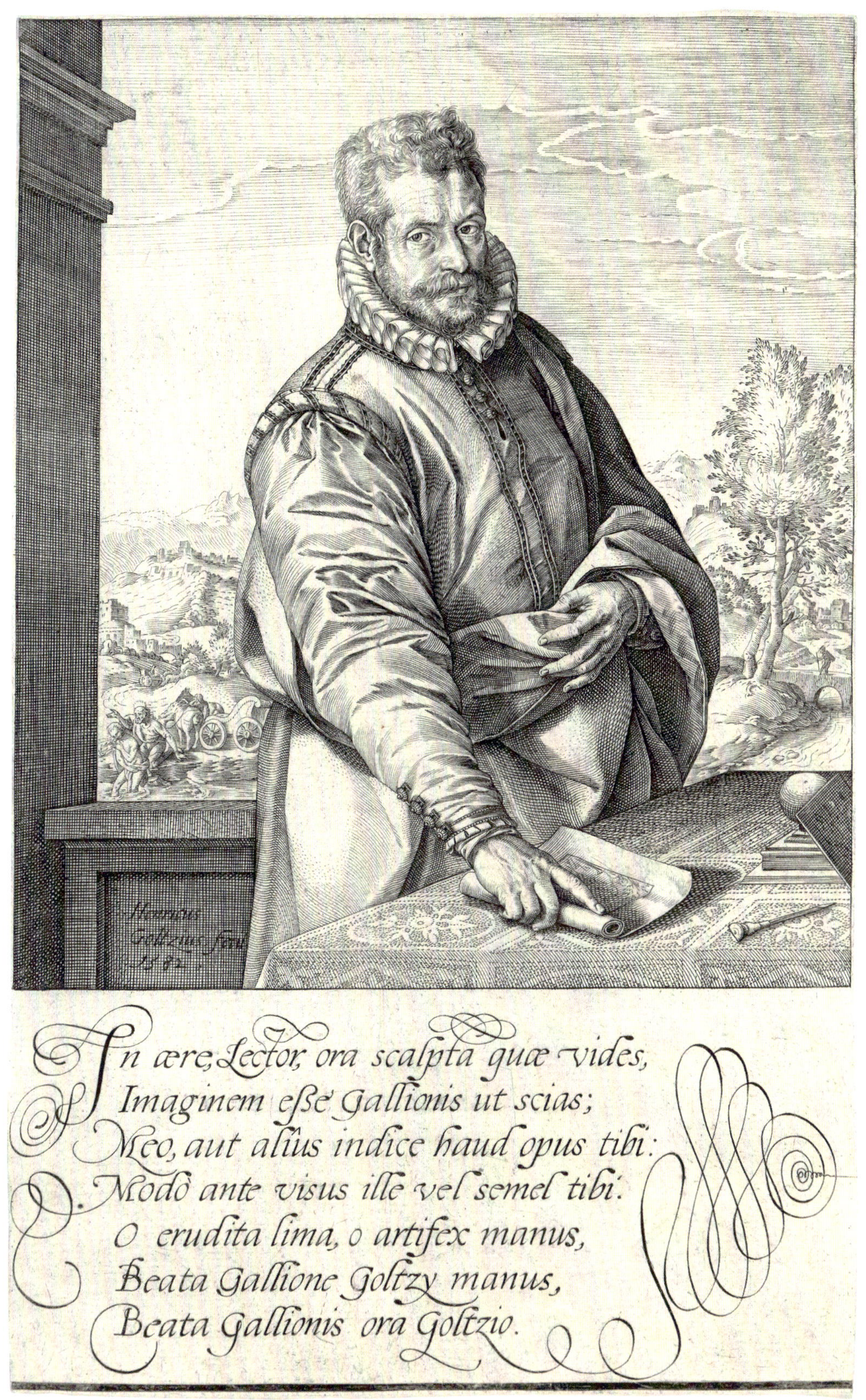

Fig. 5. Hendrick Goltzius. *Philips Galle (1537–1612), Pupil of Coornhert from Haarlem, Engraver and Publisher in Antwerp from 1570; The Baptism of the Eunuch in Background Left*, 1582. Cat. 12. Shown at actual size.

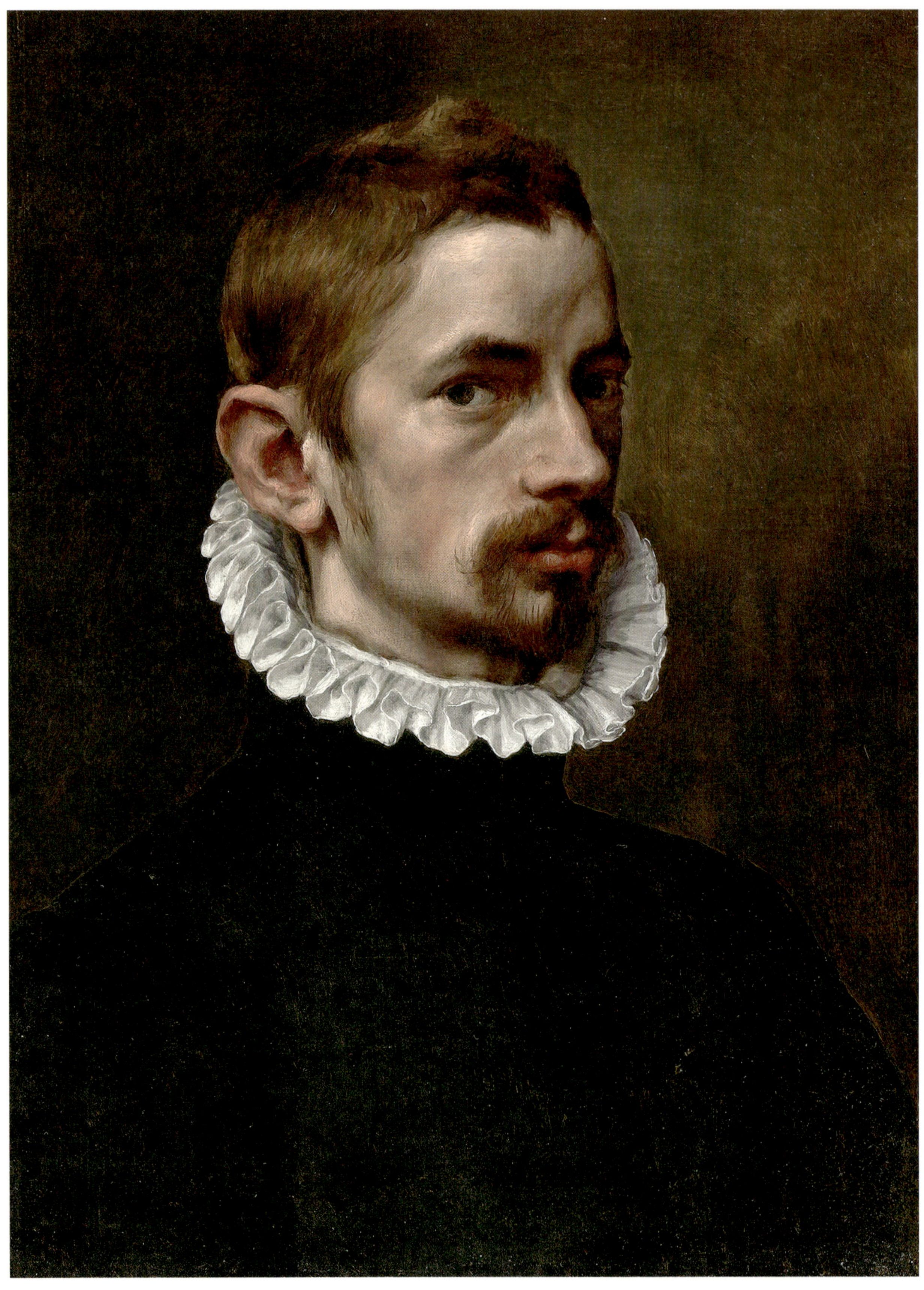

Fig. 6. Unidentified Flemish artist. *Portrait of a Man*, c. 1575. Cat. 8.

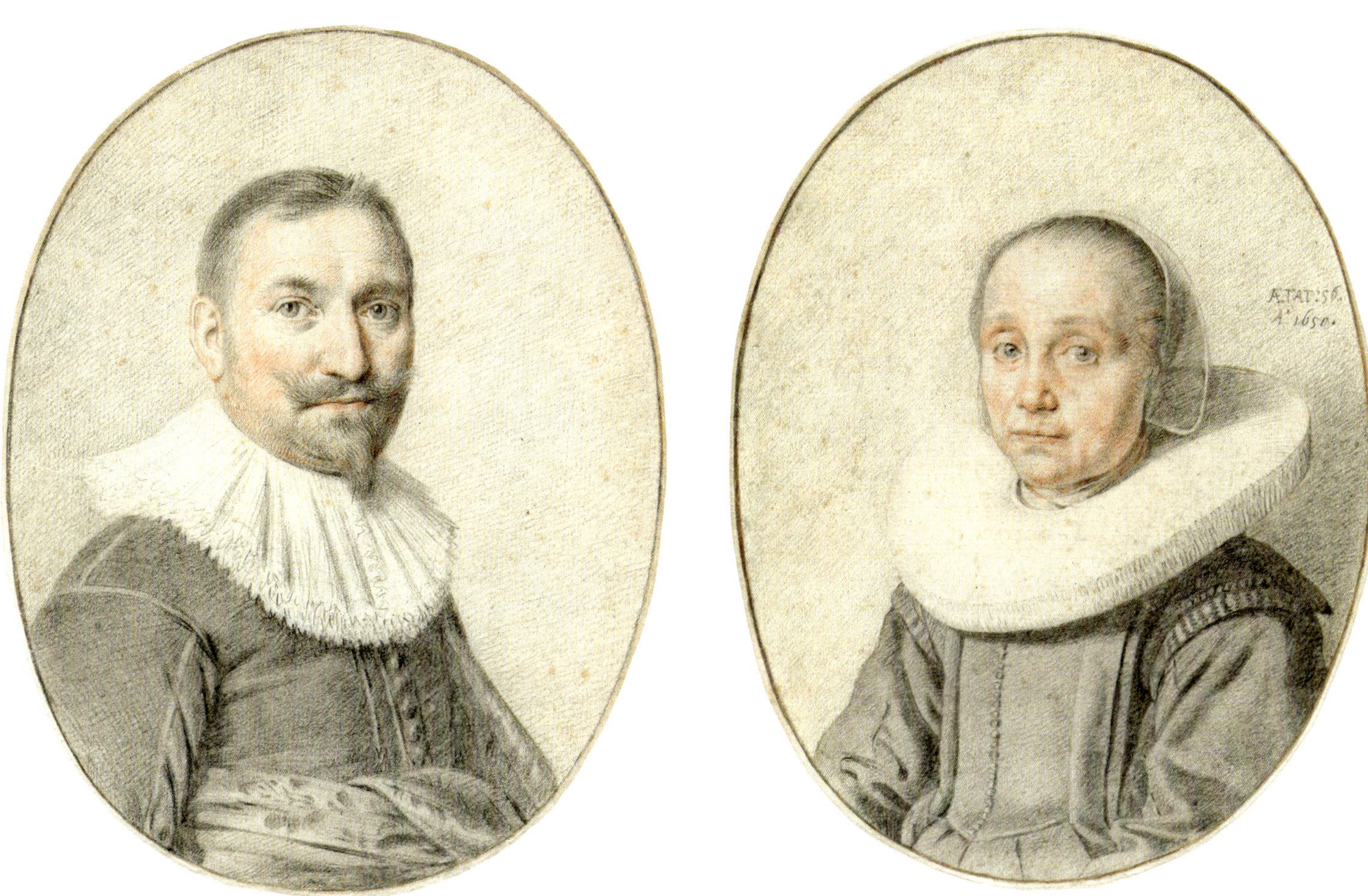

Figs. 7a and b. Jan de Bray. *Pendant Portraits of a Man and a Woman*, 1650. Cats. 100 and 101.

in sensitive portrayals that have been prized since the works were first recorded in the collection of the noted early eighteenth-century connoisseur Jeronimus Tonneman.[15] The drawings have not been connected to any known paintings and thus stand as autonomous works of art.

Even though wax offers the most lifelike representation of flesh, portraits in this medium never achieved widespread appeal outside of popular amusements and certain devotional settings, particularly within the Roman Catholic Church.[16] Despite their modest size and relatively unadorned state, the portraits of Bartholomeus and Ursula Lother (figs. 8a and b) exemplify the unique properties of wax portraiture. Wax portraits can be modeled volumetrically, and their surfaces reflect light much like skin. In their portability, painted

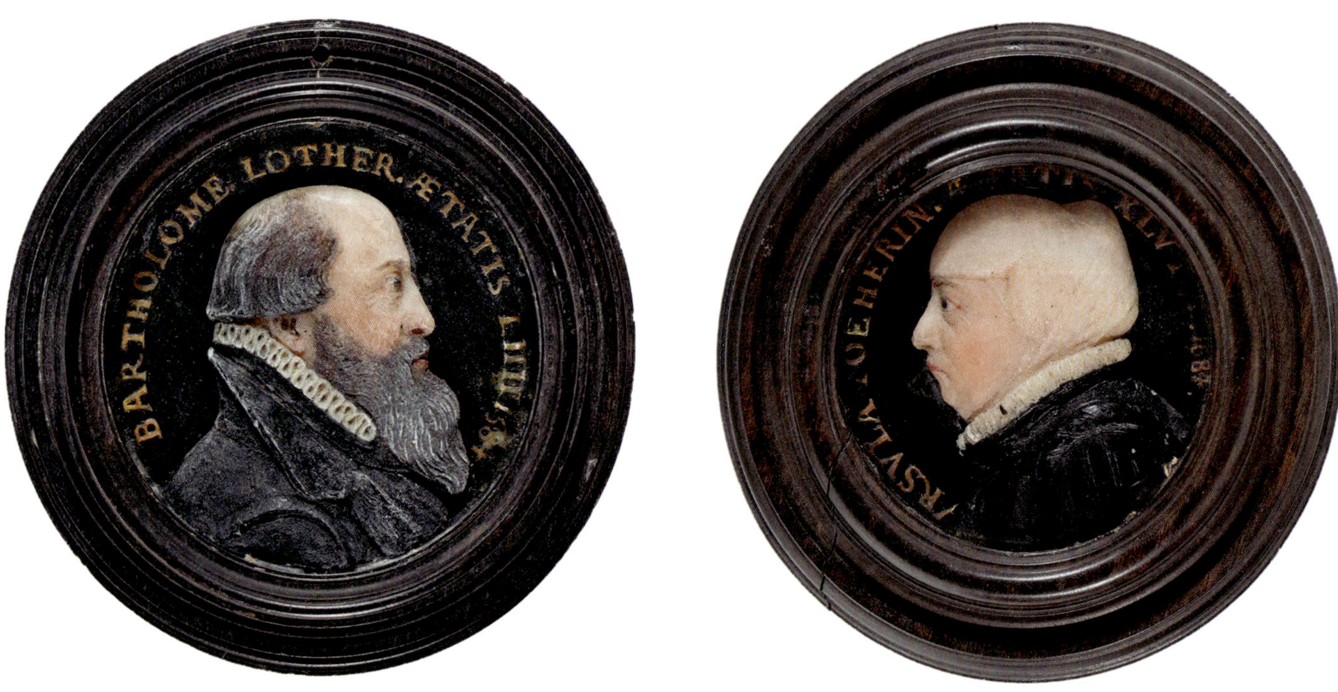

Figs. 8a and b. Unidentified German artist. *Portraits of Bartholomeus and Ursula Lother*, 1584. Cats. 9 and 10.

portrait miniatures recall wax portraits and were, in England just prior to Van Dyck's time, the art objects that manifested the greatest native refinement. Nicholas Hilliard and Isaac Oliver were among the genre's most accomplished practitioners, and their legacy was carried on by artists such as Samuel Cooper, for example, in his *Portrait of a Gentleman* (fig. 9). Miniature portraits could be carried easily or even worn; their inherent intimacy made them especially well suited to serve as lovers' gifts or memorials to the departed.[17]

Sculptural portraits, meanwhile, can depict their subjects at an intimate or a grand scale and may represent an individual frontally, in profile, or from various angles simultaneously. When a sculpture is made through a casting process, as is generally the case with portraits in bronze, the likeness may be reproduced and disseminated, making the absent present in many places at once. This also holds true of portrait medallions and portraits featured on coinage. As with Jean Warin's portraits of Anne of Austria and her young son, the future Louis XIV

(fig. 10), the diameter of medals can conform to the width of the human palm; the weight and texture of these objects further encourage their handling and contemplation.

In surveying the types of portraiture commonly produced in the seventeenth century, we can better appreciate why Van Dyck or Rembrandt (or indeed any artist) would choose to make a portrait print. Portrait prints use the descriptive potential of a specific technique—etching, engraving, woodcut, lithography—each with its own creative restrictions and freedoms. They combine the inherent goals of portraiture with an increased ease of reproducibility, portability, and the incorporation of text or visual framing devices. To give a more impressive physical presence, in the seventeenth century portrait prints were sometimes printed on silk or mounted on panels; they could also be affixed to the inner surfaces of chests.[18] They were sent from one place to another to convey information about the physical appearance of an important person or to publicize the work of a notable portraitist.[19]

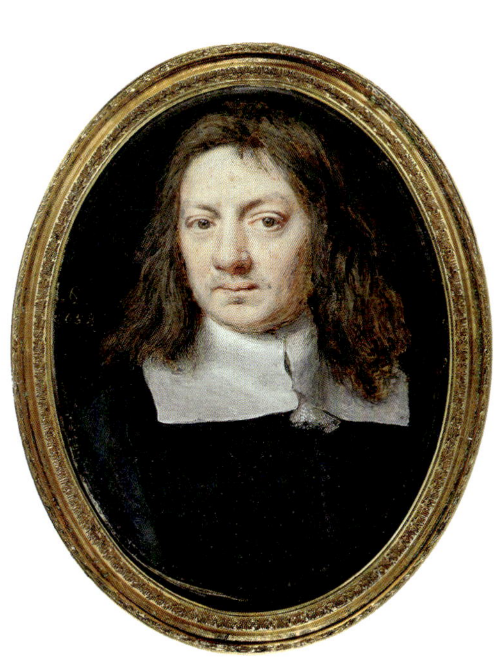

Fig. 9. Samuel Cooper. *Portrait of a Gentleman*, 1658.
Cat. 88. Shown at actual size.

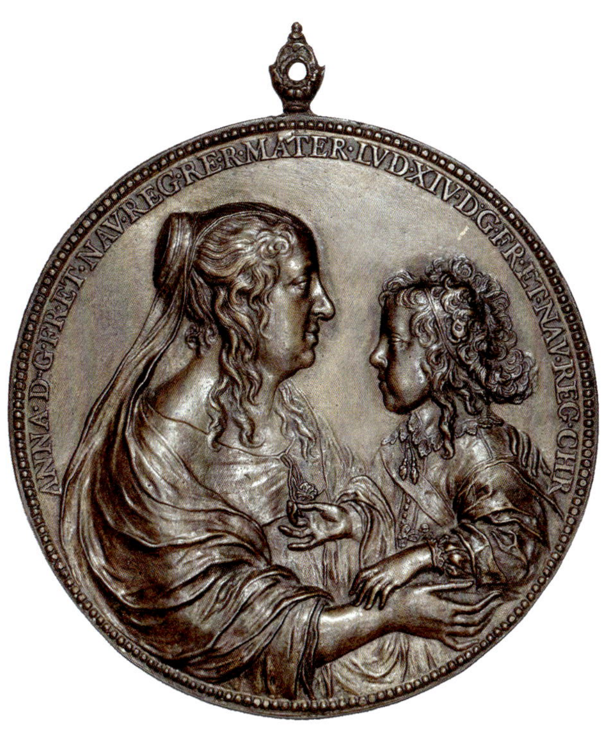

Fig. 10. Attributed to Jean Warin. *Portrait Medallion: Anne of Austria and Her Son, the Future King Louis XIV*, 1638/48. Cat. 86.

Portrait prints accompanied broadsides and spread both the fame and infamy of political figures.[20] In short, compared with other forms of portraiture, portrait prints can better affirm identity, confer authority, confirm celebrity, and express membership in a community.[21]

Perhaps most importantly, portrait prints were (and are) beautiful things to see and delightful things to touch. By the seventeenth century, print collecting was regarded as a discrete category of art collecting, separate from the practice of building libraries and increasingly within the precinct of connoisseurship.[22] Print collecting was also just then becoming a subject of discussion in art historical treatises. In his discussion of numismatics, the English diarist John Evelyn made special mention of portrait prints:

> But that which I would chiefly bespeak to the Curious of Prints, should amongst the rest be a Collection of the Heads and Effigies of Famous and Illustrious Persons, such as were

either done Originally from the Life, or from the best Painters that were so; and I do in particular recommend it to the Studious of Medals, as what may in great Part, and with no great Expence, supply what one cannot hope to procure and obtain in more rich and lasting materials; as also in as much as besides the Heads and Pourtraits, they seldom or never appear without Inscriptions of the Names, Qualities, Virtues, most signal Works and Actions of the Persons whom they represent, which makes up the defect of Reverses.[23]

Within only a few years of Evelyn's publication, the French biographer and theorist Roger de Piles wrote the first treatise dedicated to the appreciation of prints. One chapter describes the value of portrait prints for various collectors, including architects, theologians, travelers, and military figures. For those interested in history, he listed the categories that are most useful and recommended an order for organizing them:

First, the portraits of sovereigns who govern a country, the princes and princesses who are their descendants, those who have had a certain considerable position in state government, the church, the military, or the university: those who have gained esteem in the different professions and who have taken part in historical events. These portrait prints are accompanied by a few lines of text that remark on the character of the person, his birth and death, and his remarkable actions.[24]

As Evelyn's and de Piles's remarks both reflect, the collector of portrait prints had an opportunity to engage with history—more specifically, to assemble a body of objects whose subjects represented individual actors in a historical narrative. As de Piles suggested, they could be organized by country of origin and time period, or they could be grouped—and even selected—according to vocation. For instance, the collection of Robert Sonnenschein, given to the Art Institute in 1941, includes around two hundred portrait prints devoted to the medical profession, including representations of Hippocrates and the seventeenth-century English physician William Harvey.[25] This is perhaps not surprising given that Sonnenschein was himself a physician and a professor of laryngology. Sonnenschein seems to have been motivated by the desire to place himself within a history that reflected his own intellectual interests; one can imagine how exciting it could be to surround oneself with peers from foreign places and earlier times. Yet his collection represents an end to the widespread practice of collecting prints in this manner. After the early twentieth century, the project of gathering a group of portraits to represent the history of a place or profession lost its appeal.

In the eighteenth century, the vogue for collecting portrait prints spiked with the 1769 publication of James Granger's *Biographical History of England*; many owners of the book felt compelled to extra-illustrate the text with portrait prints.[26] By the early nineteenth century, massive collections of portrait prints such as that of Mark Masterman Sykes had been assembled; his collection, which included thousands of subjects, was so vast that its sale took place over several months, with the largest sections devoted to portrait prints.[27] Walter Tiffin's

collection of mezzotint portraits of English subjects included over 1,200 examples, which were listed alphabetically by the name of the sitters.[28] In 1868 the print collection of Alfred Morrison was catalogued by M. Holloway. In this case, the contents were arranged by artist, not sitter, though the vast majority of the collection was made up of portrait prints. Among the nearly three thousand examples, thirty entries are found under Van Dyck's name, with many more listed under various artists who executed prints based on Van Dyck's designs. In cataloguing Van Dyck's portrait etchings, Holloway distinguished between different states, noting, for example, that Morrison owned both a first state (fig. 11) as well as the second state of the portrait of landscape painter and draftsman Joos de Momper, which was further realized by Lucas Vorsterman.[29]

But the impulse to amass prints representing every member of the worthy world did not always go hand in hand with a passion for high-quality impressions. *The Print Collector* of 1844 offers the following warning: "It should be recollected, however, that the great majority of this class of prints are, so far as regards the English school at least, most wretched performances as works of art, not worthy of the name."[30] Sonnenschein, for example, formed his collection with a greater interest in portrait prints as portals to history than as works of art.

Among the many remarkable facets of Van Dyck's portrait print series, the *Iconography*, was that it appealed to the groups of collectors who were alternately motivated by the subjects and by the objects themselves. While the series, in its more fully realized state, engages the historian's curiosity about artists and collectors of early seventeenth-century Europe, the less finished versions of his portrait prints—those etched by the artist himself—fall comfortably within the tradition of innovative printmaking. Peter Lely, one of Van Dyck's successors in the field of portraiture, was also one of the most important print collectors of the time. His collector's mark, featuring the initials *P.L.,* was stamped onto each of his prints at the time of his death in 1680; based on surviving prints with this mark, it is evident that he possessed a considerable number of proof impressions of Van Dyck's etchings.[31] Also active in the seventeenth century was the French print publisher and dealer Pierre II Mariette, whose own distinguished

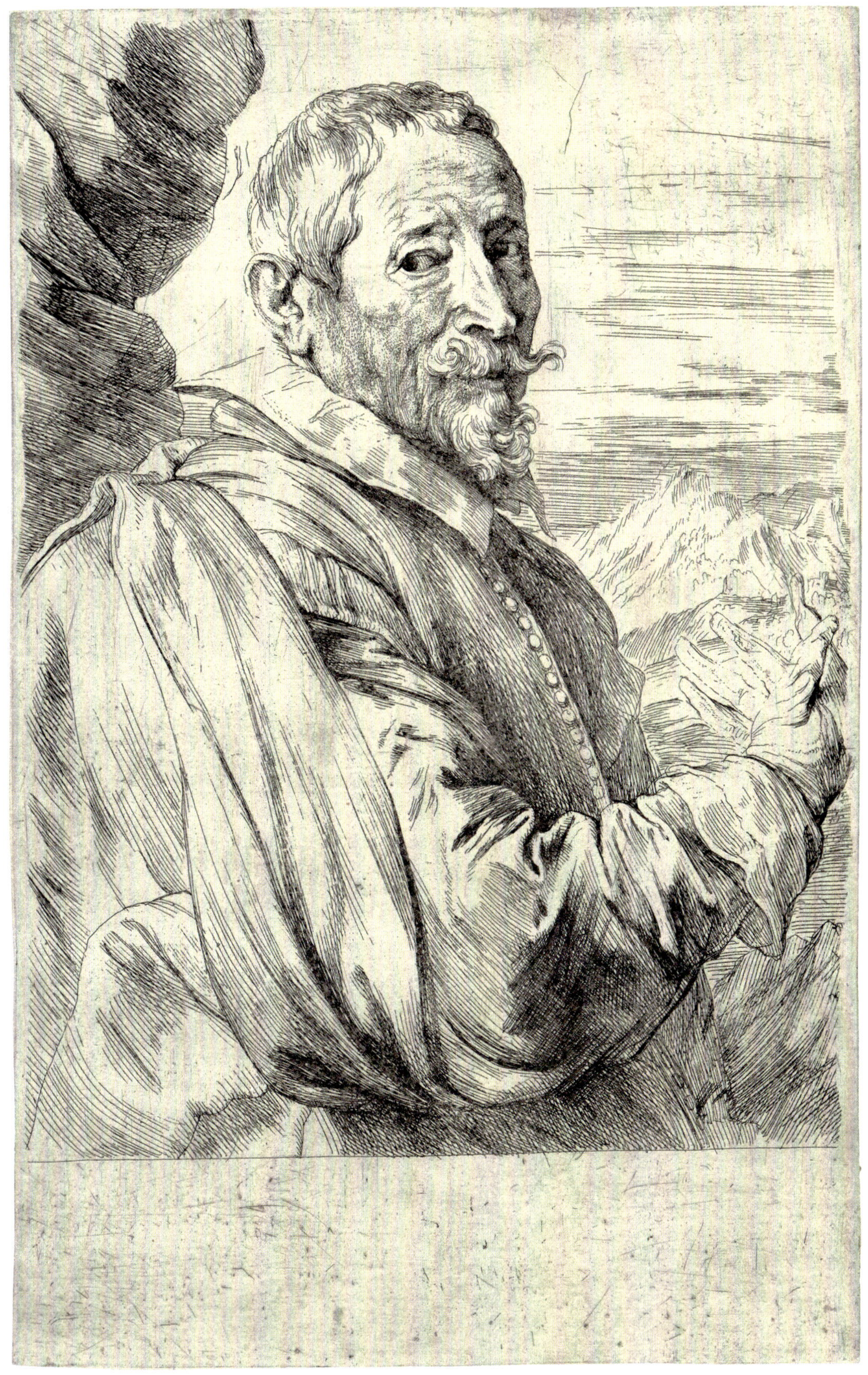

Fig. 11. Anthony van Dyck. *Joos de Momper*, 1630/33. Cat. 48.

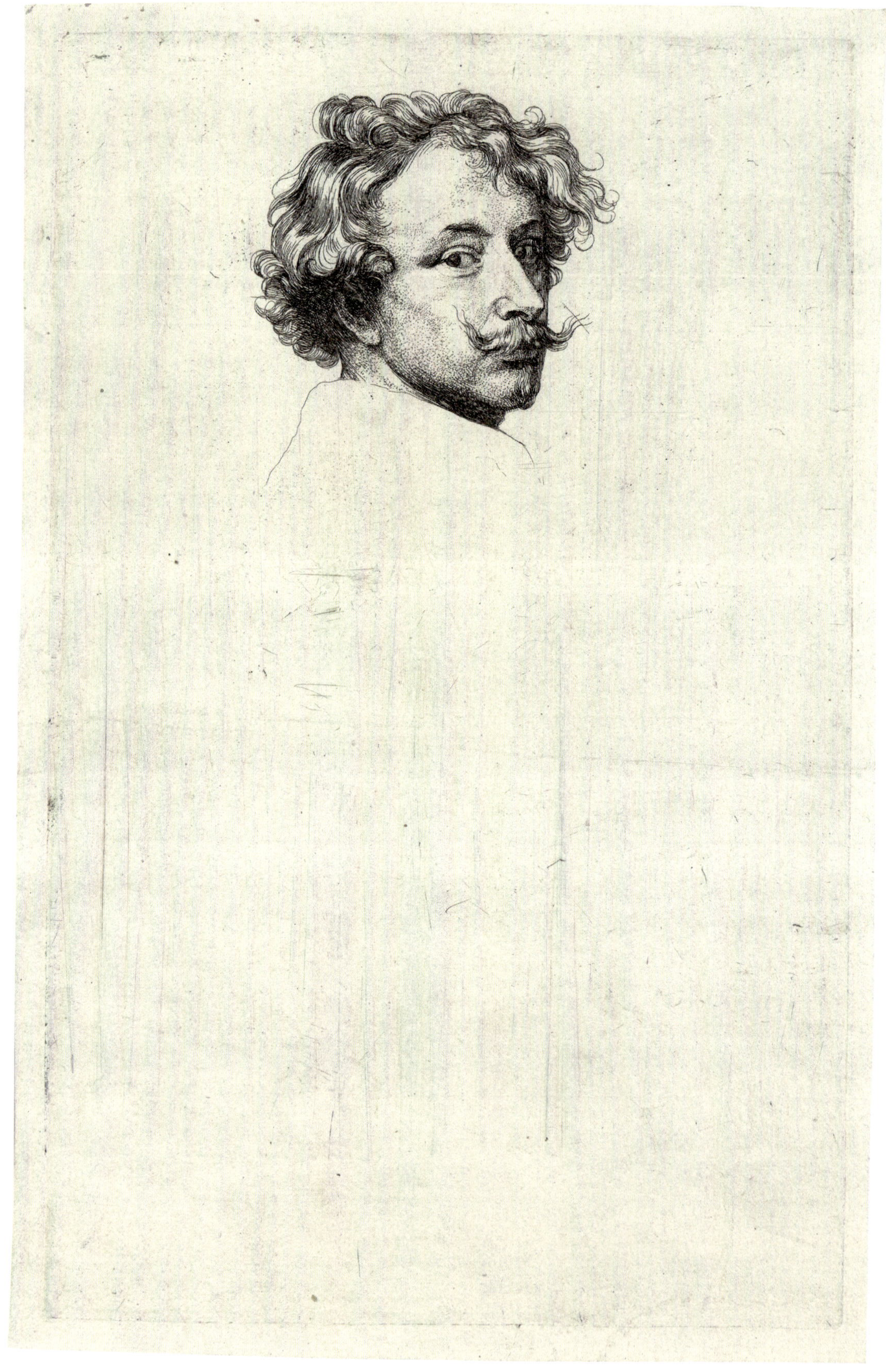

Fig. 12. Anthony van Dyck. *Self-Portrait*, 1630/33. Cat. 43.

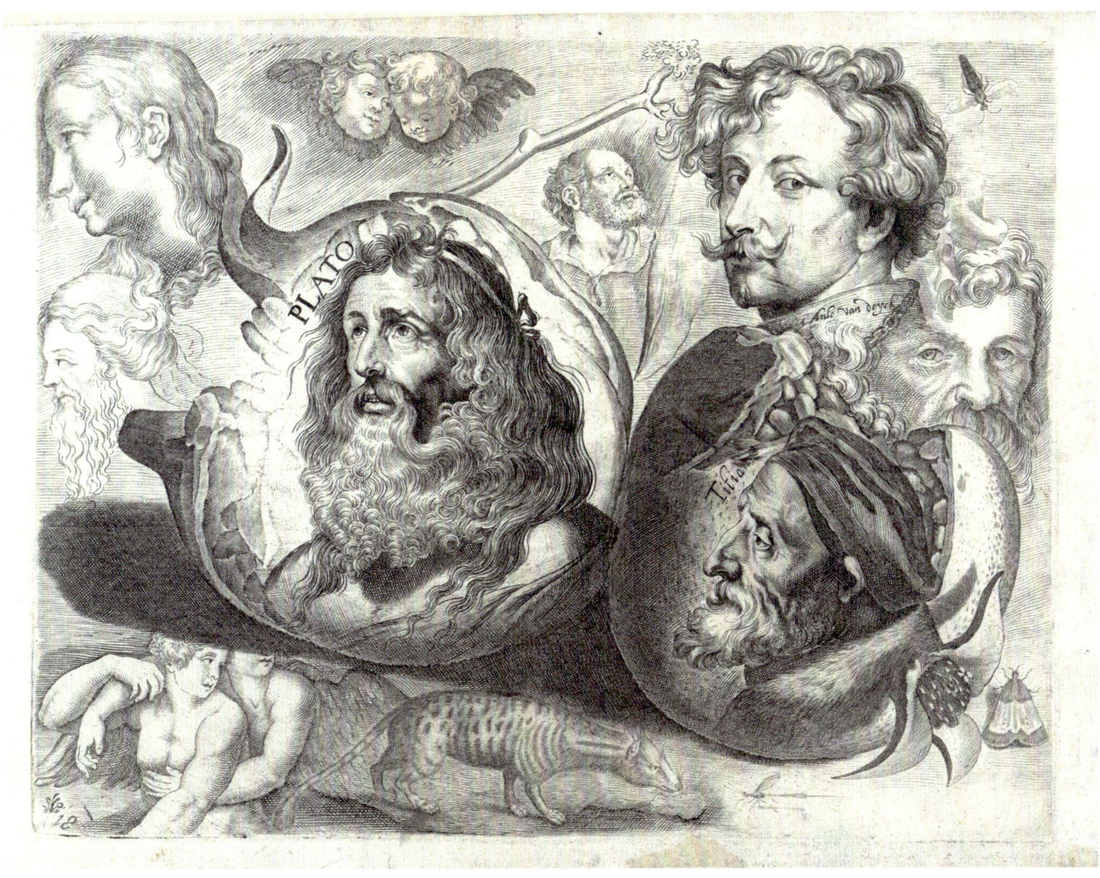

Fig. 13. Michiel Snijders (Dutch, 1610–1672). *Study Sheet from a Printed Drawing Book with Copies after Titian and Van Dyck*, n.d. Engraving; 184 × 241 mm. Rijksmuseum, Purchased with the support of the F.G. Waller-Fonds, RP-P-1996-81.

collection also included impressions of Van Dyck's unfinished etchings.[32] More than one hundred years later, in 1799, the print collection of Charles Rogers was sold in part over the course of three weeks; the sale of portrait prints by Van Dyck, described as "mostly proofs," took an entire day.[33] The demand for Van Dyck's etchings continued through the early twentieth century, diminishing only in recent decades.

One aim of this publication and exhibition is to revive interest in Van Dyck's etchings; indeed, many of the prints by the artist in the Art Institute's collection have not been exhibited for almost ninety years. These works not only mark an intersection of collecting practices, but also herald the modern and contemporary interest in self-portraiture—and in an unapologetically unfinished aesthetic. Van Dyck's greatest triumph in the medium is indeed his own unfinished self-portrait (fig. 12).

Here, as in a number of his painted self-portraits, the artist has turned his back on the viewer; in a spontaneous moment, he looks over his shoulder to give some casual acknowledgment of a world outside himself.[34] Van Dyck's head occupies the upper third of the composition, with the remainder of the printed field left dramatically blank. Astonishingly, this vast unprinted area contrasts with the compact and convincing description of the facial features and hair, which are conveyed with easy and irregular etched lines, while the tonality of the skin is achieved through precise, though not stiff, stippling. As Van Dyck would have wished, the work became highly desired among collectors almost immediately, and just as quickly it was quoted in still-life paintings and, rather wonderfully, in a late seventeenth-century series of model prints for drawing students (see fig. 13).

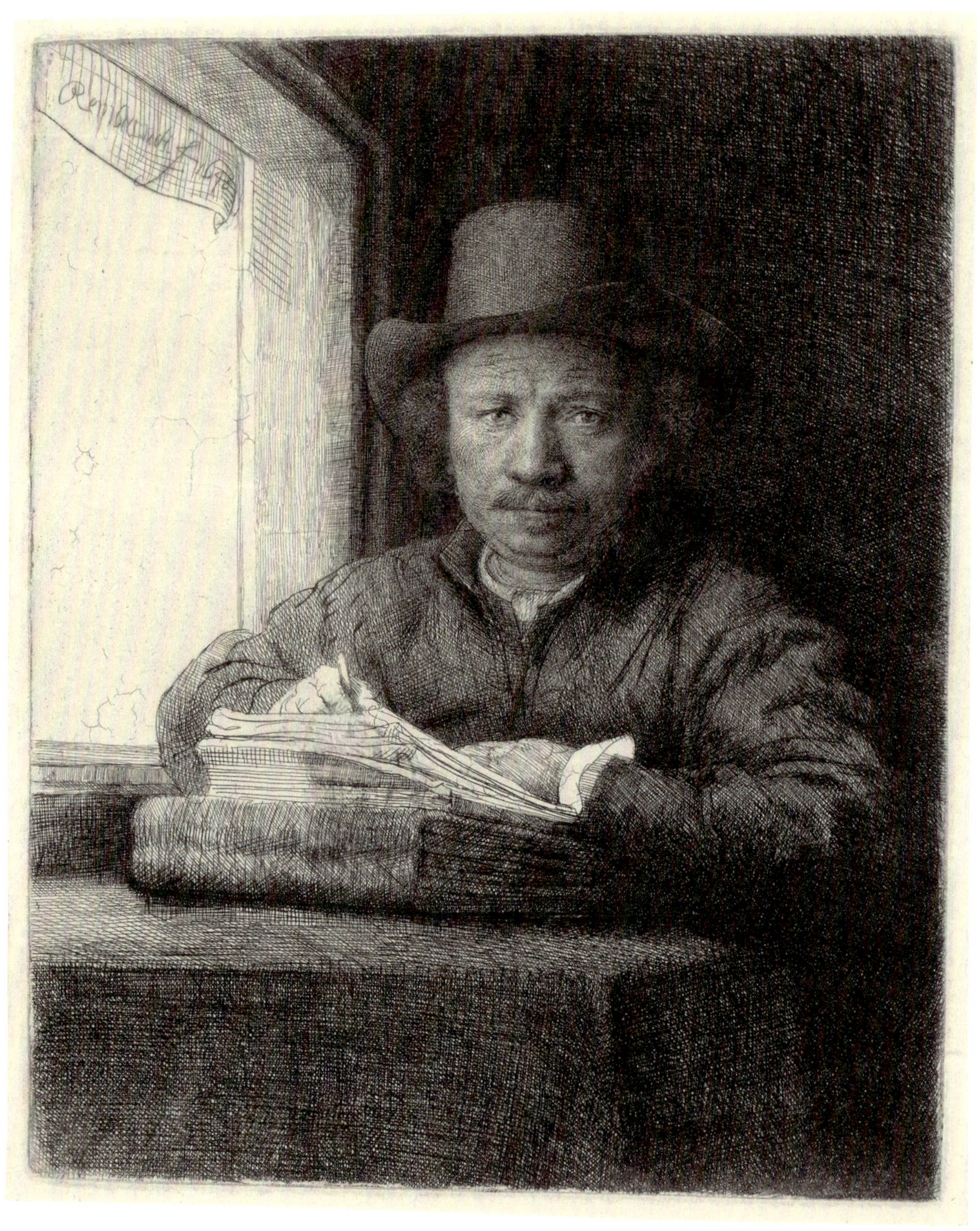

   Fig. 14. Rembrandt van Rijn. *Self-Portrait Etching at a Window*, 1648. Cat. 75. Shown at actual size.

Van Dyck's innovative use of the portrait print inspired both artists of his own time and many in the eighteenth, nineteenth, and twentieth centuries. His most immediate and profound impact can be seen in the etchings of Rembrandt, whose innovation in the genre has remained a spark for successive generations of artists even as the audience for Van Dyck's etchings have found an increasingly narrow audience of Old Master print scholars and enthusiasts. But, as others have rightly pointed out, Van Dyck's fresh approach to the portrait print indicated a path for Rembrandt, who responded to the challenge with a searching investigation of his own face.[35] In his most premeditated printed self-portrait (fig. 14), Rembrandt presented himself seated at a table, next to a window, with an etching needle in hand. Although earlier self-portraits (cats. 69–70) show the artist exploring more nonchalant poses, here he sits nearly square to the picture plane and addresses the viewer with an earnest pride in his vocation. While Van Dyck's unfinished self-portrait seems dashed off, the product of irrepressible talent, Rembrandt's displays the labor required to achieve the convincing effect of light striking unevenly across his face and clothes, the surface of the table, and the wall at the back of the scene. In the Art Institute's print (the second state of four), the view through the open window remains undescribed, indicating only a light source or, more metaphorically, the invisible working of Rembrandt's mind as he pauses from his creative endeavor. In portrait prints like these, artists asserted that they deserved a place in the canon of laudable public figures and, at the same time, engaged in a dialogue about the expressive limits of their medium. As the exhibition and the essays in this catalogue submit, the legacies of Van Dyck and Rembrandt are abundantly present in the continuing vitality of the portrait print, a genre whose power and beauty has still more to offer historians, collectors, and artists.

Notes

1. For more on Boilly's career, including a discussion of other examples of his trompe l'oeil paintings of prints of different genres, see Annie Scotte-De Wambrechies and Florence Raymond, eds., *Boilly (1761–1845)*, exh. cat. (Palais des Beaux Arts de Lille/Nicolas Chaudun, 2011), pp. 252–65, cats. 182–89. To my knowledge, this specific painting has not been extensively discussed in scholarly literature, but it has been published previously; see Jacques Seligmann et Fils, *Exposition L.-L. Boilly*, exh. cat. (Jacques Seligmann, 1930), p. 27, cat. 71; and Saint Louis Art Museum, *A Gentleman Collects*, exh. cat. (Saint Louis Art Museum, 2002), p. 14. I am grateful to Susan Tallman for our discussion of this work and its reflection on the status of the portrait print. Regarding the relationship between painting and lithography, as well as painting and photography, in the nineteenth century, see Stephen Bann, *Distinguished Images: Prints in the Visual Economy of Nineteenth-Century France* (Yale University Press, 2013). My thanks to Jordan Bear for bringing this book to my attention in a helpful review. Bear, "Photographic Exceptionalism?," *Oxford Art Journal* 38 (2015), pp. 300–04.

2. Boilly's son Jules created a portrait lithograph of Bawr in 1835 (as part of a suite of eighteen portraits of female subjects, the so-called *Bas-bleus*), which was printed by Theirry Frères. Jean Laran and Jean Adhémar, *Inventaire du fonds français après 1800*, vol. 3 (Bibliothèque Nationale de France, 1930), p. 49, cat. 22.

3. For more on Gwyn, including her painted portraits and other printed portraits, see Catherine MacLeod and Julia Marciari Alexander, with essays by Kevin Sharpe, Diana Dethloff, and Sonya Wynne, *Painted Ladies: Women at the Court of Charles II*, exh. cat. (National Portrait Gallery, London/Yale Center for British Art, 2001), cats. 67–69. Gwyn has also been depicted in many works of popular literature and was the focus of a 2015 play by Jessica Swale, *Nell Gwynn*, produced by Shakespeare's Globe, London.

4. This work is discussed in Alan Shestack, *Fifteenth-Century Engravings of Northern Europe from the National Gallery of Art, Washington, D.C.*, exh. cat. (National Gallery of Art, Washington, D.C.,1967), cat. 244.

5. The classic monograph on Dürer remains Erwin Panofsky, *The Life and Art of Albrecht Dürer* (Princeton University Press, 1943).

6. As Andrée Hayum has convincingly argued, Dürer chose to show Erasmus, and by extension himself, as a man whose significance arose through the culture of printing. Hayum, "Dürer's Portrait of Erasmus and the Ars Typographorum," *Renaissance Quarterly* 38, 4 (Winter 1985), pp. 650–87. For a broader discussion of the portraits of Erasmus in painted and printed form, as well as humanist portraits more generally, see Antoine Bodar, "Erasmus en het geleerden portret," in *Nederlandse Portretten: Bijdragen over de Portretkunst in de Nederlanden uit de Zestiende, Zeventiende en Achttiende Eeuw*, ed. H. E. Blasse-Hegeman et al., Leids Kunsthistorisch Jaarboek 8 (SDU Uitgeverij, 1990), pp. 17–68.

7. This is discussed, among other places, in Paul Zanker, *The Power of Images in the Age of Augustus*, trans. Alan Shapiro (University of Michigan Press, 1988).

8. The figure in the engraving was based on a pen-and-brown-ink drawing by Isaac Oliver; for further information on this work, see Harold Barkley, *Likeness in Line: An Anthology of Tudor and Stuart Engraved Portraits*, exh. cat. (Victoria and Albert Museum/Her Majesty's Stationery Office, 1982), cat. 5; and Antony Griffiths, with the collaboration of Robert A. Gerard, *The Print in Stuart Britain, 1603–89*, exh. cat. (British Museum, 1998), cats. 1 and 2.

9. The capital letters in the chronogram *MIserICorDIae* provide the roman numeral date of MDCIII, or 1603, the year of Elizabeth's death, after which time the print must have been made.

10. For a discussion of this group of related portrait prints, see Jan Piet Filedt Kok, "Artists Portrayed by Their Friends: Goltzius and His Circle," in "Ten Essays for a Friend: E. de Jongh 65," special issue, *Simiolus: Netherlands Quarterly for the History of Art* 24, 2/3 (1996), pp. 161–81.

11. Following the translation given in ibid., p. 164.

12. While the genre of the portrait print has been used many times as an organizing principle for exhibitions, its ability to convey meaning as distinct from other forms of portraiture has rarely been discussed. For a survey of the genre, see Constance Harris, *Portraiture in Prints* (McFarland, 1987). For an important contribution to the interpretation of early modern portrait prints, see Peter Parshall, "Portrait

Prints and Codes of Identity in the Renaissance: Hendrik Goltzius, Justus Lipsius, and Michel de Montaigne," *Word and Image* 19, 1–2 (2003), pp. 22–37. Portrait prints are also discussed in Griffiths, *The Print in Stuart Britain*.

13. For further discussion of this painting, see Till-Holger Borchert and Koenraad Jonckheere, *Portrait de la Renaissance aux Pays-Bas*, exh. cat. (BOZAR/ Palais des Beaux-Arts, 2015), cat. 47.

14. A 2015 exhibition at the Morgan Library and Museum, New York, focused on portrait drawings and included a number of independent works as well as preparatory studies. *Life Lines: Portrait Drawings from Dürer to Picasso* (June 1– September 8, 2015).

15. Regarding the biography and collecting practice of Tonneman, see Mària van Berge-Gerbaud, Marjolein Menalda, Michiel C. Plomp, and Carel van Tuyll van Serooskerken, *Hartstochtelijk Verzameld: Beroemde tekeningen in 18de-eeuwse Hollandse collecties*, exh. cat. (Fondation Custodia and Uitgeverij Thoth, 2001), especially cat. 8; and the related volume Michiel C. Plomp, *Hartstochtelijk Verzameld: 18de-eeuwse Hollandse verzamelaars van tekeningen en hun collecties* (Fondation Custodia and Uitgeverij Thoth, 2001).

16. David Freedberg, "Verisimilitude and Resemblance: From Sacred Mountain to Waxworks," in *The Power of Images: Studies in the History and Theory of Response* (University of Chicago Press), pp. 192–245.

17. For more on Samuel Cooper and English miniatures of the seventeenth century more generally, see John Murdoch, *Seventeenth-Century English Miniatures in the Collection of the Victoria and Albert Museum* (Victoria and Albert Museum/Her Majesty's Stationery Office, 1997).

18. Jan van der Waals, *Prenten in de Gouden Eeuw: Van Kunst tot Kastpapier*, exh. cat. (Museum Boijmans Van Beuningen, 2006), cats. 15 and 32, among other examples.

19. In a letter from 1626, Peter Paul Rubens expressed his frustration about not being able to access "the portraits of Master Michel, engraved on copper in Holland." As Ruth Magurn suggested, he is likely referring to the Dutch painter Michiel Jansz. Mierevelt. Willem Delff, among others, was engaged in producing reproductive prints after Mierevelt. One example that predates Rubens's cited letter is the 1623 portrait of Christian II, Duke of Brunswick (Hollstein 14). One may presume that Rubens was especially eager to receive these prints in part to observe the work of Mierevelt, a contemporary portraitist. But he may also have been eager to see such prints for the information they conveyed. Not having had the opportunity to meet, say, the Duke of Brunswick, Rubens awaited the receipt of these prints in order to become acquainted with the physical appearance of such men and women of import. As with many of his contemporaries, Rubens pursued those things or people that merited discovery, and when a firsthand encounter was not possible, a print could provide a valuable surrogate. Rubens to Pierre Dupuy, November 12, 1626, Magurn, trans. and ed., *The Letters of Peter Paul Rubens* (Harvard University Press, 1955), notes to letter no. 95.

20. See Maureen Warren's essay in this volume. For a case study of the various printed portraits featuring Admiral Maarten Harpertz. Tromp, see Van der Waals, *Prenten in de Gouden Eeuw*, cats. 166–75.

21. The subject of portraiture is vast, and it will not be possible here to include all relevant citations. Some useful references include John Pope-Hennessy, *The Portrait in the Renaissance*, A. W. Mellon Lectures in the Fine Arts, Bollingen series 35 (Bollingen Foundation, 1966); Blasse-Hegeman, *Nederlandse Portretten*; Richard Brilliant, *Portraiture* (Reaktion, 1991); Joseph Leo Koerner, *The Moment of Self-Portraiture in German Renaissance Art* (University of Chicago Press, 1993);

Katlijne Van der Stighelen, Hannelore Magnus, and Bert Watteeuw, eds., *Pokerfaced: Flemish and Dutch Baroque Faces Unveiled* (Brepols, 2010); and Borchert and Jonckheere, *Portraits de la Renaissance aux Pays-Bas*. In addition to these texts, two issues of *Word and Image* (19, 1–2) were devoted to early modern European print and medal portraits; these publications arose from a symposium held at Dartmouth College in 2000 related to the exhibition *The Power of Appearances: Renaissance and Reformation Portrait Prints and Medals* at the Hood Museum.

22. On early print collecting, see Peter Parshall, "Art and the Theater of Knowledge: The Origins of Print Collecting in Northern Europe," *Harvard University Art Museums Bulletin* 2, 3 (Spring 1994), pp. 7–36; and William W. Robinson, "This Passion for Prints: Collecting and Connoisseurship in Northern Europe During the Seventeenth Century," in Clifford S. Ackley, *Printmaking in the Age of Rembrandt*, exh. cat. (Museum of Fine Arts, Boston, 1981), pp. xxvii–xlviii.

23. John Evelyn, "Of Heads and Effigies in Prints and Taille-douce: Their Use as They Relate to Medals," in *Numismata* (London, 1697), p. 257. I am grateful to Nicholas Stogdon for referring me to this passage.

24. In the original French: "Prémiérement les Portraits des Souverains qui ont gouverné un Païs, les Princes & Princesses qui en sont descendus, ceux qui ont tenu quelque rang considerable dans l'Etat, dans l'Eglise, dans les Armes, dans la Robe: ceux qui se sont rendus recommandables dans les différentes Professions, & les Particuliers qui ont quelque part dans les Evénemens historiques. Ils accompagnent ces Portraits de quelques lignes d'écriture, qui marquent le caractére de la Personne, sa Naissance, ses Actions remarquables, & le tems de sa Mort." Roger de Piles, *Abregé de la vie des peintres* (1699; repr., Olms, 1969), pp. 86–87. For further discussion of de Piles and other theories of print collecting at the turn of the eighteenth century, see Antony Griffiths, "Print Collecting in Rome, Paris, and London in the Early Eighteenth Century," *Harvard University Art Museums Bulletin* 2, 3 (1994), pp. 37–68.

25. Inv. nos. 1941.191–390. Sonnenschein also donated a large group of bookplates, personal papers, and portraits in different media, including photographs, to the University of Chicago Special Collections Research Center.

26. The most spectacular example is the so-called Bute-Grainger in the Huntington Library, San Marino (library catalogue number 283000, 36 volumes). For more on this subject, see Lucy Peltz, "A Friendly Gathering: The Social Politics of Presentation Books and Their Extra-Illustration in Horace Walpole's Circle," *Journal of the History of Collections* 19, 1 (2007), pp. 33–49; and Robert A. Shaddy, "Grangerizing: 'One of the Unfortunate Stages of Bibliomania,'" *Book Collector* 49, 4 (2000), pp. 535–46.

27. *A Catalogue of the Highly Valuable Collection of Prints, the Property of the Late Sir Mark Masterman Sykes, Bart*, 5 parts, sale cat. (Sotheby's, London, 1824). The Art Institute's Ryerson and Burnham Libraries owns an annotated copy of this volume, which includes individual prices for prints as well as notations for their purchasers.

28. Walter F. Tiffin, *Catalogue of a Collection of English Portraits in Mezzotint . . .* (Salisbury: Bennett Brothers, Printers, Journal Office, 1883). Once again, I am indebted to Nicholas Stogdon for his reference to this publication.

29. M. Holloway, *The Collection of Engravings, Formed between the Years 1860–68 by Alfred Morrison with an Index to Portraits* (London: Holloway and Son, 1868), p. 88.

30. John Maberly, *The Print Collector: An Introduction to the Knowledge Necessary for Forming a Collection of Ancient Prints* (London: Saunders and Otley, 1844), pp. 64–65.

31. A large group of these ex-Lely collection impressions were published together in *The Portrait Etchings of Anthony van Dyck*, sale cat. (Knoedler, 1934); the self-portrait listed in this catalogue is now in the Fogg Art Museum, Harvard University (inv. no. 2008.25.1), and the portrait of Willem de Vos is now in the Ursula and R. Stanley Johnson Family Collection, Chicago. The Art Institute owns portrait prints designed by Van Dyck that were once owned by Lely (*Hendrick van Balen* [1959.34] and *Theodore van Thulden* [2014.1135]), but these are not examples of proof impressions made by Van Dyck himself. For a discussion of Lely as a collector of works on paper, see Diana Dethloff, "Sir Peter Lely's Collection of Prints and Drawings," in *Collecting Prints and Drawings in Europe, c. 1500–1750*, ed. Christopher Baker, Caroline Elam, and Genevieve Warwick (Ashgate/Burlington, 2003), pp. 123–39.

32. The Art Institute's collection includes two examples: *Paul de Vos* (cat. 58) and *Desiderius Erasmus* (cat. 46).

33. Thomas Philipe, *Catalogue of the Capital and Extensive Collection of Prints, Books of Prints, of Charles Rogers . . .*, sale cat. (London: G. Hayden, 1799), n.p. For more on Charles Rogers as a collector and the fate of his collection, see Antony Griffiths, "The Rogers Collection in the Cottonian Library, Plymouth," *Print Quarterly* 10, 1 (March 1993), pp. 19–36.

34. Van Dyck made several self-portraits, some as early as during his teenage years. Around the time of the self-portrait etching made circa 1630, he also painted a few self-portraits in rapid succession, including the famous *Self-Portrait with a Sunflower* (c. 1633, Duke of Westminster, Eaton Hall) and a double portrait with Endymion Porter (c. 1635; Museo del Prado, Madrid, inv. no. 1489); another painted self-portrait from this period was a major acquisition by the National Portrait Gallery, London, in 2014. The source for Van Dyck's self-portrait etching has been the recent subject of some debate. A painting with a similar composition, which has been known for many years, was sold at Lempertz in Cologne in May 2012 as a copy after a lost original, but the attribution has been reconsidered by leading Van Dyck painting scholars, and the work was put on view in the Minneapolis Institute of Art in 2015 (Martin Bailey, "Van Dyck Self-Portrait Confirmed as Genuine," *Art Newspaper* 24, 266 [March 2015], p. 4), although full written documentation of the reattribution and of the supporting evidence is still forthcoming. More generally, Van Dyck's painted self-portraits have been well studied in scholarly literature. In addition to the various entries in exhibition catalogues and the catalogues raisonnés by Barnes and Larsen, see also Walter A. Liedtke, *Flemish Paintings in the Metropolitan Museum of Art* (Metropolitan Museum of Art, New York/Getty Trust, 1984) vol. 1, pp. 67–71; and John Peacock, *The Look of Van Dyck: The Self-Portrait with a Sunflower and the Vision of the Painter* (Ashgate, 2006).

35. Stephanie Dickey, "Van Dyck in Holland: The Iconography and Its Impact on Rembrandt and Jan Lievens," in *Van Dyck 1599–1999: Conjectures and Refutations*, ed. Hans Vlieghe (Brepols, 2001), pp. 289–303.

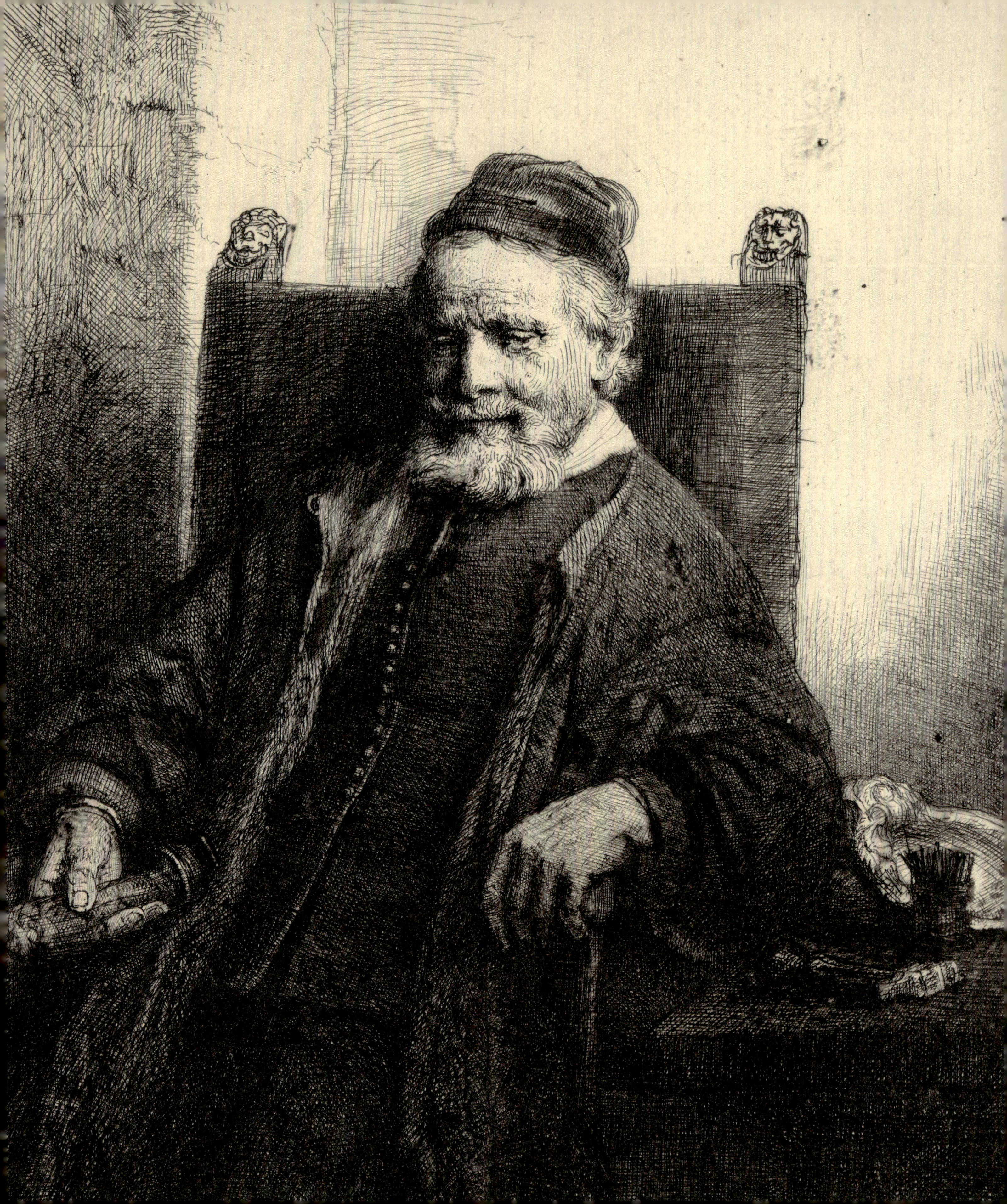

Van Dyck's Legacy

THE ARTIST AS SUBJECT AND THE VITALITY OF THE PORTRAIT PRINT

Victoria Sancho Lobis

It is the common wonder of all men, how among so many millions of faces, there should be none alike.

Thomas Browne, 1642

VAN DYCK AND THE *ICONOGRAPHY*

In the last decade of his life, Anthony van Dyck began a print-making project that would fundamentally alter the conventions of portraiture. This series of over one hundred portrait prints, eventually known as the *Iconography*, featured monarchs, diplomats, and scholars; rather unusually, it also included artists, architects, and collectors.[1] Beyond simply choosing to portray his peers and friends, Van Dyck also indirectly elevated the status of the artist by employing consistent strategies of representation for all of his sitters—regardless of social station. These strategies included specific and lifelike descriptions of facial features, jaunty positioning of the figure in relation to the implied viewer, placement of the face in the upper third of the composition, and the use of a half-length format. This was especially important given the contested role of visual artists at the time. Over the course of the seventeenth century, artists

such as Peter Paul Rubens, Van Dyck, and Diego Velázquez sought to be recognized as practitioners of the liberal arts equal to poets and philosophers, who had long been venerated for their work.[2] As opposed to being associated with trade guilds (and submitting to the requisite taxation and regulation), these artists sought court appointments and membership in knightly orders, which conferred noble status and greater financial freedom. The aesthetic goals of Van Dyck's print series fit squarely within this broader agenda.

The prints for the *Iconography* emerged through a combination of etchings produced by Van Dyck himself and designs (drawn and painted) that he conceived for other printmakers to execute. Although the series was never published in toto during his lifetime, its coherent aesthetic indicates that he intended it to be understood as a unified artistic statement.[3] Still, Van Dyck's motivations and specific ambitions for the project remain mysterious. Virtually no documentary evidence directly related to the series survives, and there are certain questions that will likely never be answered, such as precisely how many subjects the artist meant to include and in what order he wanted the prints to appear. Further, Van Dyck's own etchings circulated as individual prints during his lifetime, taking the form of both fully realized compositions and almost abstract fragments; it is therefore difficult to determine whether he preferred one of these modes of presentation over the other or if he thought of them as serving congruent, equally useful functions.

By the early 1630s, when the first prints began to appear, Van Dyck had already achieved international acclaim as a painter. The impetus for the series could therefore not have emerged out of a desire to attain recognition as an artist. A more likely goal would have been to cement the fame he had earned and perhaps also to assert his theories of portraiture, the genre for which he had been celebrated by monarchs, regents, and grandees in England, Flanders, Holland, and Italy. Scholars have also speculated that Van Dyck undertook the ambitious project with an eye to matching the prolific publication of prints by Rubens, his mentor and former employer.[4] Writing later in the seventeenth century, Dutch artist and theorist Samuel van Hoogstraten advised painters "to make their art available" through the production of prints: "Let your works come out freely in print, so that your name will fly over the world more quickly."[5] Van Dyck's enterprise certainly provided one strong example of how prints could allow artists to reproduce and circulate their work in a format that was more portable and generally more affordable than paintings.

While it is true that Van Dyck could have conceived the *Iconography* as a means of gaining prominence in the broader community of art enthusiasts and scholars, his focus on portrait prints allowed him to codify his innovations in the field of portraiture. The project also provided him an opportunity to express his ideals for the genre through the specific graphic languages of etching and engraving. When one looks more closely at the etchings Van Dyck produced for the series, it becomes clear that he used it to disrupt the prevailing standards for portrait prints. This essay examines Van Dyck's specific contributions to, as well as his indelible impact on, the genre of the portrait print. As the following discussion of the artist's immediate predecessors in addition to his direct and more distant followers will demonstrate, Van Dyck's *Iconography* constitutes a pivotal moment in which the portrait print came to be viewed not only as a method for the memorialization of an individual likeness but also as a vehicle for artistic expression.

Several distinguishing features of Van Dyck's portrait etchings can be observed in his print of the Flemish painter Jan de Wael (figs. 1–2), including dramatic state changes, an unfinished and experimental aesthetic, and the employment of a printed composition to recast a previous painted description. During his second period of work in Antwerp, the city of his birth, the artist completed a double portrait of De Wael and his wife, Geertruid de Jode (fig. 3).[6] The canvas is nearly life-size, and it includes some of the hallmarks of Van Dyck's portraits, to wit, the column positioned at De Wael's back and the cascading red drape behind De Jode. Despite Van Dyck's customary success in uniting figures in double portraits, the description of De Wael's face suggests that it was he, not De Jode, who truly captured the artist's attention. Isolated as a single figure in Van Dyck's etching, De Wael commands the focus of the viewer with a gaze that is both arresting and somehow vulnerable. In the second state of the print (fig. 1), the sitter's left arm and hand have been burnished out of the composition; only the face remains thoroughly rendered, set off and framed by the loose, unstarched folds of his ruff.[7] In combination with the longer lines of the contours of the face, nose, and head, Van Dyck used expressive individual marks to describe the furrows of the brow; the creases at the corners of the eyes; and the wiry strands of hair in the beard, mustache, and temples. Additional shading and texture are rendered through stippling and short, hatched lines at the sides of the face. Below the ruff, the costume is left in only abbreviated form with long, freely etched lines to denote the volume occupied by the body underneath the clothes. A series of loose circles at the chest suggests the absent buttons.

In a later state (fig. 2), the left arm and hand reappear, and an inscription names De Wael as a painter of human figures (*Antwerpiæ Pictor Humanarum Figurarum*). On canvas Van Dyck rarely repeated the exact position or representation of a sitter, even when he portrayed the same individual on multiple occasions; this continued in his printmaking, as can be seen in the depictions of De Wael. Though the pose in the print was clearly derived from the double portrait, it is not entirely the same. As we have seen, the subject's right hand and arm are

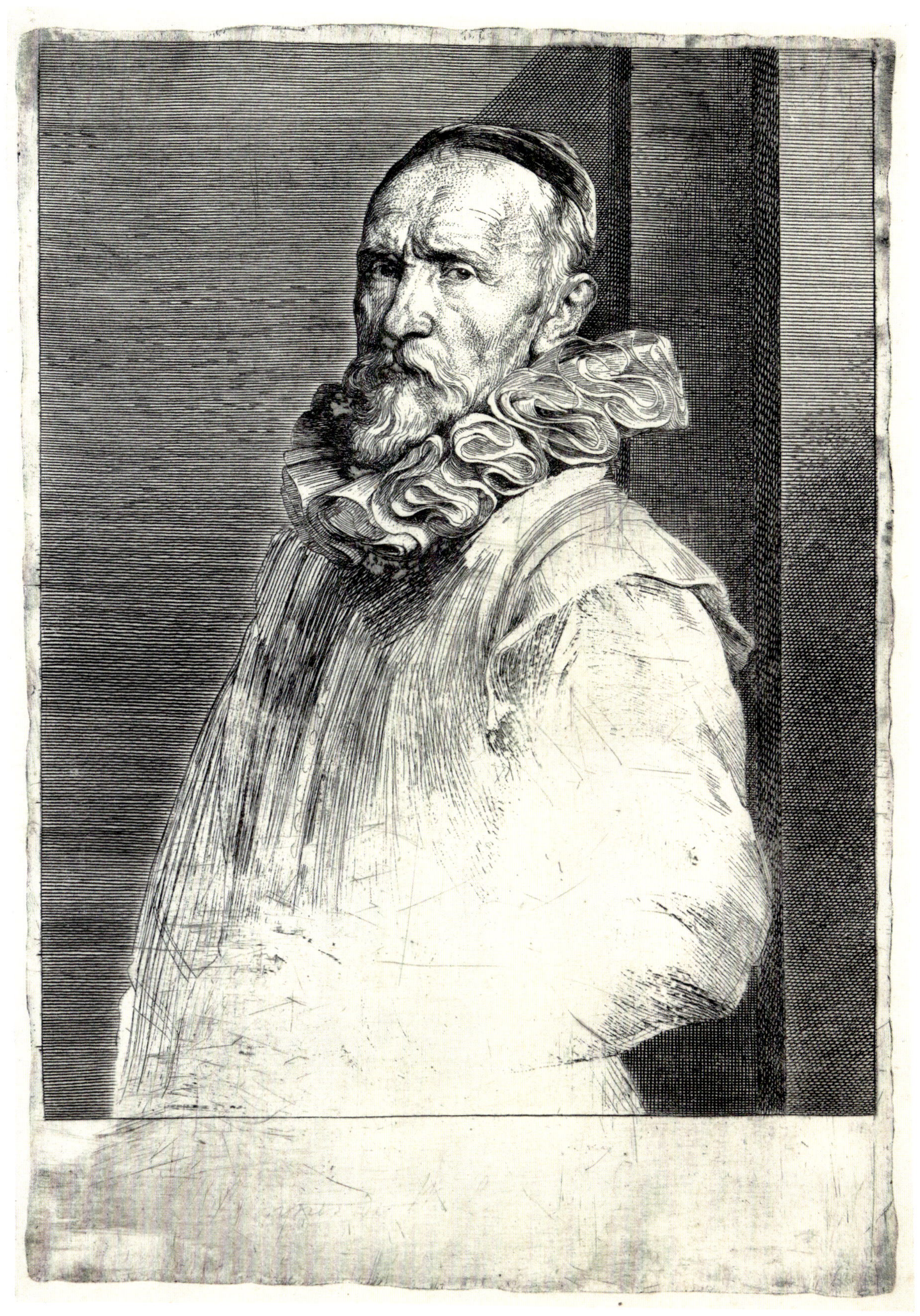

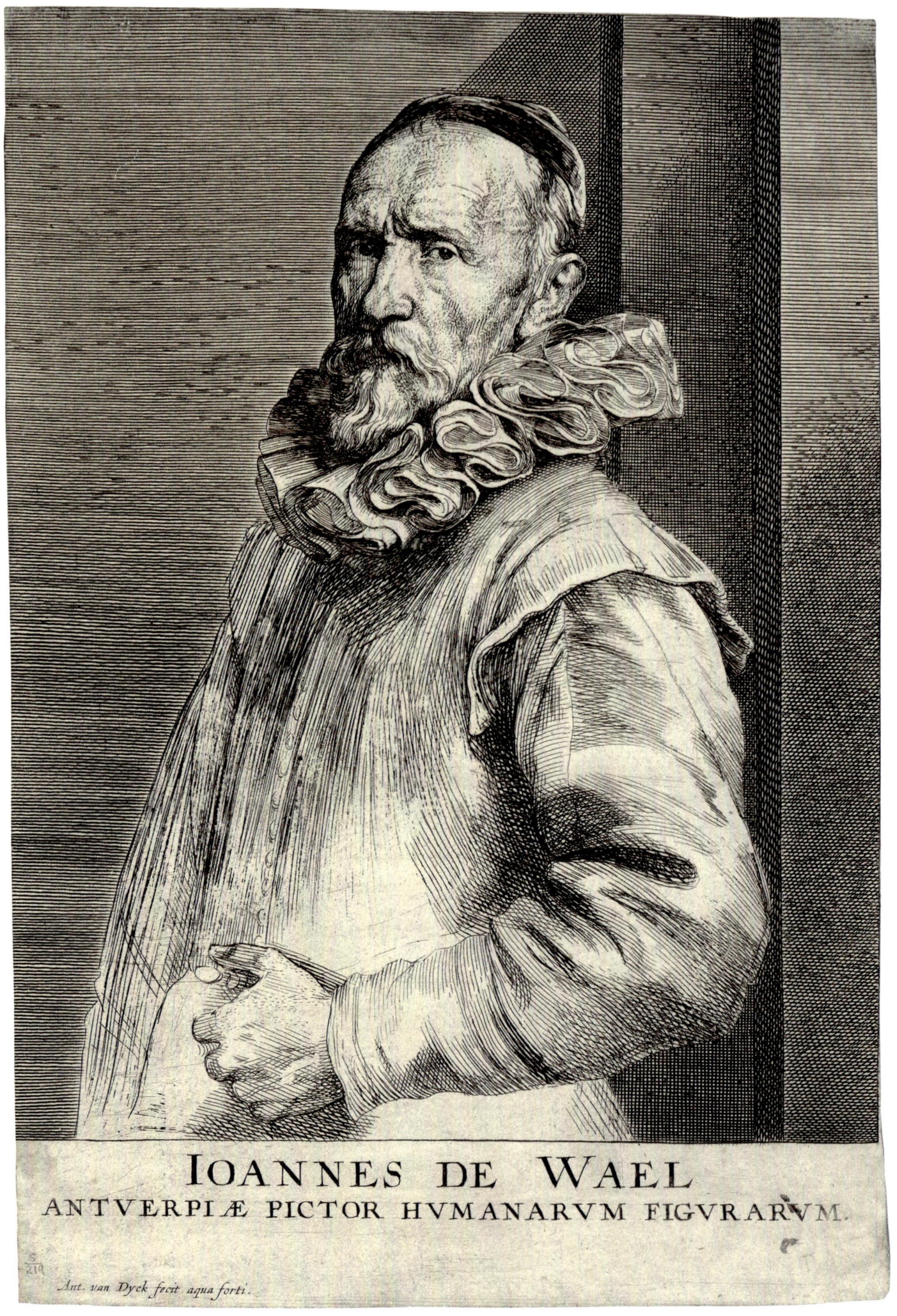

Fig. 2. Anthony van Dyck. *Jan de Wael*, 1630/33. Cat. 61.

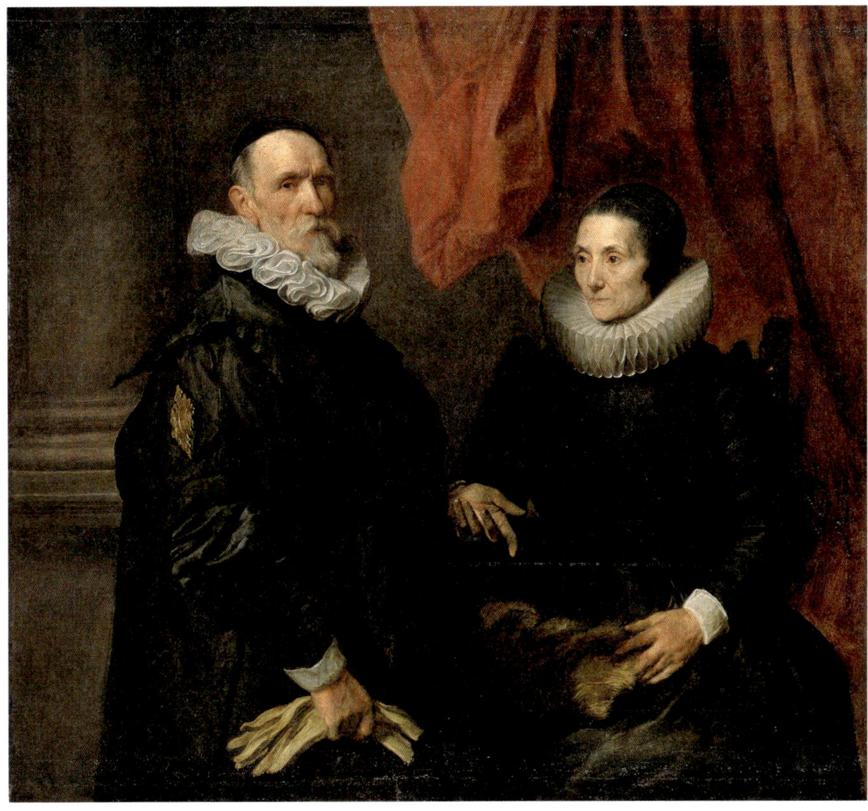

Fig 3. Anthony van Dyck. *Portrait of Jan de Wael and His Wife, Geertruid de Jode*, 1629.
Oil on canvas; 125.3 × 139.7 cm (49¼ × 54¾ in.). Bayerische Staatsgemäldesammlungen,
Alte Pinakothek, Munich.

completely excluded; moreover, the position of his left arm is more akimbo than extended, and the left hand no longer holds a pair of gloves. The setting has also been changed; where there is a stately column in the painting, in the print Van Dyck used a more abstract rendering of a beam or doorjamb.

Curiously, it is on the basis of the print—with its clarifying inscription—that the subjects of the double portrait could be identified. Though of obvious significance to Van Dyck, De Wael is excluded from artistic biographies of the seventeenth century, and even today little is known about his oeuvre. Contemporary scholars have learned that De Wael was active in his native Flanders and also in Italy, where he received the young Van Dyck on his travels there in the early 1620s.[8] De Wael's sons, Cornelis and Lucas, were also living in Italy at that time, and it appears that they adopted Van Dyck as an honorary family member. Van Dyck's choice to include De Wael as a subject in the *Iconography*, then, suggests an interest in memorializing the artists he knew personally, preserving their identities alongside those of the more celebrated aristocrats and regents of his day.

THE PROMOTION OF ONE'S PEERS

Prior to the *Iconography*, such series of portrait prints—and to a great extent portrait prints in general—had been used to commemorate political figures or intellectual leaders.[9] The concept itself can be traced to antiquity, when literary biographies were collected in unillustrated compendiums such as those by Plutarch, Varro, and Suetonius. The Renaissance interest in individual identity and expression led to the revival of this tradition in the form of such fourteenth-century

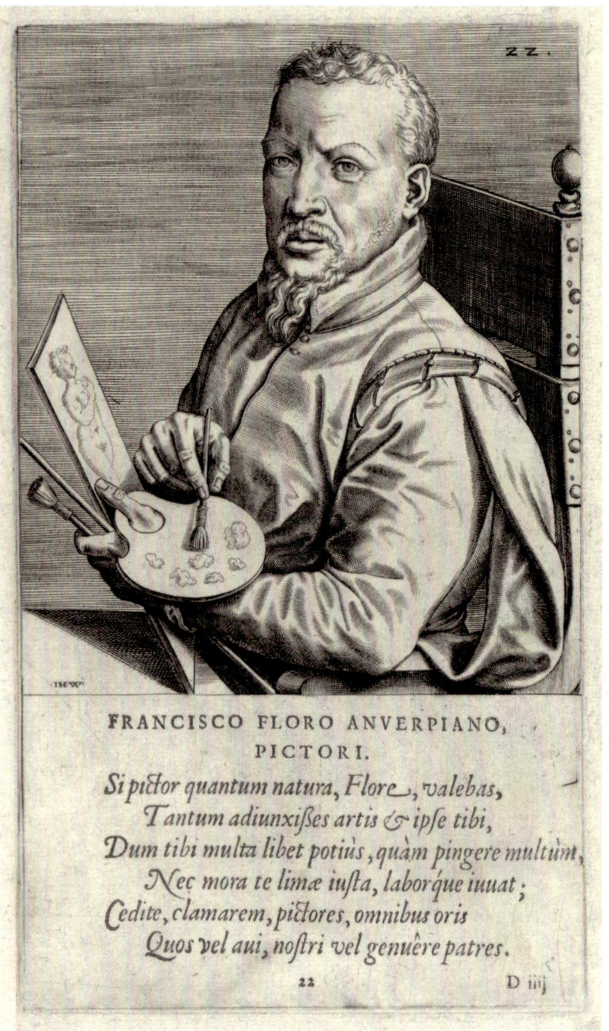

Fig. 4. Johannes Wierix (Flemish, 1539–1620). Published by Hieronymous Cock and Volcxken Diericx. *Portrait of Frans Floris*, plate 22 from *Pictorum Aliquot Celebrium Germaniae Inferioris Effigies / Francisco Floro Anwerpiano, Pictori*, 1572. Engraving on paper; 225 × 132 mm. British Museum, 1879, 0510.454.

biographical collections as Petrarch's *De viris illustribus* and Boccaccio's *De mulieribus claris*, both of which treat eminent historical and literary personalities.[10] By the middle of the sixteenth century, artists became the subjects for such works, most significantly in Giorgio Vasari's *Lives of the Artists*, the second edition of which, published in 1568, was enhanced with printed portraits. In Antwerp just four years later, Hieronymous Cock's widow, Volcxken Diericx, published his collection of twenty-two artists' portraits together with verses by Dominicus Lampsonius (see fig. 4); this was Cock's second portrait series, his first being a set depicting contemporary European rulers published in the late 1550s. Cock's prints were subsequently reused in 1610 by Hendrick Hondius for his expanded series of artists' portraits.[11] While Van Dyck's project shares with these precedents a desire to name and commemorate individual artists, what distinguishes the *Iconography* from earlier efforts is not only its more ambitious scope but also its insistence on the power of the printed image to stand on its own, relatively free of text.

A more immediate precursor to the *Iconography* is an interrelated group of portrait prints made in the circle of Hendrick Goltzius.[12] Among these is Aegedius Sadeler's double portrait of Bartolomeus Spranger and his recently deceased wife, Christina Müller (fig. 5), one of the most compelling and elaborate portrait prints to depict an artist.[13] The ambitiously large work features a different conceit for each of the principal subjects, who are surrounded by ten mythological and allegorical figures. Spranger points with his left hand toward the likeness of Müller, which is contained within an oval frame at the center of a large funerary monument.

Spranger and Müller are described through a similar use of engraving—primarily with parallel sinuous lines and diagonally oriented crosshatching to indicate shadows. The supporting allegorical figures are rendered using thicker lines and moiré patterning to define volumes. While the depictions of the couple derive from an earlier work, the designer of the print remains unknown.[14] It is possible that Sadeler invented this composition as part of his tribute to Spranger; the inscription in the text plaque below the composition states that the artist "made public the private tears of Bartolomeus Spranger out of admiration for Spranger's art and out of love for those who love him."[15]

Goltzius created a memorial portrait print (fig. 6) soon after the death of his teacher Dirck Volckhertz. Coornhert, the Dutch humanist and printmaker. Life-size in scale and austere in ornament, the portrait is a profound demonstration of Goltzius's ability to represent facial features through the restrictive graphic language of engraving. The text within the oval frame declares that the work was drawn from life (*ad vivum depictus*), a claim supported by the presence of moles

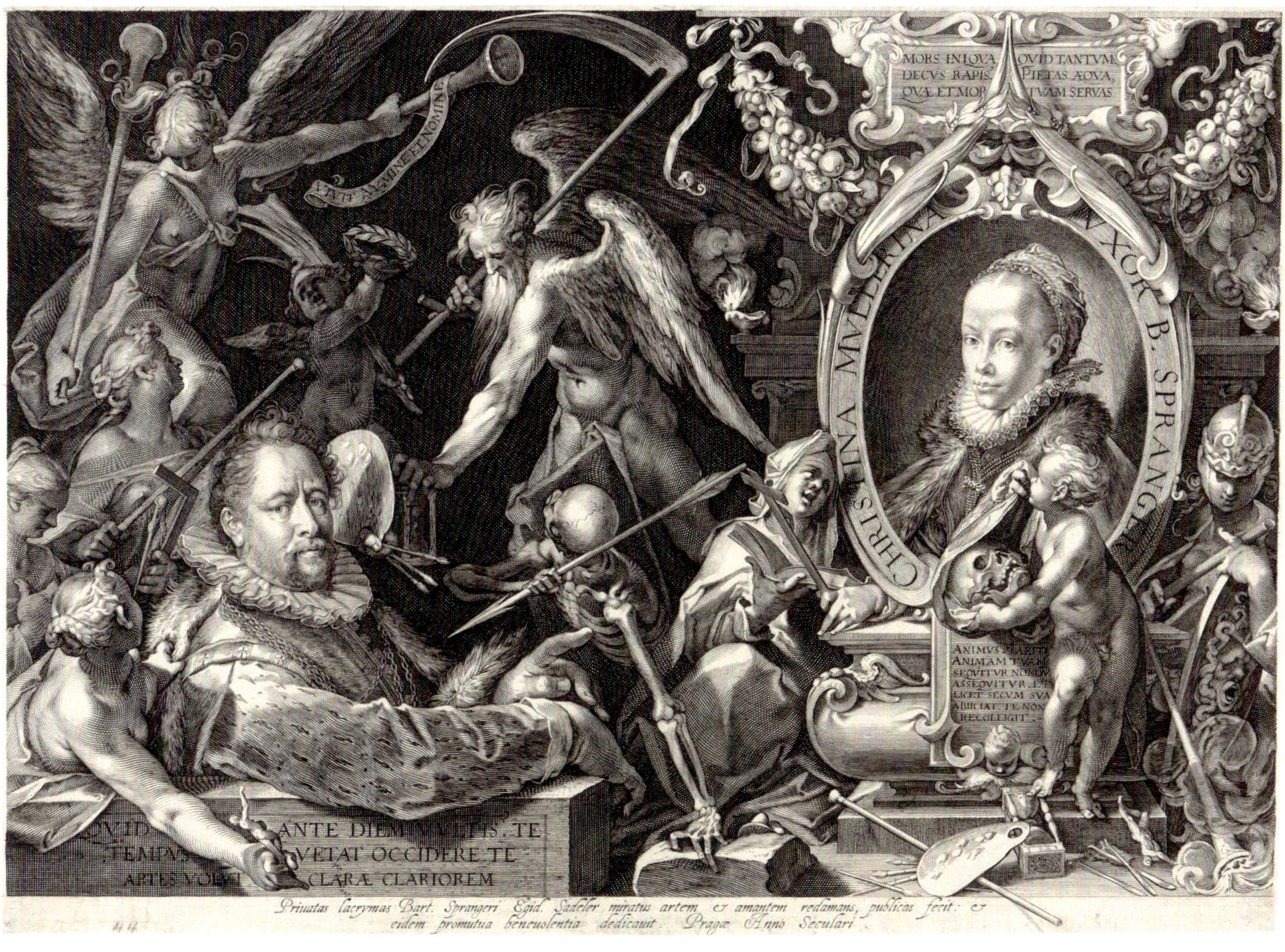

Fig. 5. Aegidius Sadeler. *Portrait of Bartolomeus Spranger with an Allegory of the Death of His Wife, Christina Müller*, 1600. Cat. 21.

and other imperfections on Coornhert's face. The print is a tour de force of the engraving technique, particularly impressive in the alternation of dense networks of crosshatching in different directions with the total absence of printed line; combined, these passages convey the strong presence of light cast on the subject's rippling mounds of flesh and the bunching fabric of his plain doublet. The exquisite and poignantly rendered face emerges from a combination of irregular curving lines—used to describe the wavy strands in the beard and the sparse ringlets at the back of the head—as well as the dot-and-lozenge pattern to define the volumes of the mouth

and cheeks. Goltzius emphasized his successful illusionism by situating the figure in front of a text frame, a choice that is underscored by the shadow cast over the words at the left.[16] Decades later, his follower Jan Muller would provide an analogous portrayal of Goltzius (fig. 7), itself based on a late self-portrait; though comparable in its monumental size and convincing representation, it is broader in the quality of line used throughout.

With the *Iconography* Van Dyck embraced the spirit of this group of friendship portraits, combining its technical innovation with a uniform aesthetic and the more expansive

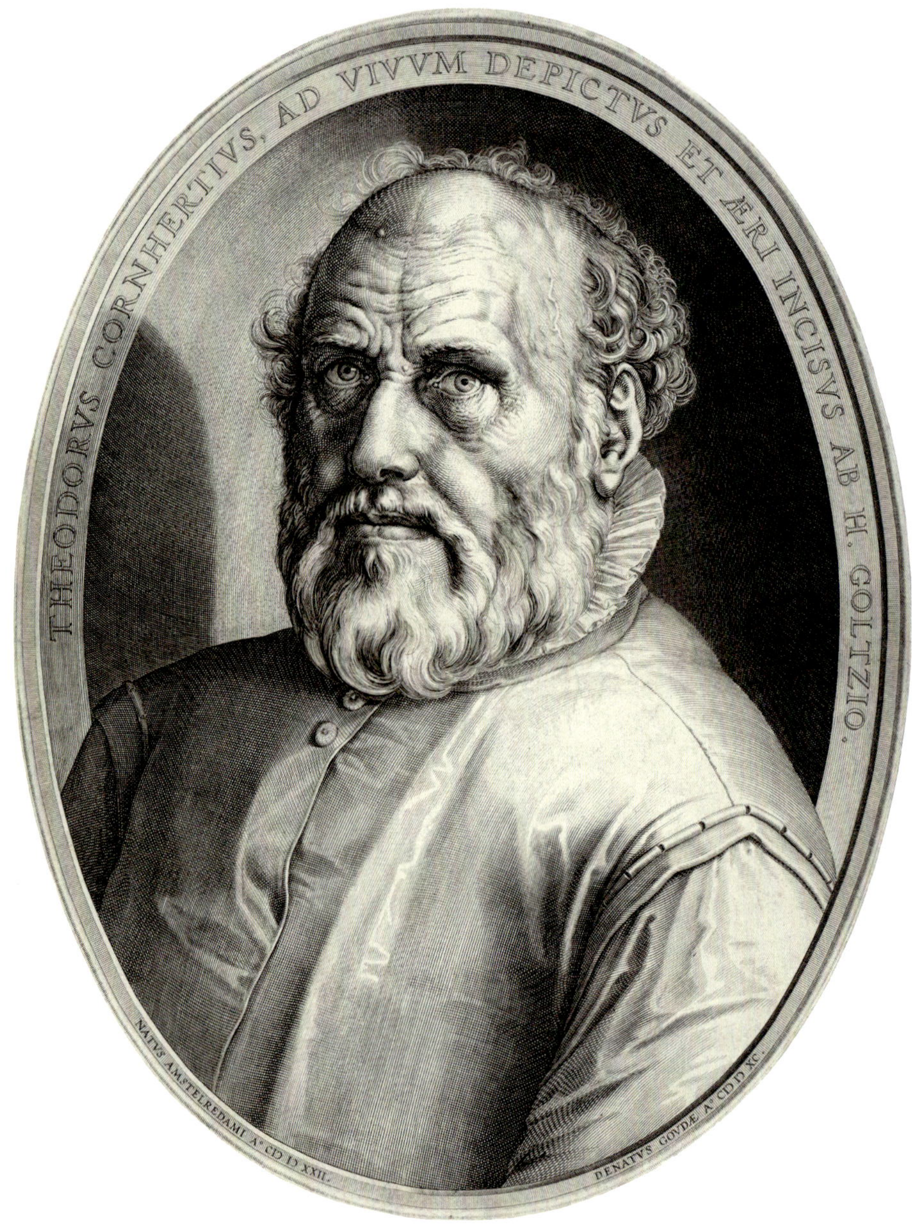

Fig. 6. Hendrick Goltzius. *Dirck Volckertsz. Coornhert (1522–1590), Author, Secretary of the City of Haarlem, Printmaker, Goltzius's Teacher*, 1591. Cat. 15.

context of a large series. Of the fifteen etchings Van Dyck created himself, almost all portray artists with whom he had a personal relationship.[17] In addition to De Wael, whom he knew especially well because of his travel to Italy, he etched portraits of artists Jan Brueghel the Elder (cat. 44), Lucas Vorsterman (fig. 8), Paulus Pontius (fig. 9), and Frans Snyders (p. 60, fig. 23)—all of whom were associated with Van Dyck during their time working within the orbit of Rubens in Antwerp. In the portraits of Vorsterman and Pontius, Van Dyck used similar devices to different ends. Each sitter looks out of the picture plane to the viewer's left—over his right shoulder, which is closer to the space of the viewer—and is

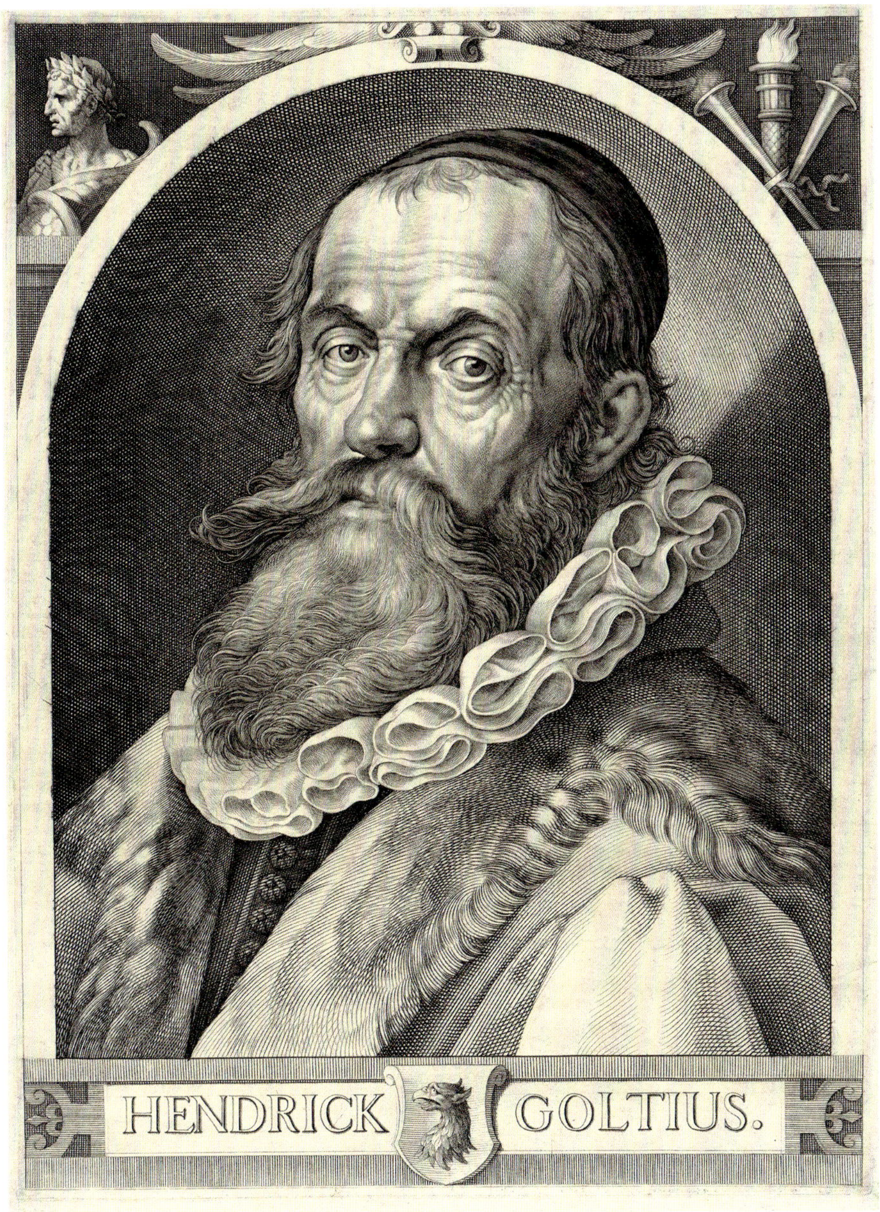

Fig. 7. Jan Harmensz. Muller. After Hendrick Goltzius.
Portrait of Hendrick Goltzius, c. 1617. Cat. 27.

shown in half-length, following the convention of the series. Finally, both use their right arms and hands—in Vorsterman's case to hold closed a draped overcoat, in Pontius's to indicate something unseen below. Despite the consistencies in the figures' positions, Van Dyck's description of each man's facial features results in dramatically different characterizations.

Vorsterman's firmly pursed lips, together with wide eyes whose gripping focus is further enhanced by the angular hatching around the brow and cheekbones, assert an intensity of character that is equal parts confidence and disdain. Pontius's face, on the other hand, with its soft creases under the eyes and gently upturned corners of the mouth, expresses a

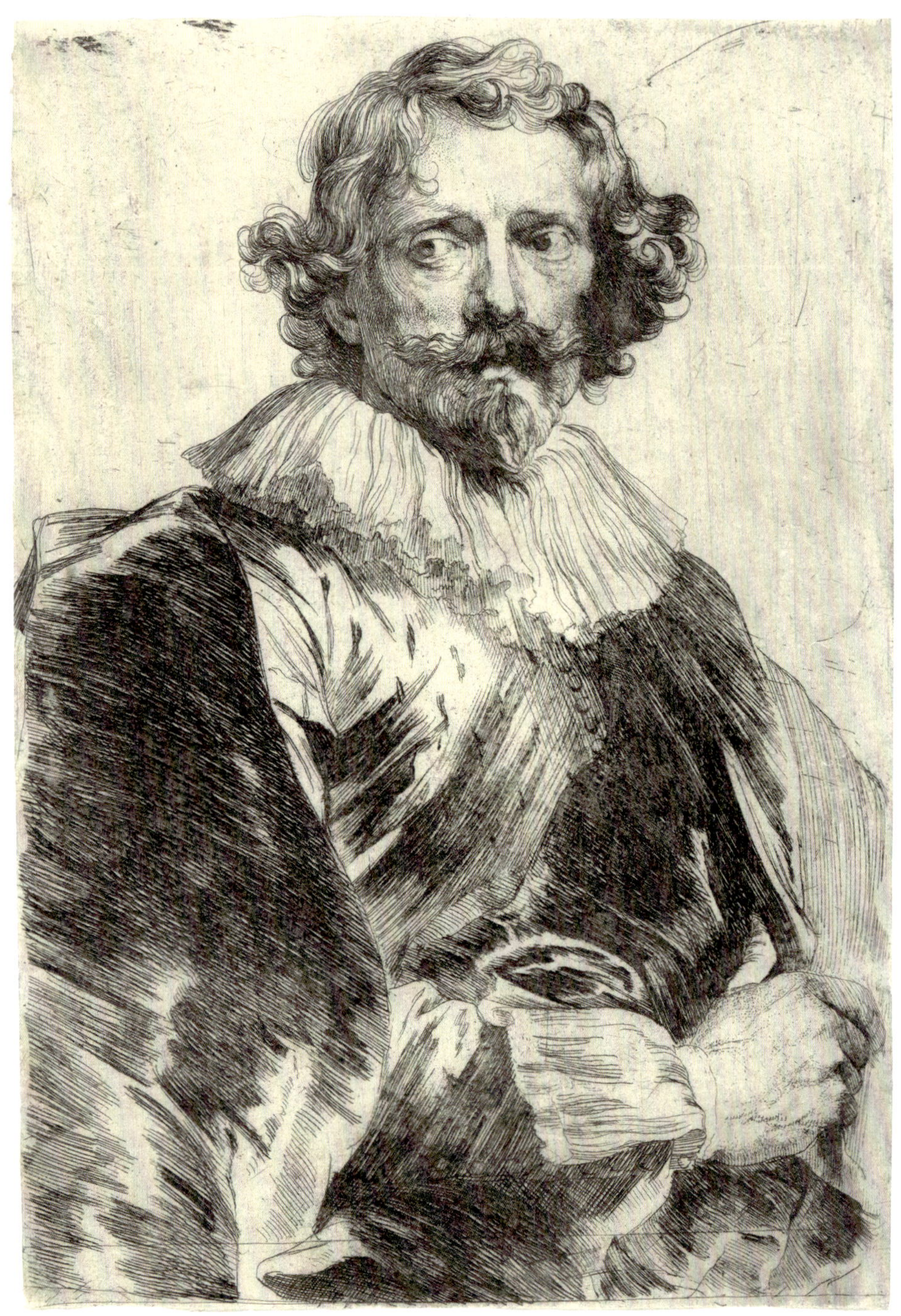

Fig. 8. Anthony van Dyck. *Lucas Vorsterman*, 1630/33. Cat. 55.

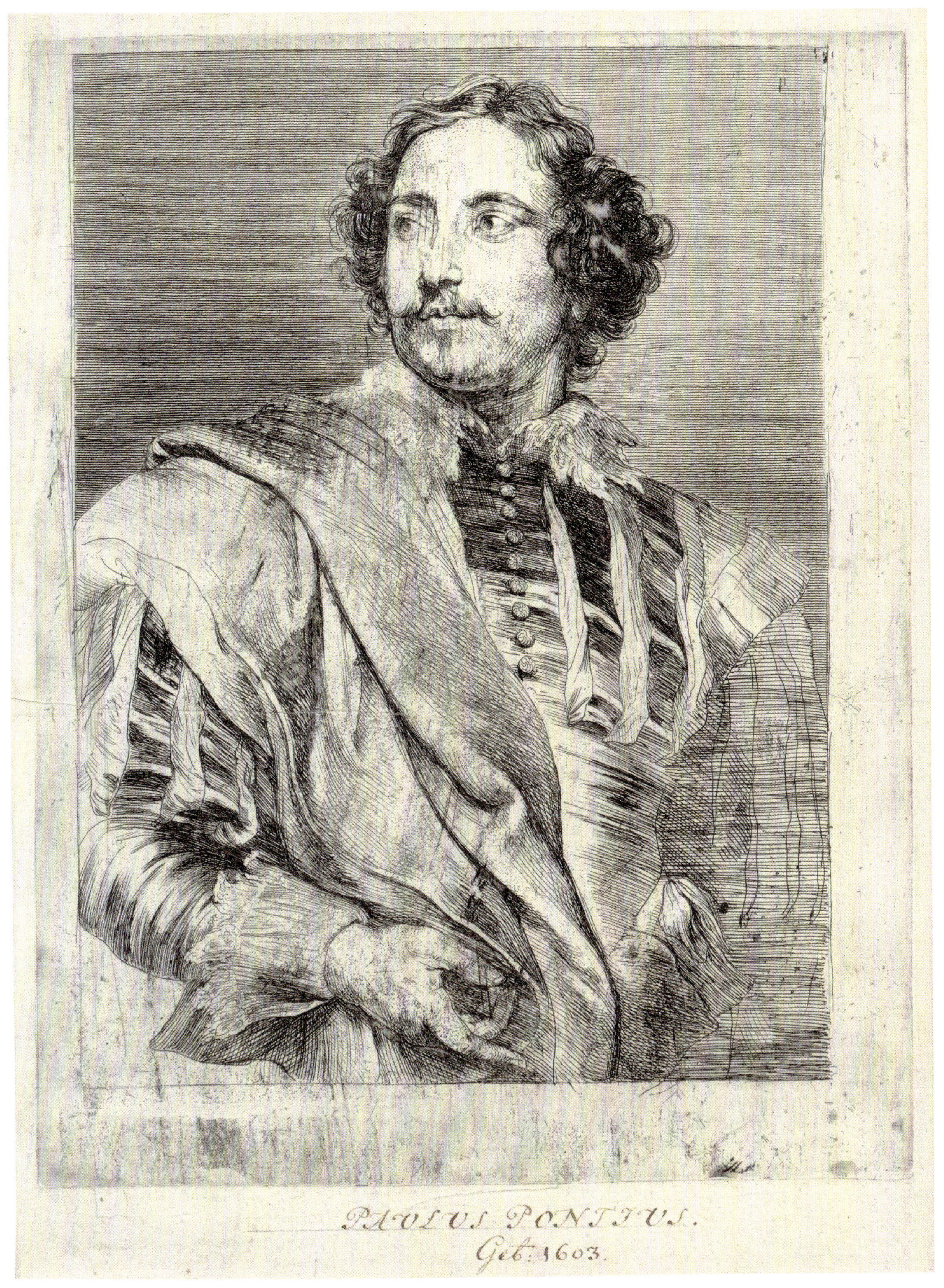

Fig. 9. Anthony van Dyck. *Paulus Pontius*, 1630/33. Cat. 50.

gentleness of demeanor and a quiet fearlessness. Indeed, in these two portrait prints we see how Van Dyck could express a depth of personality in his treatment of the face alone.

The generation of artists immediately following Van Dyck, including Rembrandt van Rijn and his contemporaries, also found among their peers compelling subjects for innovative portrait prints. Jan Lievens emulated Van Dyck in his style and choice of subjects, as can be seen in his portrait of the French-born lutenist Jacques Gaultier (fig. 10), one of only a few prints made by the artist and his first formal portrait print.[18] Lievens and Gaultier met while both were working in the court of the English king Charles I from 1632 to 1635, overlapping during that time with Van Dyck, who had returned to London early in 1632 to serve as the king's principal painter.[19] Though rather stiff in its description of Gaultier's facial features and general posture compared with Van Dyck's etchings, Lievens's portrait does reflect a shared desire to ennoble the sitter: the dedicatory text indicates that it was created as an expression of "true friendship."[20] If the friendship of the artist and his subject was the impetus for the work, Gaultier's popularity at court and beyond also assured a ready market for Lievens. Charles I's patronage of the arts—both visual and performing—was of international renown, and his discerning taste has long been celebrated.[21] Lievens's portrait print, then, could be seen as serving three simultaneous functions: the promotion of the sitter, a fellow artist; the promotion of the artist by association with the court of Charles I; and, for the print's owner, the declaration of his own status within the inner circle of the English king.

Rembrandt never left the Netherlands and therefore would have come into Van Dyck's orbit during the latter's stay in The Hague in 1631–32, when Van Dyck made a portrait study of the humanist and statesman Constantijn Huygens, who was also a patron and promoter of both Rembrandt and Lievens.[22] While it cannot be proven that Van Dyck and Rembrandt ever met, Rembrandt's interest in Van Dyck's work is evident through a comparison of their oeuvres, and further, through a well-known reference in Rembrandt's bankruptcy inventory of 1656. Among the possessions that Rembrandt was obliged to put up for sale were works by other artists, the listing of which provides crucial insight into his

sources of inspiration. Within the art room (*kunst caemer*) the following is recorded: "A book full of portraits such as those by Van Dyck, Rubens, and various other old masters."[23] Van Dyck's influence on Rembrandt is apparent in the latter's use of state changes, experimentation with degrees of finish, and interest in portraying his artistic peers as well as himself. Compared with the sitters of his painted portraits, with whom he often had brief and merely contractual interactions, the subjects of his portrait prints were typically people he really knew.[24] One example was Jan Lutma, whom Rembrandt depicted in a poignant etching of 1656. In the Art Institute's early state of this print (fig. 11), the background has not been fully realized; only the recession of the wall is indicated by a dramatic shift from the shadow-cast plane at the composition's far left to the bright passage perpendicular to it. This first state was produced in fairly large numbers; nearly fifty impressions have been documented in museum collections, not including counterproofs, of which there are also several.[25] Eyes cast down, arms resting on both sides of a high-backed armchair, Lutma seems pleasantly lost in thought. The stippling in the forehead and short lines in the eyes and cheeks recall techniques employed by Van Dyck. Lutma's son, who took up the silversmithing trade and also created a small group of portrait prints, provided a fascinating contrast to Rembrandt's portrayal (fig. 12). In his portrait, the younger Lutma embraced the ancient tradition of the portrait bust and cast his father in the role of a poet or emperor.[26]

While in his portrait of Lutma—as well as in his depictions of the physician Ephraim Bonus (cat. 74) and the Mennonite preacher Cornelis Claesz. Anslo (cat. 72)—Rembrandt embraced the ennobling characterizations commonly found in Van Dyck's portrait etchings, in other cases he made several interesting departures from the model set by Van Dyck. For example, Rembrandt's 1651 portrait of the print and map dealer Clement de Jonghe—in which the artist was able to convey character despite hiding portions of the sitter's face in shadow—provides a stark contrast to Van Dyck's emphasis on facial expressions and facial features.[27] Rembrandt positioned the subject close to the space of the viewer, with no object or text to intervene. Despite this immediacy, De Jonghe's hat and overcoat mask the contours of his head and body; he is close

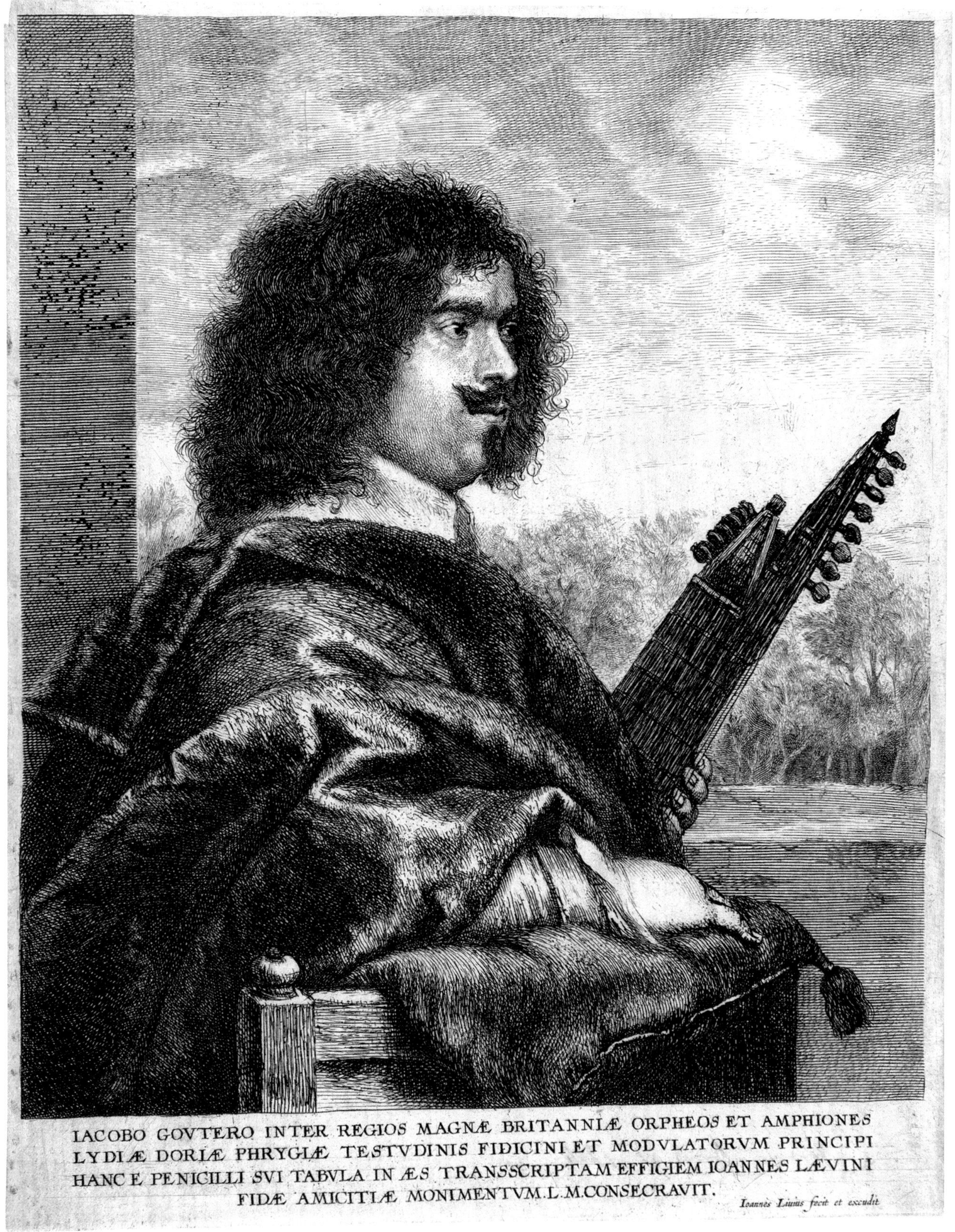

Fig. 10. Jan Lievens. *Portrait of Jacques Gaultier*, 1632/35. Cat. 84.

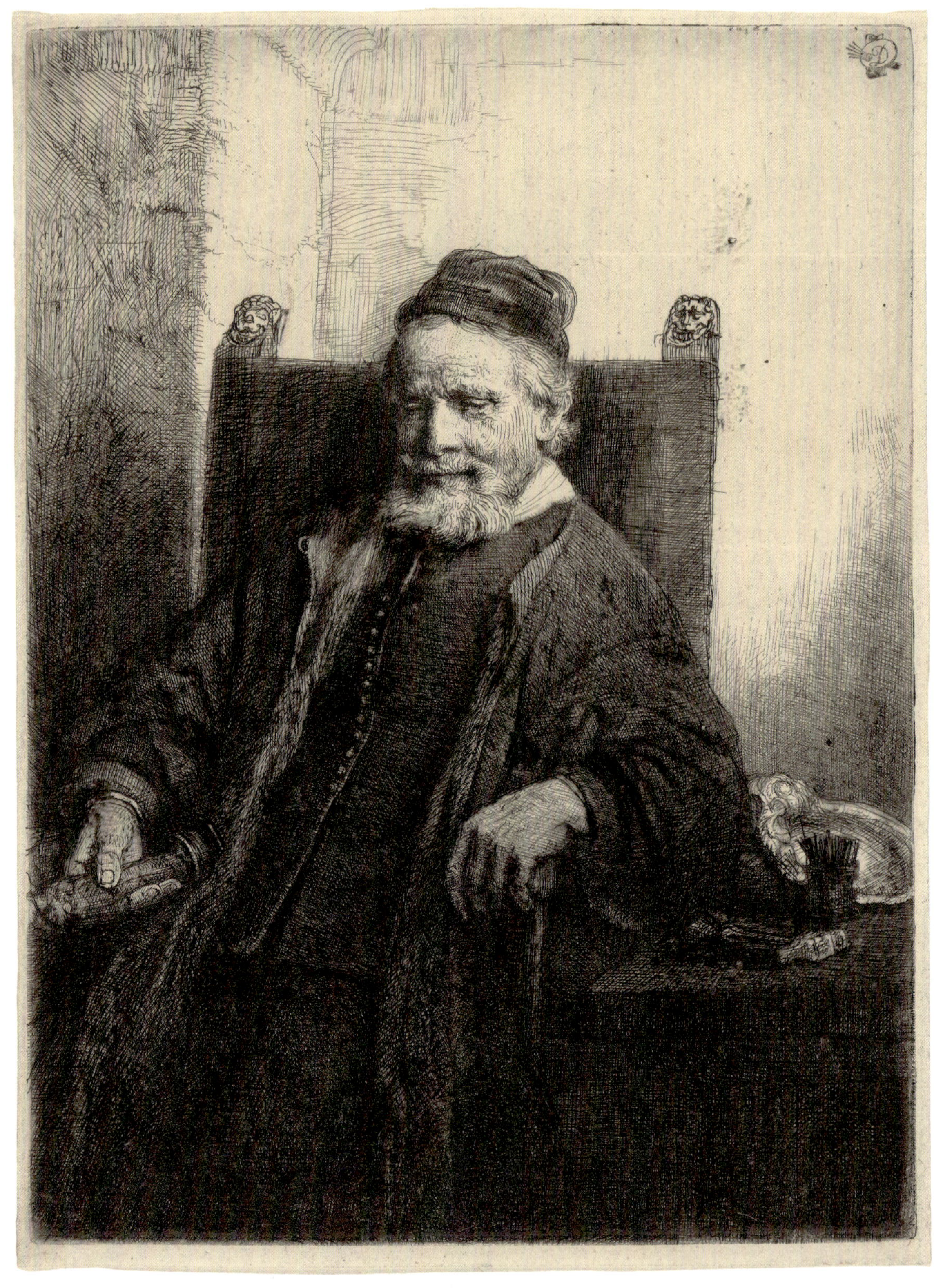

Fig. 11. Rembrandt van Rijn. *Jan Lutma, Goldsmith*, 1656. Cat. 78. Shown at actual size.

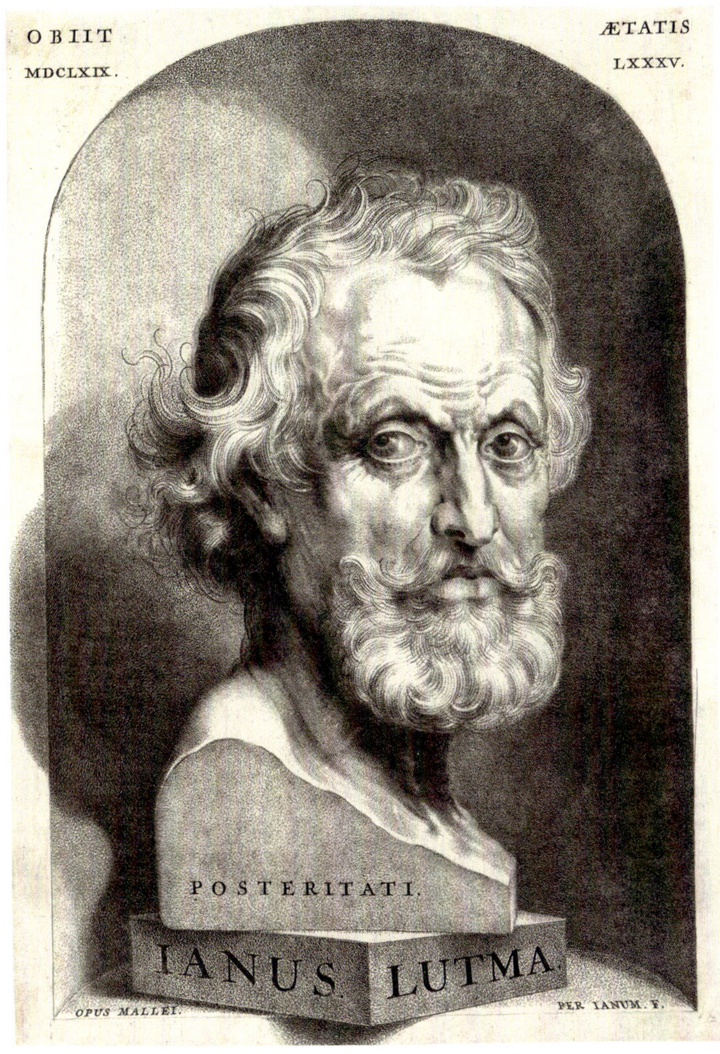

Fig. 12. Jan Lutma II. *Father Lutma*, 1669/81. Cat. 97.

but remains inaccessible. In the first state (fig. 13), the wall behind De Jonghe is described only vaguely. In the third state (fig. 14), an archway has been drawn in, making the relationship between figure and ground both tighter and more explicit, as if the chair has been placed closer to the wall. The shadows cast on the face are darker, with the light more restricted and directional compared with the more diffuse treatment of light in the earlier state. Here De Jonghe appears suspicious, even menacing; by obscuring the subject's face, Rembrandt calls into question the primary function of portraiture: Is the artist meant to capture the sitter's likeness or rather evoke a sense of his spirit? This portrait may also be viewed as a reflection on the relationship between subject and artist, who were connected through their professions. At some point during Rembrandt's lifetime, De Jonghe took possession of seventy-four of Rembrandt's etching plates. We can infer that De Jonghe was not only aware of Rembrandt's profound financial difficulties, but also that he intervened to allay the artist's debts, however insurmountable.[28] The intimacy implied by this portrait suggests not only Rembrandt and De Jonghe's shared knowledge of the art trade but also the growing appeal of unconventional portrait prints.

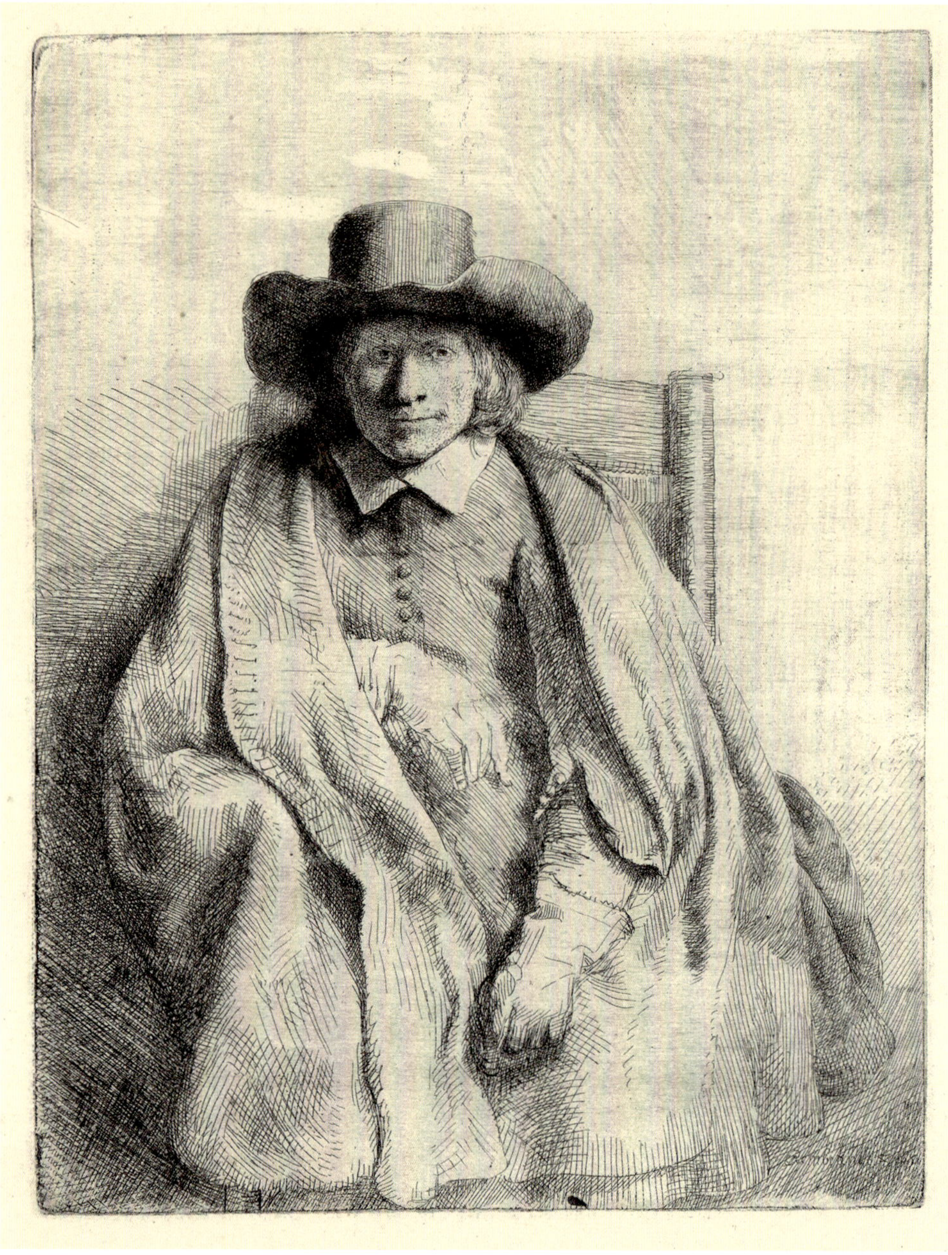

Fig. 13. Rembrandt van Rijn. *Clement de Jonghe, Printseller*, 1651. Cat. 76.

The Art Institute's impression of the third state of Rembrandt's portrait of De Jonghe was in the hands of the nineteenth-century painter and printmaker James McNeill Whistler, a leading figure in the Etching Revival. In addition to his early exposure to Rembrandt's etchings through the collection of his brother-in-law, Seymour Haden, Whistler also came in contact with the print toward the end of his life via Edward G. Kennedy, a dealer and the first cataloguer of his etchings. Whistler was so overcome by the print that he felt compelled to write directly on its mount: "Without flaw! Beautiful as a Greek marble—or a canvas by Tintoret. A masterpiece in all its elements—beyond which there is

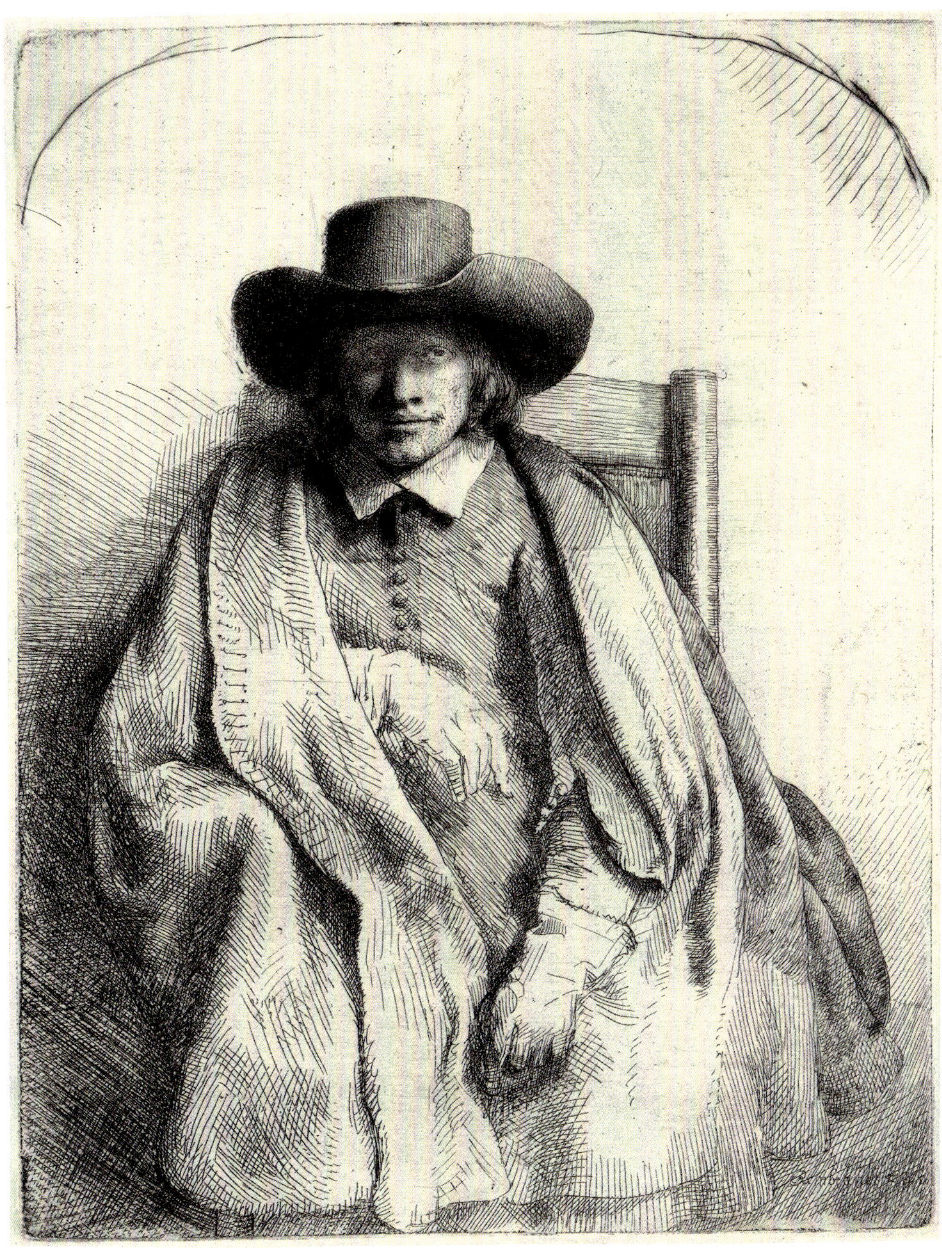

Fig. 14. Rembrandt van Rijn. *Clement de Jonghe, Printseller*, 1651. Cat. 77.

nothing."[29] Like Rembrandt and Van Dyck before him, Whistler employed printmaking to capture a personal relationship with an artistic peer. Like fellow members of the Etching Revival movement, Whistler engaged with the medium in part to reassert its status as a fine art. His etched portrait of the sculptor-musician Just Becquet (fig. 15)

describes its subject sitting to play the cello. Whistler placed the figure in direct confrontation with the viewer, choosing to situate Becquet's face at the very upper limit of the composition and leaving—in all six states of the print—the instrument and the sitter's body incomplete.[30] Whistler's interest in Rembrandt goes well beyond contact with a single print.

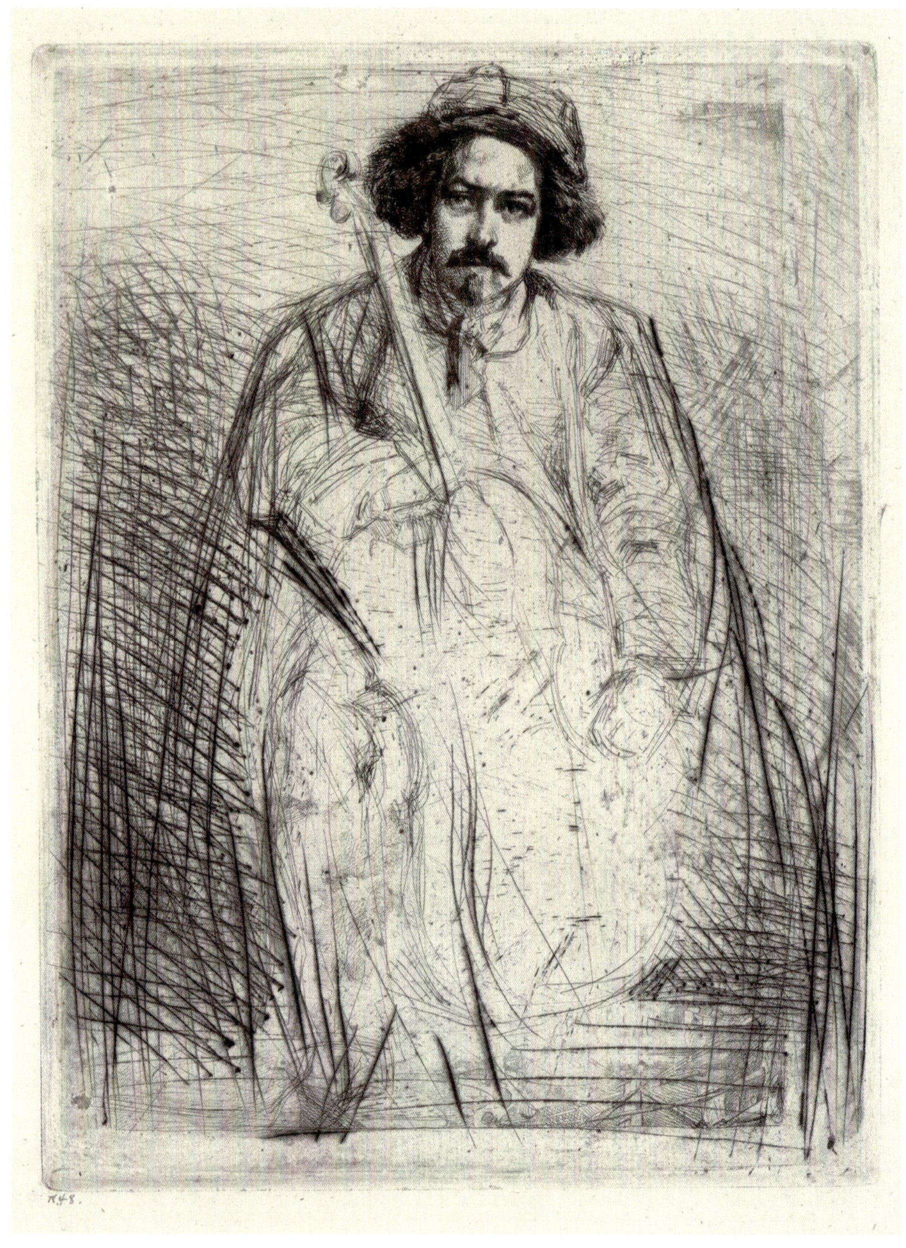

Fig. 15. James McNeill Whistler. *J. Becquet, Sculptor*, 1859. Cat. 127.

Early in his etching career, he was exposed to Haden's collection of Rembrandt etchings, still considered one of the best ever assembled. In his portrait of Becquet and in his regular use of state changes, selected wiping, and varied paper choice, Whistler employed some of the strategies used to best advantage by Rembrandt and to a lesser extent Van Dyck.

In his elaborate portrait of leading art dealer and critic Edmond de Goncourt (fig. 16), which in later states includes fully realized costume details and additional symbolically charged objects, Félix Bracquemond similarly evoked familiarity with the subject while experimenting both with highly finished passages describing the face and with the blank

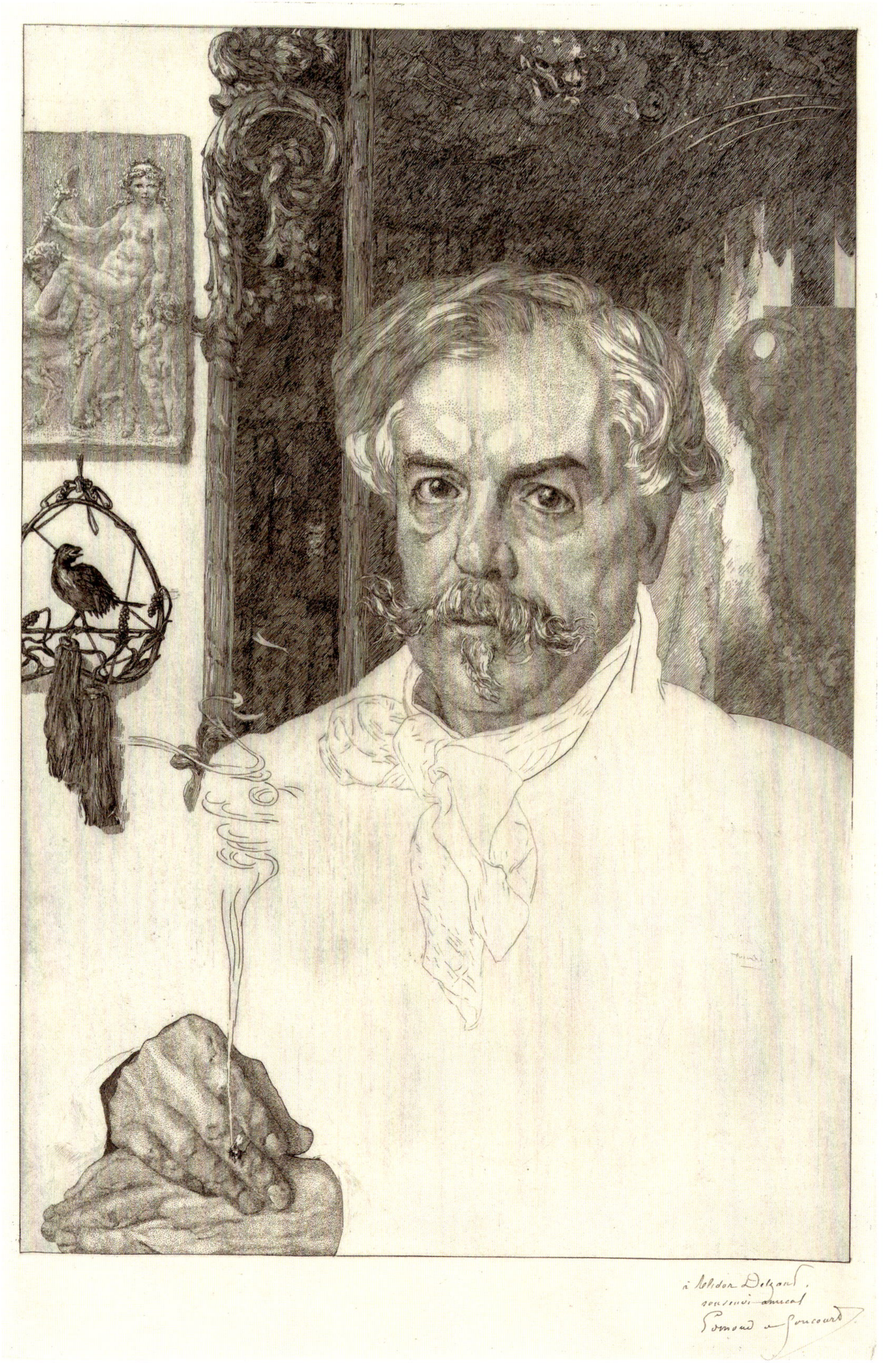

Fig. 16. Félix Bracquemond. *Portrait of Edmond de Goncourt*, 1882. Cat. 125.

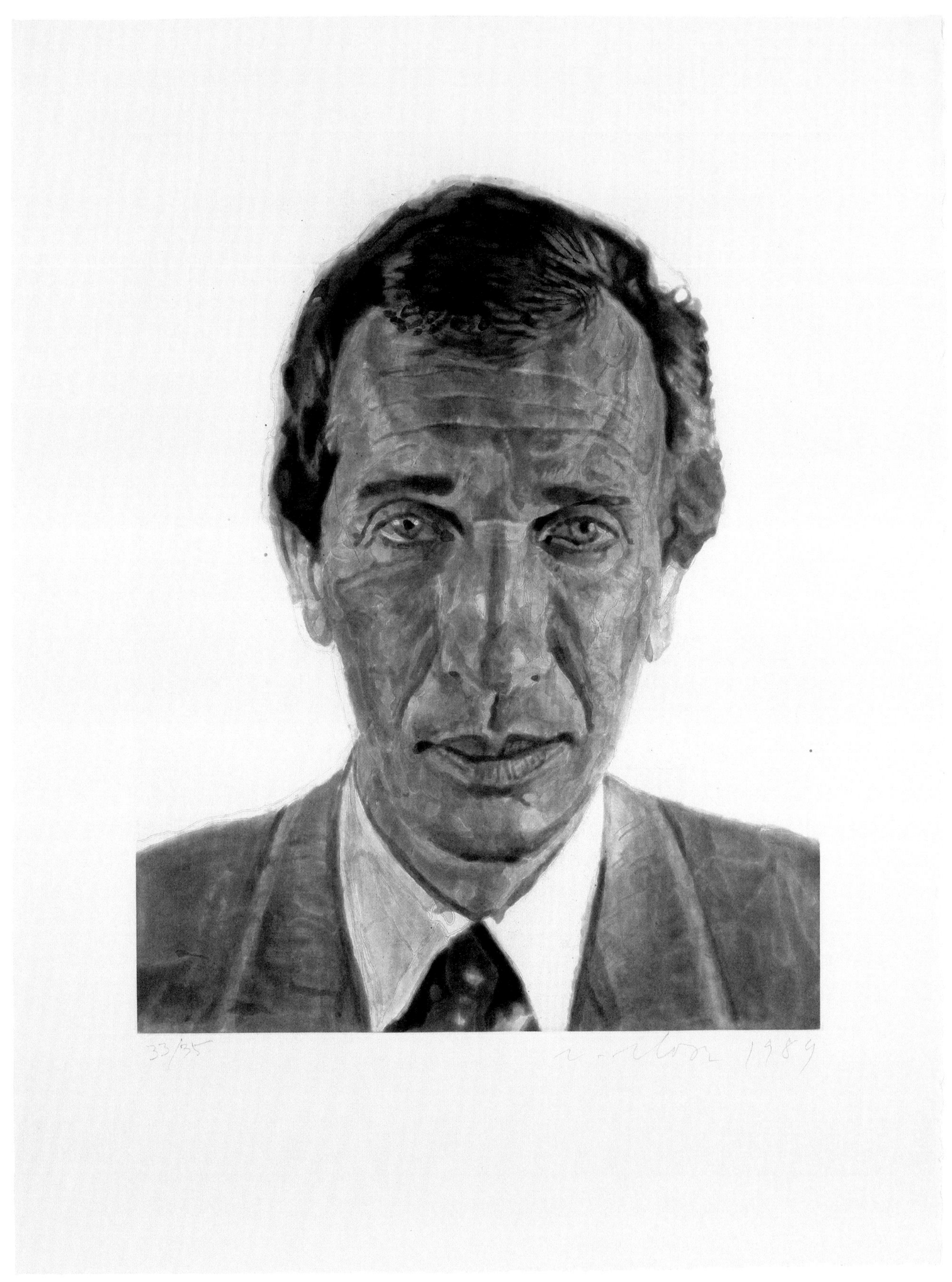

Fig. 17. Chuck Close. *Arne*, 1989. Cat. 137.

expanses of the reserve in the center of the composition. As did Van Dyck with a number of the early states of his portrait prints, it seems that Bracquemond considered the early states of his portrait of Goncourt successful enough to warrant printing multiple impressions.[31] The Art Institute's impression of the first state was dedicated to the artist's friend and fellow collector Alidor Delzant; this inscription underscores how portrait prints—from the circle of Goltzius through later centuries—have served both as gestures of friendship within artistic communities and as a means of mutual promotion.[32]

Indeed, the tradition of artists depicting other members of their creative communities in portrait prints has endured to the present day. During Van Dyck's time, the status of the artist was pointedly at stake, but for Whistler and others of the nineteenth and twentieth centuries, the impulse to create such likenesses may have had more to do with familiarity and shared experience. One striking example from recent decades is Chuck Close's etched portrait of Arne Glimcher (fig. 17), the founder of Pace Gallery and Close's dealer for more than three decades. The choice of subject echoes Rembrandt's portrayal of De Jonghe, but the work's monumentality demands the viewer's immediate attention rather differently than do Rembrandt's or Van Dyck's more intimate etched portraits. Like Bracquemond, Whistler, and others before him, Close created this portrait print not only to capture a likeness, but also to deploy the expressive reach of his craft. The artist achieved tonal variation by applying ferric chloride to the plate, using a paintbrush to deliver the acid directly and varying the length of time that it was exposed to different sections.[33] The portrait is at once a virtuosic display of technique and also a loving tribute to a friend and fellow inhabitant of the late twentieth-century New York art world.

AN EXPERIMENTAL AESTHETIC

Rembrandt and Whistler, among many others, embraced Van Dyck's practice of realizing different artistic ends through state changes in their portrait prints. Perhaps equally compelling to his followers was the raw, unfinished aesthetic of his portrait etchings, which seem to anticipate the modern taste

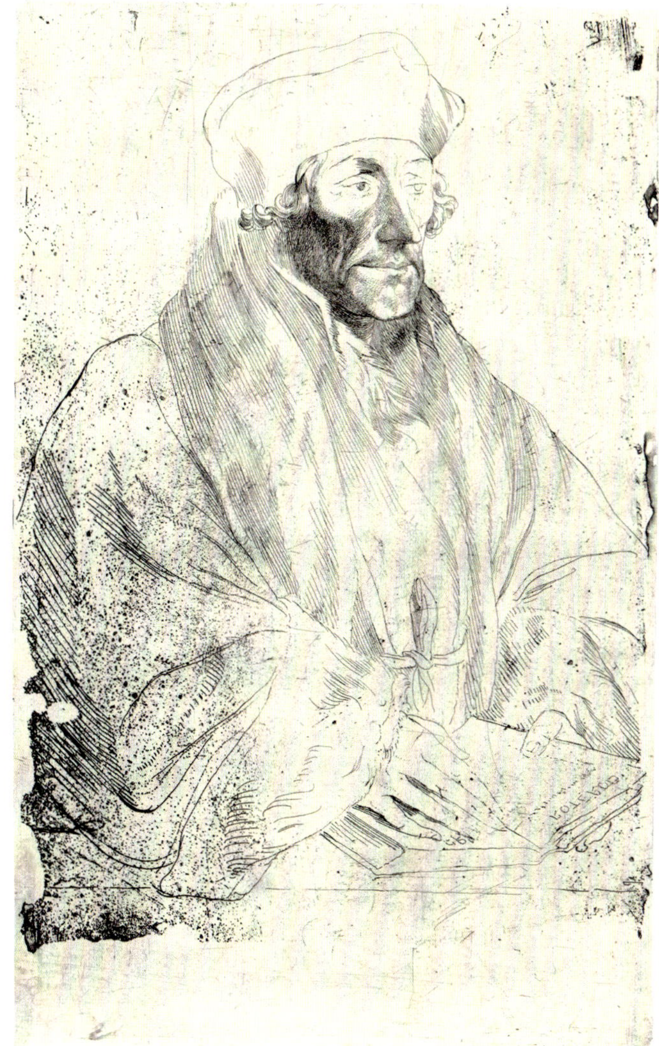

Fig. 18. Anthony van Dyck. After Hans Holbein the Younger. *Desiderius Erasmus*, 1630/33. Cat. 46.

for fragmentation and coarseness. While in his paintings Van Dyck may have achieved a celebrated level of refinement, his etchings fall far from perfection in their incomplete treatment of their subjects and also in their evident lack of technical proficiency.[34] Among the most beloved of these etchings, the portrait of Erasmus (fig. 18) displays all the shortcomings of Van Dyck's personal printmaking practice. The far left margin shows the results of foul biting (unintentional etching of the plate from an uneven application of the ground), which

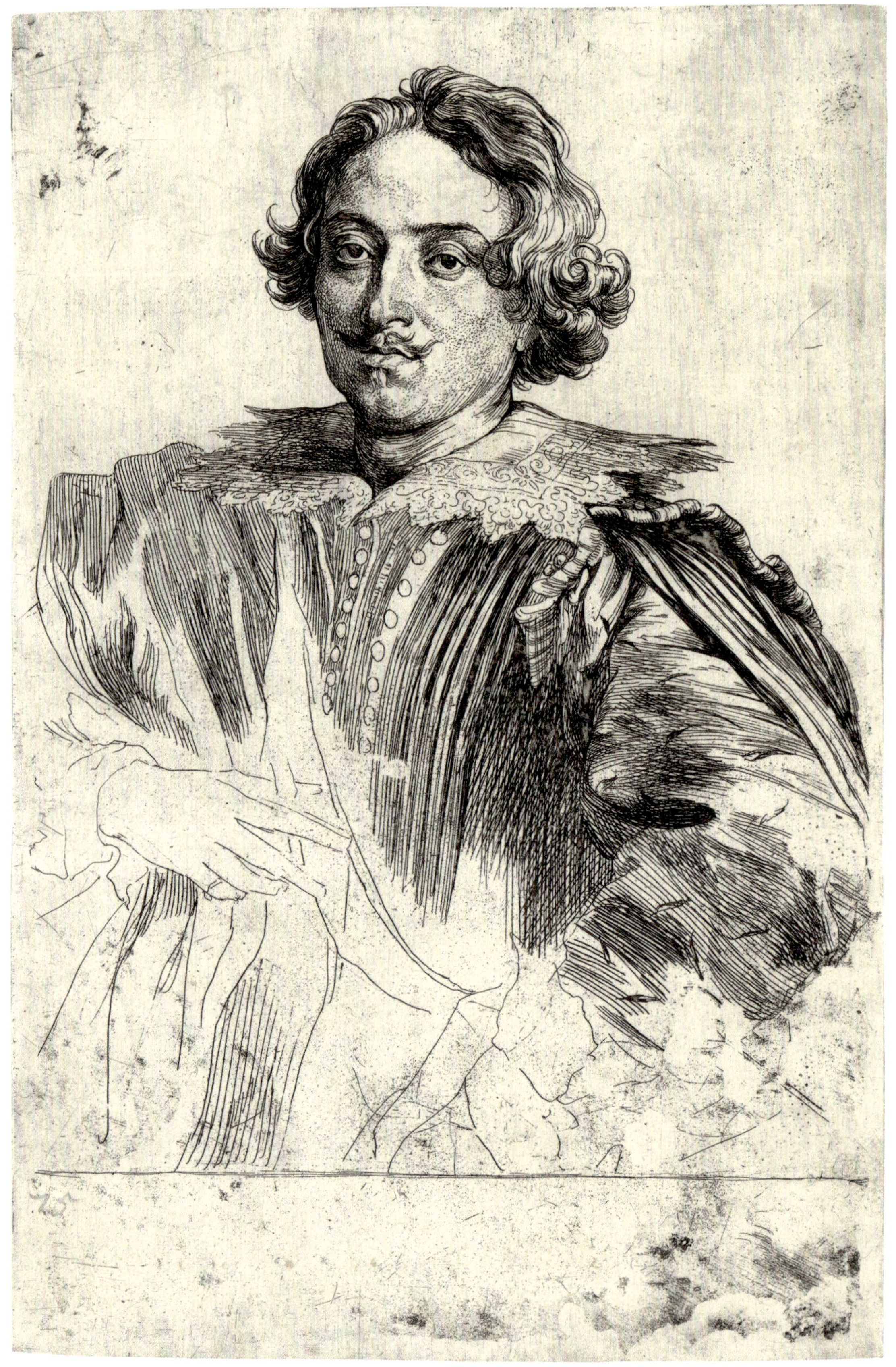

Fig. 19. Anthony van Dyck. *Justus Sustermans*, 1630/33. Cat. 54.

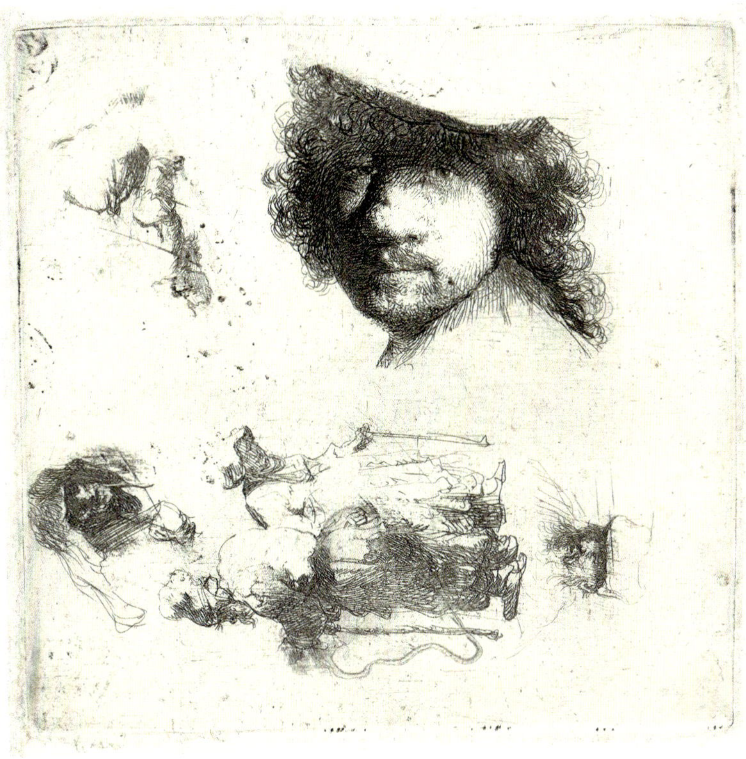

Fig. 20. Rembrandt van Rijn. *Sheet of Studies: Head of the Artist, a Beggar Couple, Heads of an Old Man and Old Woman, Etc.*, 1632. Cat. 69.

also can be seen in the portrait of Justus Sustermans (fig. 19); at the right margin, stopping-out varnish has been applied rather casually, resulting in large patches of biting where a clear margin was intended; and vertical scratches are visible in the upper register, a result of sanding of the plate with sandstone instead of polishing it with a finer, gentler substance like breadcrumbs. The most fastidious printmakers of Van Dyck's day regularly printed an unetched or unengraved plate after it had been polished to be sure that no scratches would appear in a printed impression, a habit Van Dyck clearly did not embrace. Furthermore, a number of the artist's etchings, including his portrait of De Wael, show uneven, visibly wavy plate marks, a sign that the plates had been cut before they had been pounded flat. None of these imperfections must have mattered very much to Van Dyck, who likely assumed that in later states the subjects would be not only more fully realized by his assistants but also disburdened

of their blemishes. In some cases this was indeed borne out, but a handful of Van Dyck's rather rough and unfinished prints, his portrait of Erasmus among them, found their place in the larger series without significant "improvement."[35] Of course, these are the very works that are most appealing today, and some were even celebrated by print enthusiasts in the artist's own time.

As with his choice of subject matter, Rembrandt most likely drew inspiration from Van Dyck's radical approach to the preparation of his etching plates. In a sheet of studies with a self-portrait from 1632 (fig. 20), he conceived his likeness in a pose similar to Van Dyck's unfinished self-portrait (p. 28, fig. 12) and juxtaposed it with studies of beggars drawn in a different direction and on a considerably smaller scale. As has been noted, early impressions of this print demonstrate a number of the irregularities also seen in Van Dyck's portrait etchings—most notably foul biting and an uneven plate mark.[36]

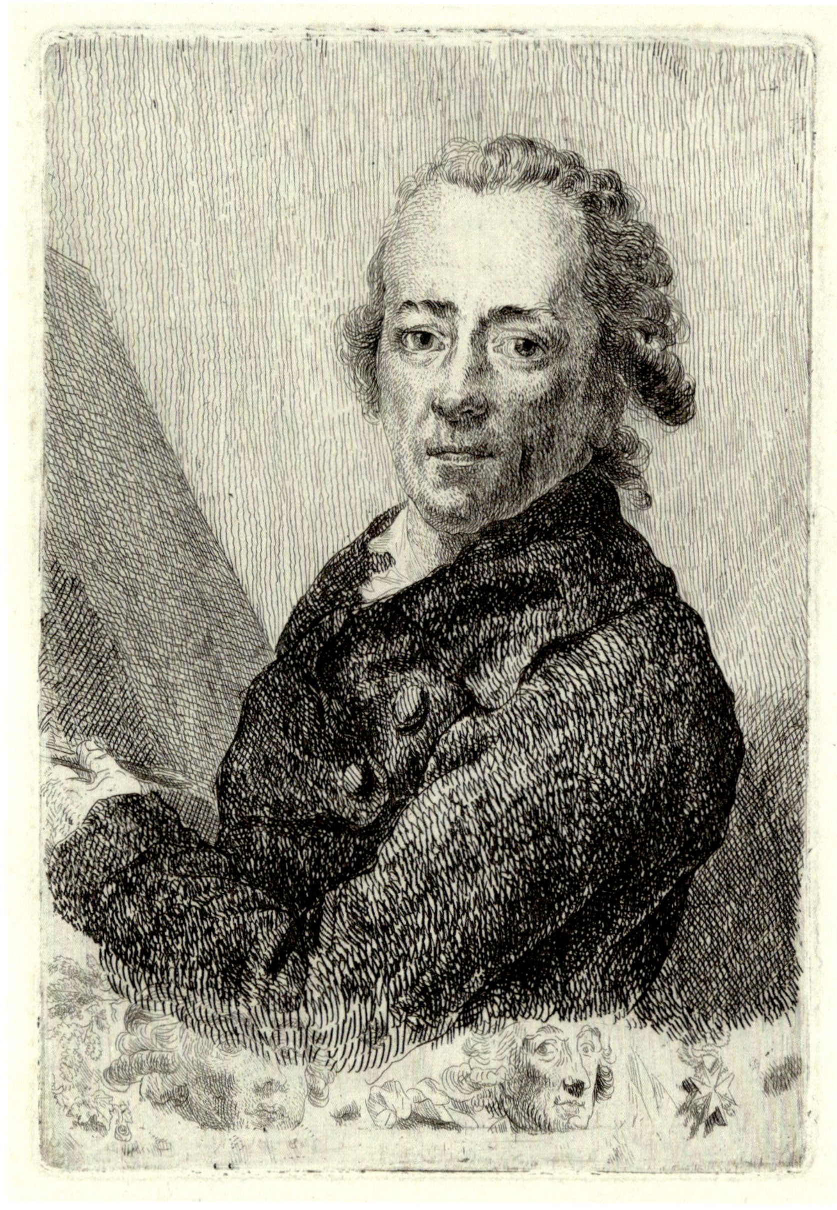

Fig. 21. Anton Graff. *Self-Portrait before an Easel*, c. 1787. Cat. 117.

More than a century later, Swiss portrait specialist Anton Graff employed a similar conceit, incorporating in an early state of a self-portrait a group of sketches at the lower margin of the plate (fig. 21). These sketches would be burnished out in later states.[37]

Several decades later Edgar Degas realized an impressive self-portrait etching (fig. 22) in which he also embraced an unfinished aesthetic, demonstrated most notably in the striking contrast between the delicate web of hatching in the face and the broad fields of foul biting found at the edges of the composition. In this print, Degas adopted a narrow, vertical format, which he would also use for what today are considered some of his most famous works.[38] Within this compressed frame, the body of the artist emerges at the lower register

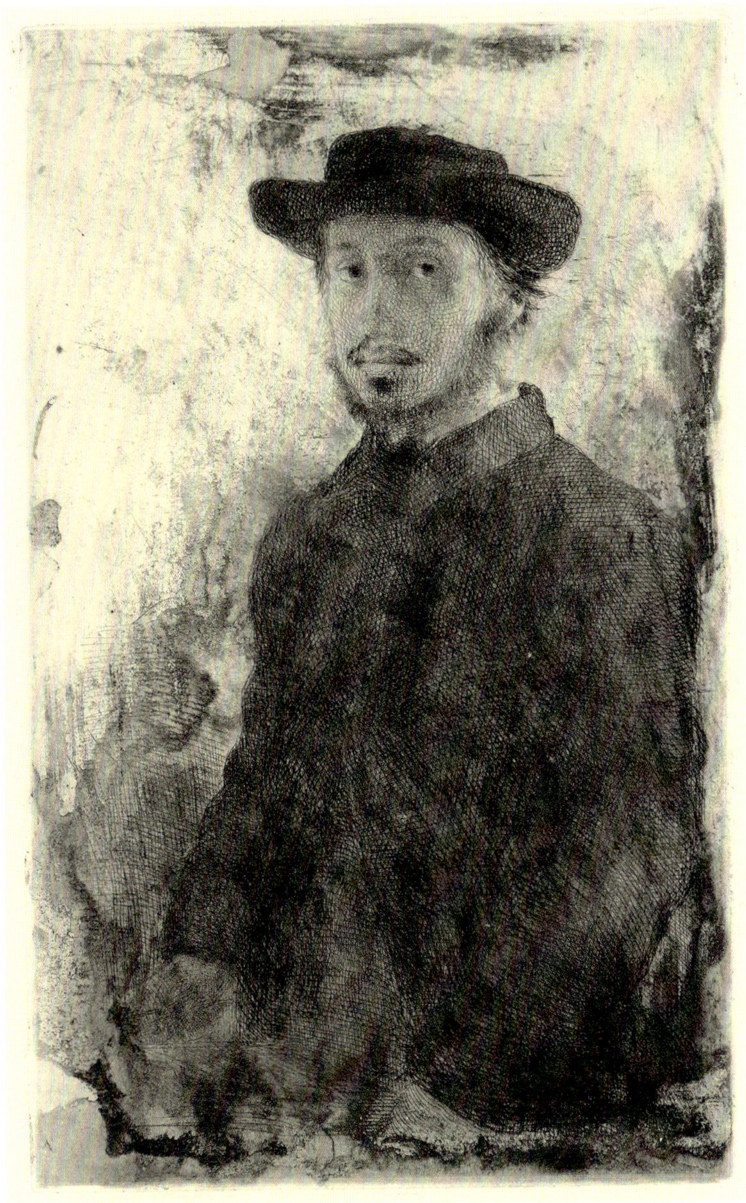

Fig. 22. Edgar Degas. *Self-Portrait*, 1857. Cat. 126.

from the indistinct field of foul biting. His right hand can only be vaguely discerned. Opposed to the careful mimesis found in the portrait engravings of Goltzius, Degas used a network of etched lines in the face to assert the artifice of his self-representation. The hatching appears as a layer set over his facial features rather than serving as the vehicle for their precise description. Effectively, Degas created a portrait of himself as an embodiment of the art of etching in its most elemental sense. While Degas's debt to Rembrandt has long been acknowledged in specific connection with this print,[39] Van Dyck's experimental approach to etching should also be credited for helping to establish an audience of print connoisseurs who could appreciate such intentionally unfinished or unresolved work.[40] In 1662, shortly after the release of the first set of

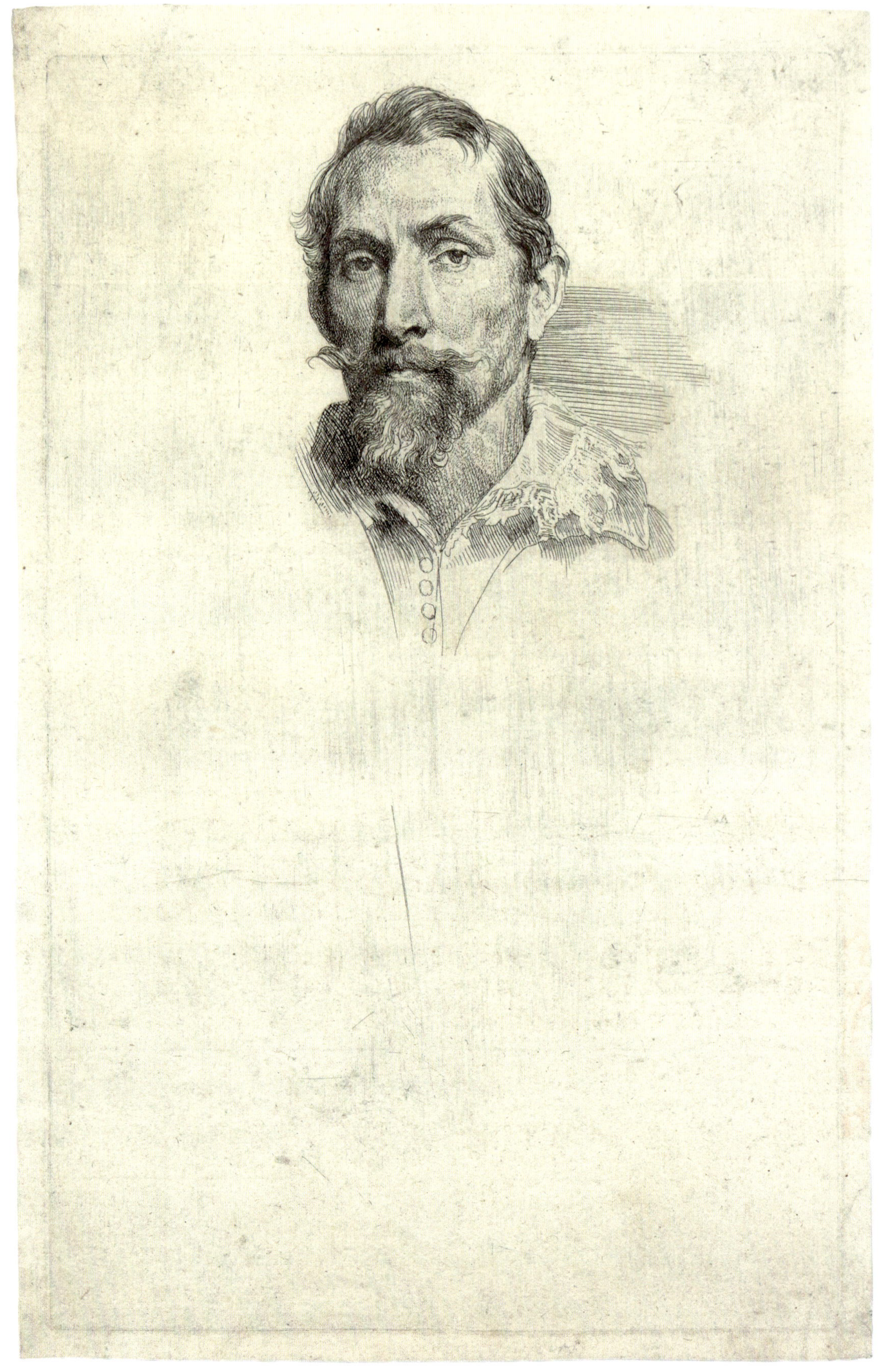

Fig. 23. Anthony van Dyck. *Frans Snyders*, 1630/33. Cat. 53.

collectively published prints from the *Iconography*, John Evelyn noted in an early treatise on the art of printmaking that Van Dyck "engraved after a new way, of etching it first, and then pointing it (as it were) with the burin afterwards," a reference to the artist's novel practice of etching in earlier states with the expectation that others would complete his compositions subsequently in a different printing medium.[41]

THE FACE STRIPPED OF ITS DECORATION

Given his choice to homogenize the subjects of the *Iconography* through the use of similarly nonchalant postures, generally half-length format, and comparable aristocratic dress, it was clearly in the treatment of his subjects' faces that Van Dyck expected to distinguish one sitter from another while conferring upon them an equal measure of elegance and grace. While all genres of portraiture demand that the artist create a faithful likeness, prints present an especially high degree of difficulty in that the artist can rely only on the quality of line, the colors of the printing ink, and the type of paper support to create a persuasive representation. Van Dyck's decision to minimize and frequently eliminate emblematic objects such as palettes, orbs, and laurel wreaths placed an even greater focus on his own ability to convey identity through physical traits. Yet he clearly flourished under such constraints. Indeed, it was Huygens, one of the artist's most famous portrait subjects, who wrote that "Van Dyck preserves head and hands, saying, the rest is for death."[42] Later in the seventeenth century, French critic Roger de Piles noted that the artist

> designed his heads and hands with the utmost perfection…
> and took his time to draw a face when it had its best looks
> on. He observed its charms and graces, he kept them in
> his mind, and not only imitated Nature, but heightened her
> as far as he could do it, without altering the likeness.[43]

By harnessing the distinct facial features of his subjects, Van Dyck was able to emphasize each as an individual rather than as a member of a particular class or profession.

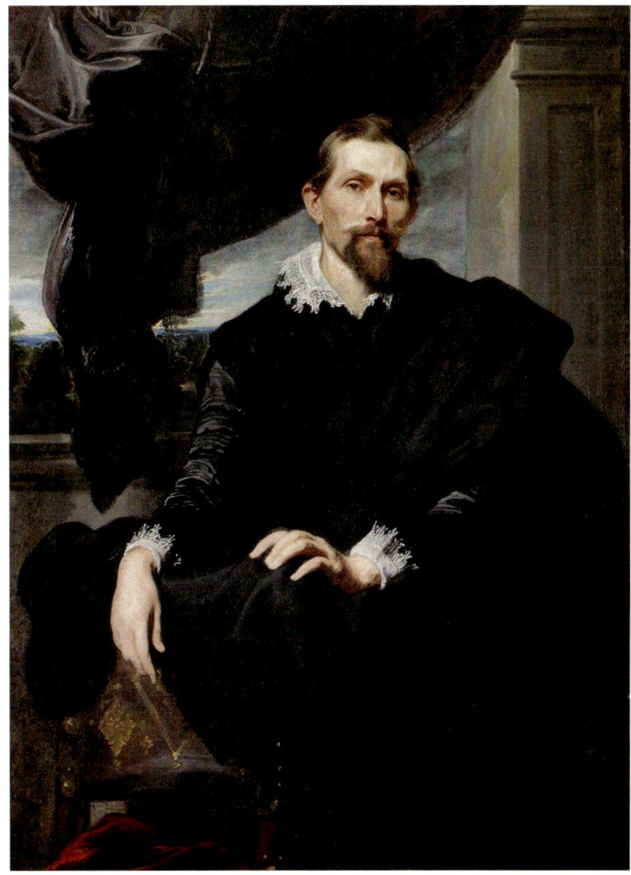

Fig. 24. Anthony van Dyck. *Portrait of Frans Snyders*, c. 1620.
Oil on canvas; 142.6 × 105.4 cm (56⅛ × 41½ in.).
The Frick Collection, Henry Clay Frick Bequest, 1909.1.39.

The portrait of Frans Snyders (fig. 23) offers one example of an etching in which Van Dyck described the sitter's face nearly to the exclusion of all other elements. Placed in the upper register of the sheet, Snyders's face and neck are set off by a fragment of his overcoat and lace-edged shirt; a series of horizontal hatched lines indicates the ground against which the volume of the face is defined. Snyders casts a tranquil gaze, his mouth closed but not tense. Like the depiction of De Wael, this etched portrait departs from a finished painted representation (fig. 24) that Van Dyck completed around 1620. In returning to Snyders as a portrait subject more than ten years later, Van Dyck stayed close to his original characterization, but he registered the sitter's more advanced age by elongating the face, making it appear slightly more drawn.

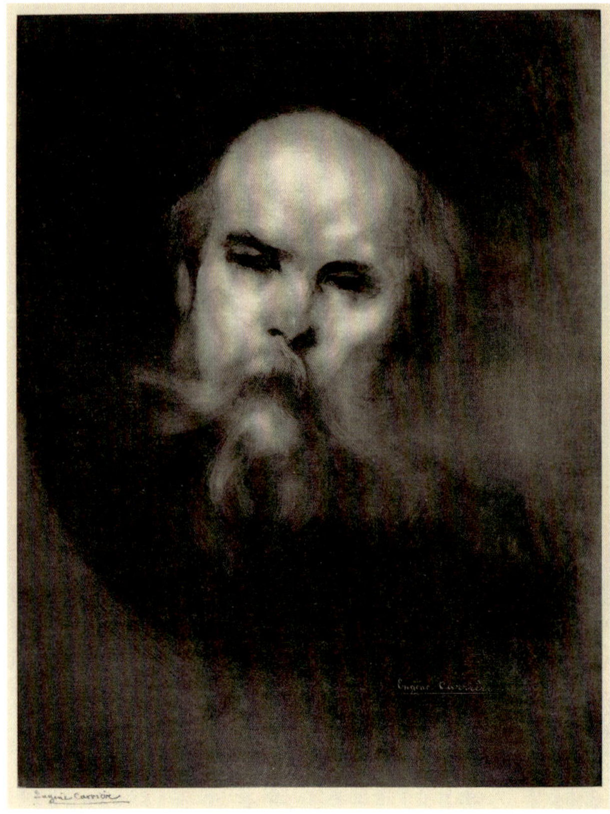

Fig. 25. Eugène Carrière. *Portrait of Paul Verlaine*, 1896. Cat. 128.

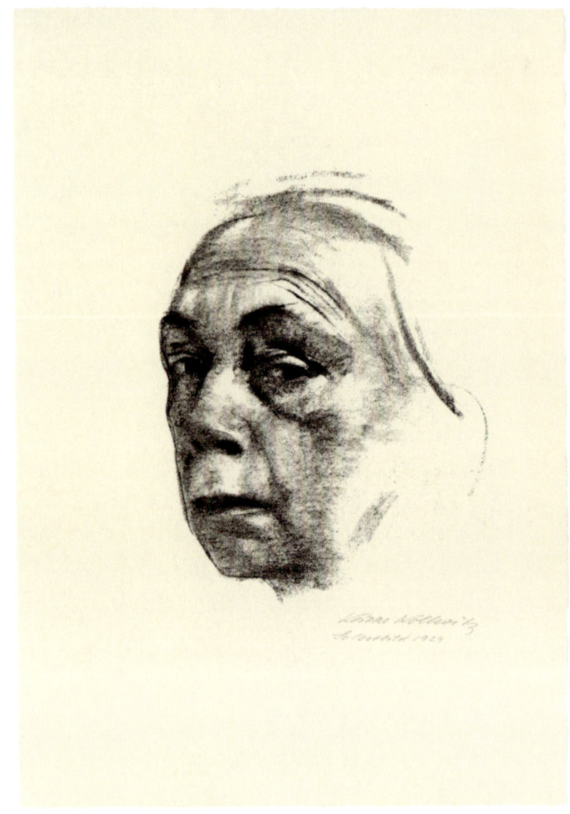

Fig. 26. Käthe Kollwitz. *Self-Portrait*, 1924. Cat. 132.

As a result, the circles below the left eye—rendered with concentric hooks of dotted stippling—also fall lower on the face, conveying a sense of world-weariness absent in the earlier painting. Later states were elaborated with engraving by Jacob Neeffs, who added a pillar behind Snyders's right shoulder as well as both of the artist's hands, which are clasped over the back of a chair. Van Dyck's "unfinished" version evidently met an eager market, as more than twenty impressions of this earlier state of the print are known to exist still today.[44]

While Rembrandt occasionally printed early states of his self-portraits in which only his face is set off against a greater field of the unprinted sheet, he did not use this dramatic device in his other portrait prints. The practice of featuring the face alone as an isolated, unadorned, and decontextualized element became more common in the nineteenth and twentieth centuries in works such as Eugène Carrière's portrait of French poet Paul Verlaine (fig. 25). In striking contrast to

Van Dyck's practice of setting the face against the unprinted reserve of his printed sheet, Carrière covered the paper support completely, describing Verlaine's face as if emerging from a rich field of billowy blackness. To achieve the desired range of tonality, Carrière used two lithographic stones and superimposed them on the same sheet. Produced decades after the advent of photography, Carrière's portrait reflects his interest in a kind of metaphysical likeness as opposed to a precise representation. Similarly dramatic is Käthe Kollwitz's moving self-portrait of 1924 (fig. 26), made especially powerful due to its life-size scale. Equally bold and perhaps even more arresting, David Alfaro Siqueiros's self-portrait of 1936 (fig. 27) presents his disembodied head at a larger than life-size scale. The placement of the edge of his face at the very borders of the zinc plate he used as his matrix presents a compelling foil to the suspended isolation seen in such Van Dyck etchings as the portrait of Snyders and the unfinished

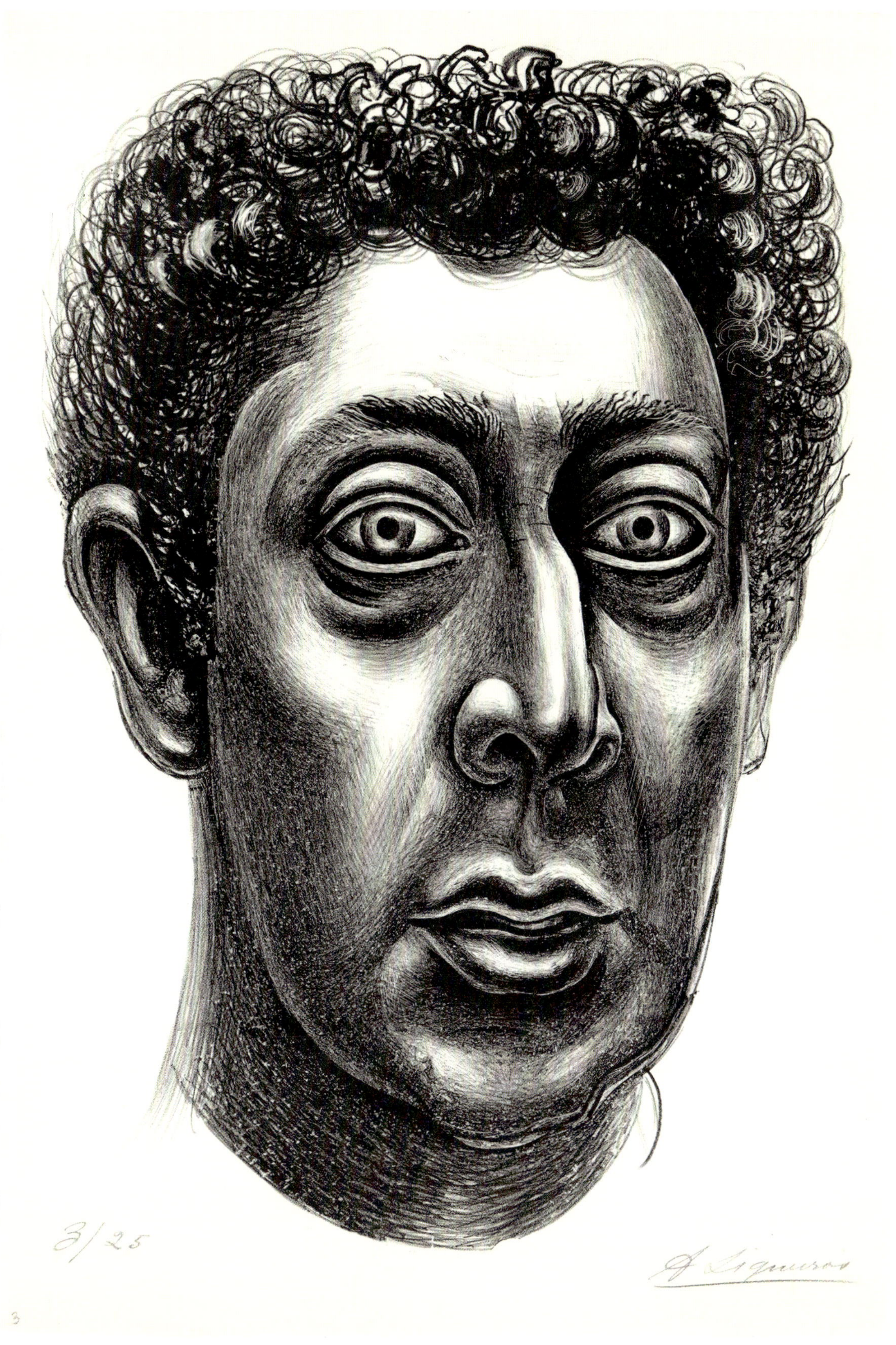

Fig. 27. David Alfaro Siqueiros. *Self-Portrait*, 1936. Cat. 134.

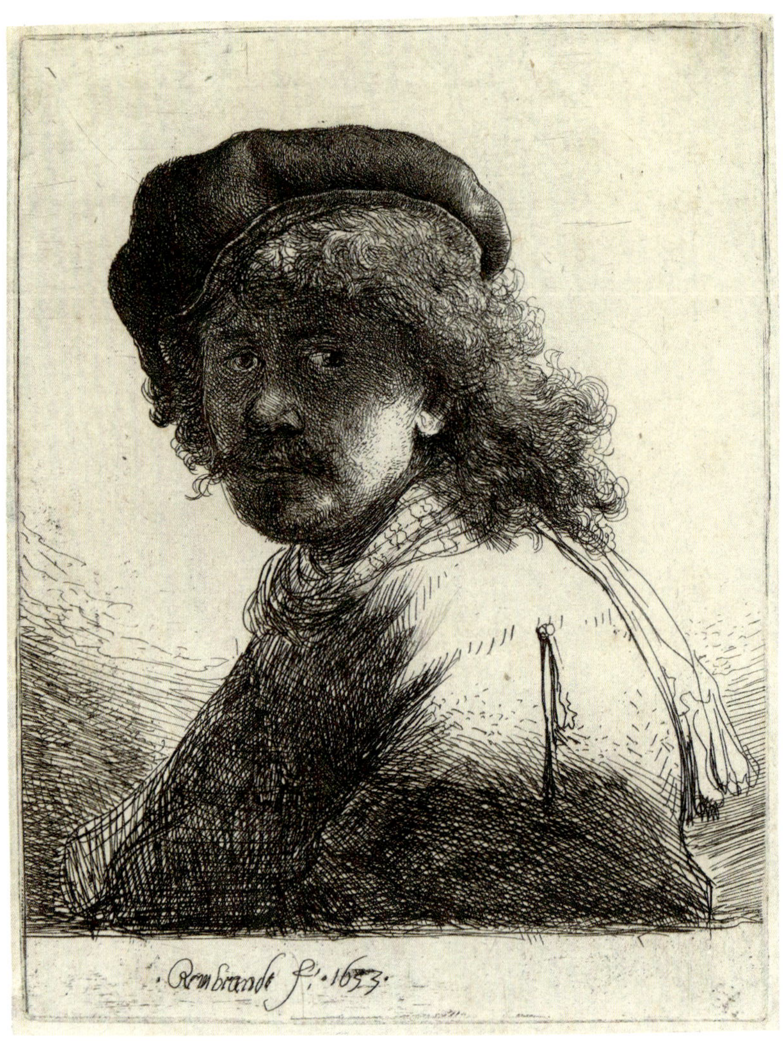

Fig. 28. Rembrandt van Rijn. *Self-Portrait in a Cap and Scarf with the Face Dark: Bust*, 1633. Cat. 70. Shown at actual size.

self-portrait. By underscoring the importance of their own faces in isolation, these artists stressed the intellectual work of visual art: their heads alone can represent them.

THE SELF AS SUBJECT

Undoubtedly, Van Dyck's greatest contribution to the history of the portrait print is the assertion that artists were worthy subjects for this reproducible genre. More specifically, the popularity of his own self-portrait etching—in its unfinished as well as reworked states—helped establish the self-portrait as an acceptable and marketable subject for prints. Rembrandt was the most immediate beneficiary of this innovation, as his career-long engagement with the genre yielded one of the most copious and varied bodies of self-representation in the history of art. Rembrandt's profound influence has made it easy to overlook Van Dyck's prior contributions to the development of portrait etching or to portrait prints more broadly. Indeed, Van Dyck's unfinished self-portrait etching

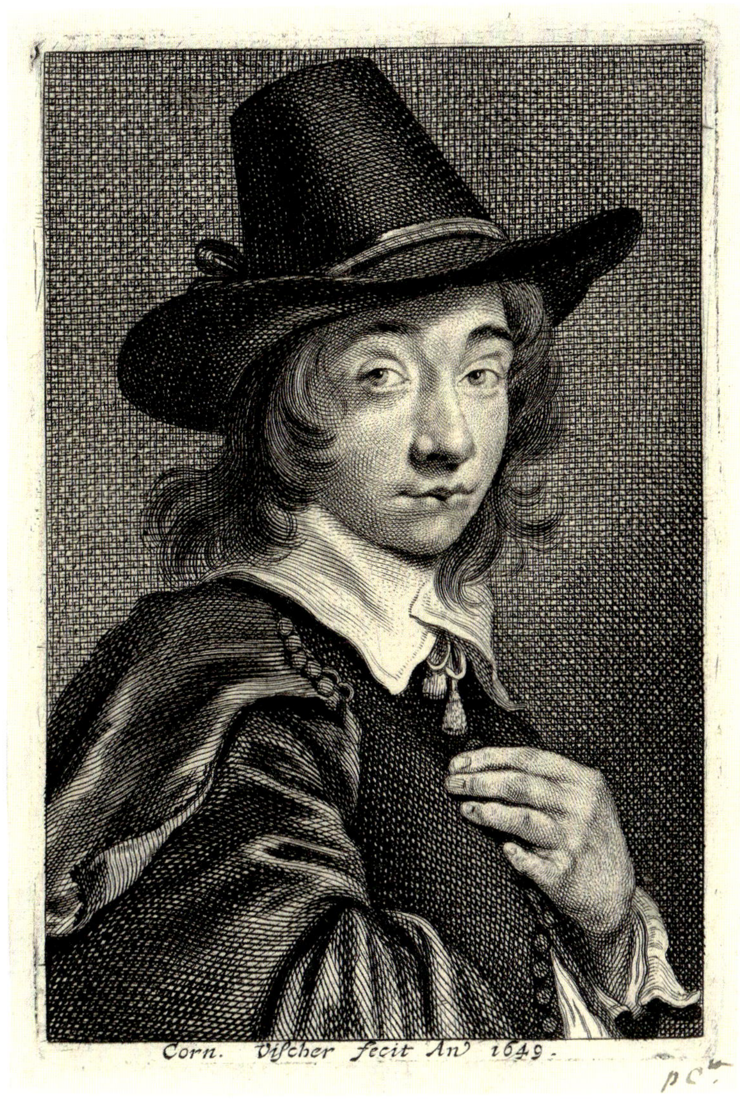

Fig. 29. Cornelis Visscher. *Self-Portrait*, 1649. Cat. 102. Shown at actual size.

bears directly on the production of a number of Rembrandt's self-portraits from the early 1630s. In one example from 1633 (fig. 28), Rembrandt similarly used a bust-length format, with his left shoulder closer to the picture plane and head turned toward the viewer.[45] Importantly, this print reverses the directional sense of Van Dyck's, as if Rembrandt referred to Van Dyck as a source while he etched his printing plate, with the change in direction emerging from the printing process. In a similar fashion, Cornelis Visscher portrayed himself in bust length, looking casually over his right shoulder with one hand on his chest (fig. 29).[46] The tradition of self-portrait prints follows abundantly from these precedents and includes exemplary works—beyond those already discussed—by artists such as Jean-Pierre Norblin de la Gourdaine, Jean-Jacques de Boissieu (cat. 119), James Ensor, Edvard Munch (cat. 130), and Emil Nolde (cat. 131).[47] Jim Dine's *Self-Portrait in a Flat Cap (Winter), First State* (fig. 30) recalls both Rembrandt and Van Dyck. While the etching plate—and the corresponding printed field—is the size of a standard sheet of letter paper, Dine chose a support three times that size. By printing in the upper

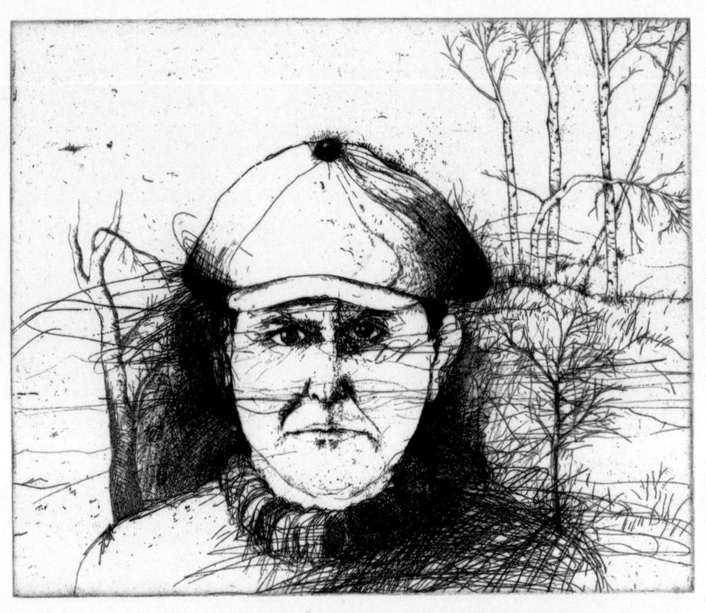

 Fig. 30. Jim Dine. *Self-Portrait in a Flat Cap (Winter)*, *First State*, 1974. Cat. 136.

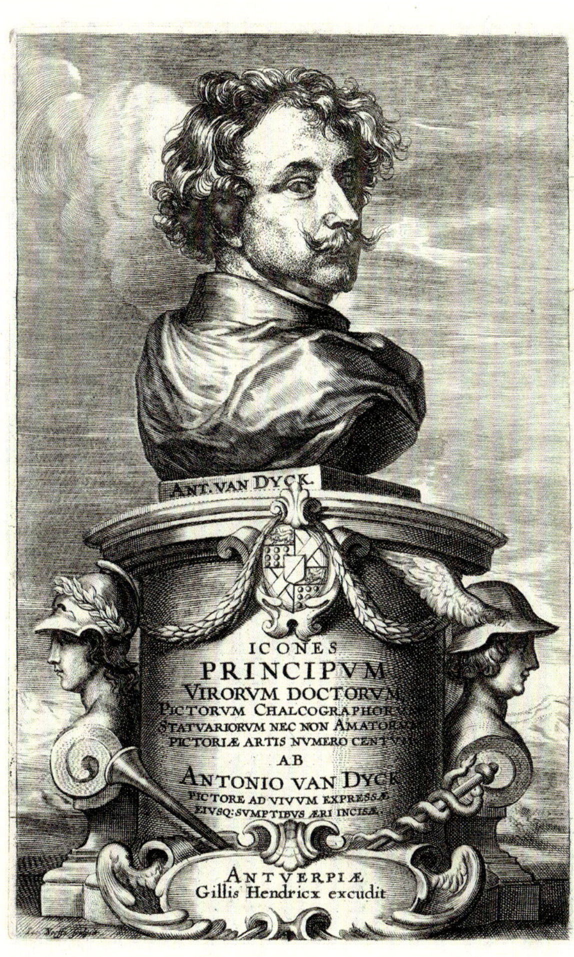

Fig. 31. Jacob Neeffs. After Anthony van Dyck.
Title Page from the "Iconography," 1645. Cat. 89.

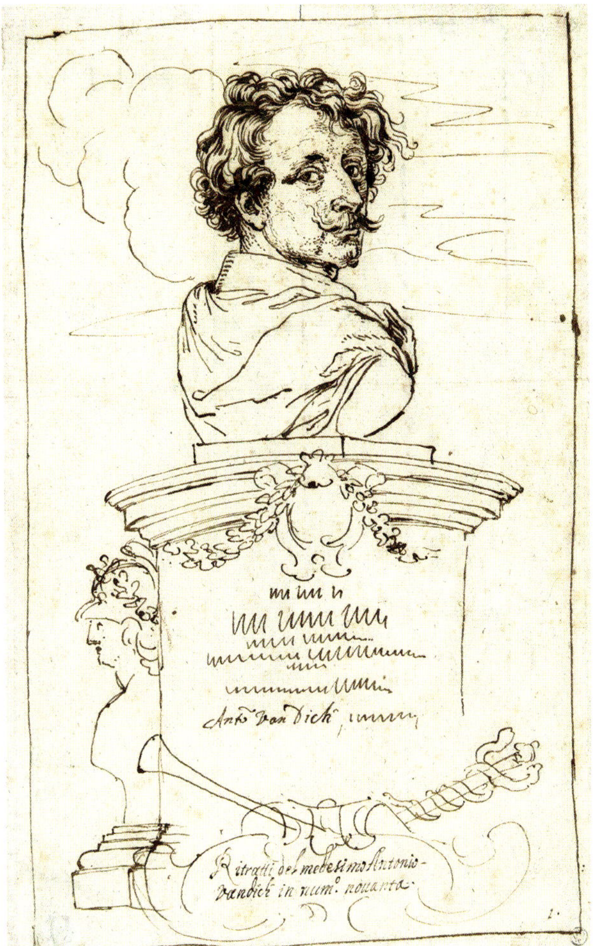

Fig. 32. Unknown artist. After Anthony van Dyck. *Title Page from the "Iconography,"* late seventeenth century. Cat. 63.

register, he further emphasized the fragmentary representation of himself, suspending his head and shoulders over a blank expanse of the reserve. In this way, he too—perhaps unconsciously—demonstrated the enduring relevance of Van Dyck's pioneering self-portrait.[48]

In later, posthumously designed states, Van Dyck's etched self-portrait incorporates text that would allow it to function as a title page for the *Iconography*. In this version of the print (fig. 31), realized by Neeffs in combination with Van Dyck's original, spare etching of the face alone, the portrait is conceived as a sculpted bust placed atop a columnar pedestal into which an inscription has been carved. The

immediate impact of this print, and indeed the series as a whole, is registered in a copy drawing by an unidentified seventeenth-century artist (fig. 32). In addition to sketching the central motif, the artist noted in Italian that the bust is a likeness of Van Dyck and that the title page introduces a series of portraits by the same, ninety in number.[49] In direct lineage with Neeffs's print, French artist Jean Lepautre also used a self-portrait as an element in what appears to be a title page (fig. 33). In the horizontal-format etching and engraving, the artist looks over one shoulder in Van Dyck's iconic pose. Set before an elaborate history subject and landscape scene, the portrait roundel is embellished with a wreath and hangs

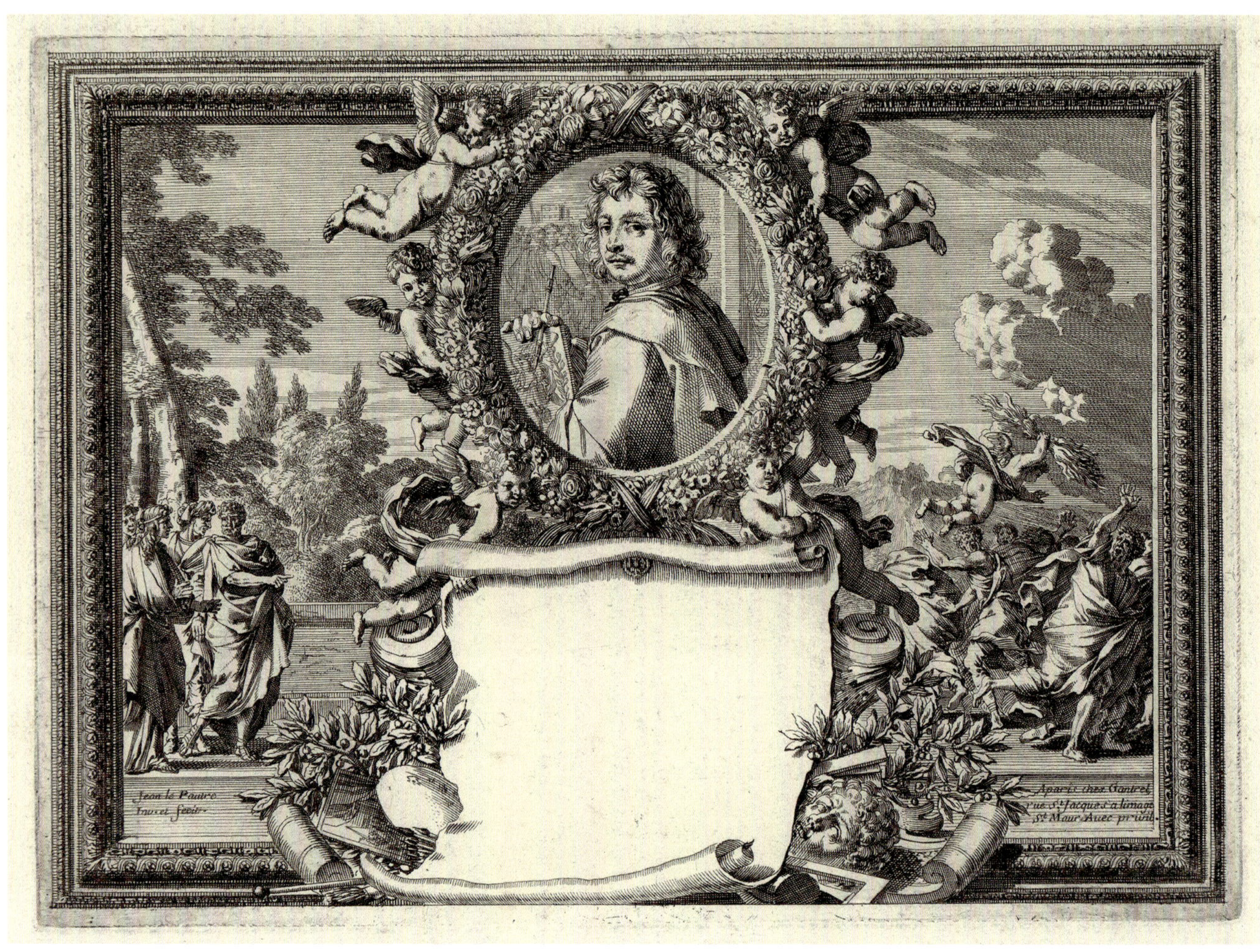

Fig. 33. Jean Lepautre. *Self-Portrait*, after 1674. Cat. 94.

above a blank cartouche, presumably designed for as-yet-unidentified text. Today Lepautre is best known for his printed representations of court festivities and performances, though he is treated as part of a collective more than as a distinct individual artistic personality.[50] The purpose of his fascinating self-portrait remains unknown. At the turn of the nineteenth century, Francisco de Goya's self-portrait in profile appeared as the first print in *Los Caprichos* (fig. 34), a series of eighty etchings with aquatint in which the artist criticized social mores and projected a dystopian fantasy world. While the series proved to be a financial failure in his own lifetime, it was eventually hailed as a groundbreaking statement of both technical and imaginative prowess and earned Goya a position of great

esteem within the history of printmaking and indeed the history of art. The placement of his own likeness as the first print of the series—one of very few self-portraits that he created in any medium—indicates that the artist wanted to insist on his authorship and his status as an intellectual.[51]

By the time Van Dyck died in 1641, far from fulfilling his artistic potential, many of the *Iconography* prints had been produced and circulated. As has been touched on in the introduction to this catalogue, seventeenth-century collectors' marks and inscriptions indicate that impressions of Van Dyck's etchings were in fact already prized by an emerging community of print connoisseurs. In the years following his death and continuing into the twentieth century, the

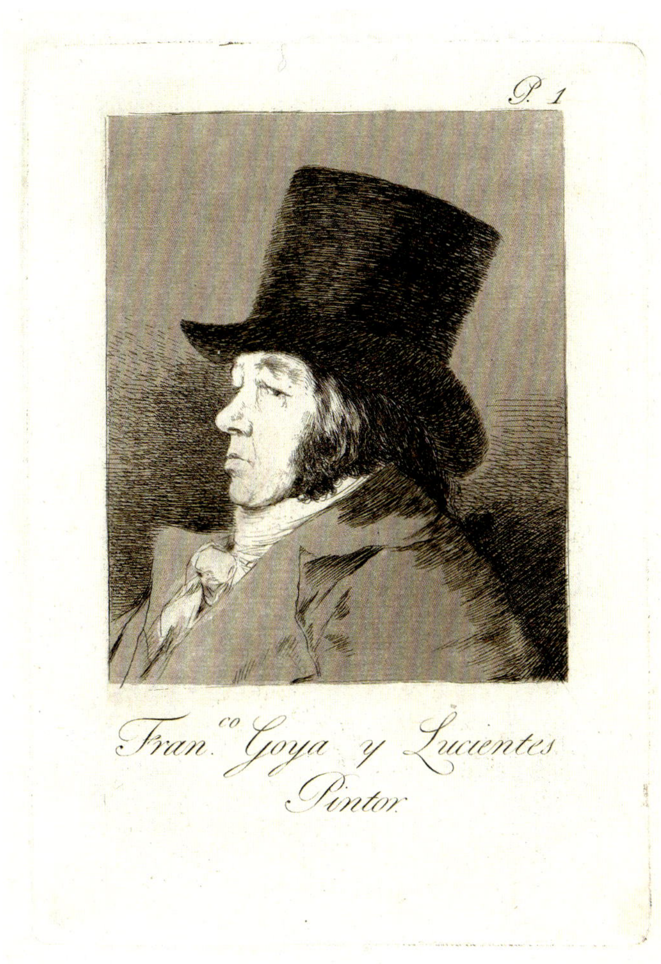

Fig. 34. Francisco José de Goya y Lucientes. *Francisco Goya y Lucientes, Painter*, plate one from *Los Caprichos*, 1797/99. Cat. 121.

portraits for the *Iconography* were printed in various editions by different publishers.[52] The plates still exist today and are held in the Chalcographie du Louvre. For many, the *Iconography* serves as a summation of Van Dyck's career as a portraitist; for others, the series provides a collection of admirable individuals, a portal into history. For artists, Van Dyck's portrait prints, especially those he etched himself, sparked a momentous shift in the aesthetic conventions of the portrait print and affirmed that artists themselves were worthy subjects for portraiture, even in the reproducible medium of printmaking.

While Van Dyck's embrace of unfinished compositions and roughly wielded techniques may have been the most

forward-looking elements of the *Iconography*, consideration of the prints in aggregate reveals his great gift for perceiving and conveying the distinct character of his subjects. Writing within two years of Van Dyck's death, Thomas Browne explored the challenges of portraiture in section two of his *Religio Medici*: "There are mystically in our faces certain Characters which carry in them the motto of our Souls, wherein he that cannot read A.B.C. may read our natures."[53] Van Dyck, perhaps above all other artists, was able to identify the specific physical features that conveyed this "motto" of the soul; in his portrait prints, those elements are described in the sparest and most immediate terms. The circulation of these works has allowed a greater audience to recognize the humanity and dignity that Van Dyck was able to impart to his subjects while preserving the most essential elements of their individuality.

Notes

Epigraph: Thomas Browne, *Religio Medici*, 5th ed. (London, 1642; London: Thomas Milbourn for Andrew Crook, 1659), p. 130. I wish to thank Jessica Wolfe for bringing this passage to my attention.

1. Among the extensive scholarship on the *Iconography*, the primary references are Friedrich Wibiral, *L'Iconographie d'Antoine van Dyck* (Leipzig: Alexander Danz, 1877); Arthur Mayger Hind, *Van Dyck: His Original Etchings and His Iconography* (Houghton Mifflin, 1915); Marie Mauquoy-Hendrickx, *L'Iconographie d'Antoine van Dyck, catalogue raisonné*, 2 vols. (Academie Royale de Belgique, 1956); Joaneath A. Spicer, "Anthony van Dyck's Iconography: An Overview of Its Preparation," in *Van Dyck 350*, ed. Susan J. Barnes and Arthur K. Wheelock, Jr. (National Gallery of Art, Washington, D.C., 1994), pp. 327–64; Carl Depauw and Ger Luijten, with contributions by Erik Duverger, Danielle Maufort, Saskia Sombogaart, and Ad Stijnman, *Anthony van Dyck as a Printmaker*, exh. cat. (Stedelijk Prentenkabinet/ Rijksmuseum, 1999); Simon Turner, *The New Hollstein: Dutch and Flemish Etchings, Engravings, and Woodcuts, 1450–1700; Anthony van Dyck*, 9 vols., ed. Carl Depauw (Sound and Vision, 2002); and Pascal Torres, *Van Dyck graveur: L'art du portrait*, exh. cat. (Musée du Louvre, 2008).

2. The status of the early modern European artist has been well studied. The classic text on this subject is Rensselaer W. Lee, *Ut Pictura Poesis: The Humanistic Theory of Painting* (Norton, 1967); other useful references include Mary Crawford Volk, "On Velázquez and the Liberal Arts," *Art Bulletin* 60, 1 (March 1978), pp. 69–86; and Julius S. Held, "Rembrandt's Aristotle," in *Rembrandt Studies* (Princeton University Press, 1991), pp. 17–58.

3. It is likely that Van Dyck began the project in the late 1620s; by the early 1630s, the first impressions of his own etchings began to appear on the market, and correspondence from 1636 suggests the artist was still engaged with the design of the prints later in the decade. One of the few pieces of documentary evidence related to this series is a letter from Van Dyck to his friend the philosopher Franciscus Junius in which he asks him to pen an epigraph for the portrait of their mutual friend Kenelm Digby. Van Dyck to Franciscus Junius, August 14, 1636, Harleian Collection, 4936, formerly British Museum, transferred to British

Library (translated and published in facsimile form in William Hookham Carpenter, *Memoir of Sir Anthony van Dyck with a Description Catalogue of the Etchings Executed by Him* [London: James Carpenter, 1844], pp. 55–56). During Van Dyck's lifetime, Martin van den Enden published eighty of the portraits, though no title page appeared with these first editions. The idea that Van Dyck's portrait prints were meant to be seen collectively is further supported by the existence today of a number of bound albums of the series, including one in the Art Institute's Ryerson and Burnham Libraries (cat. 64); I would like to thank Suzanne Folds McCullagh for bringing this volume to my attention. For references to other extant bound volumes of the various editions of the *Iconography*, see Turner's survey of editions, introduction to *The New Hollstein,* Guide to the Catalogue, pp. xxv–xlii. Other collections include impressions of these prints with the same type of manuscript annotations, which reflects the fact that print collectors of the eighteenth, nineteenth, and twentieth centuries viewed the works as being part of a series.

4. As early as 1620, while Van Dyck was still in the Rubens workshop, Rubens began issuing prints representing his painted inventions; Van Dyck may even have participated in the design of these prints, though his precise contribution to these efforts remains unclear and hinges on the attribution of a number of preparatory drawings for Rubens-related prints.

5. In the original Dutch: "Zijn konst openbaer te maken" and "Laet dan vry uwe werken in print uitkomen, zoo zal uwen naem te spoediger al de werelt over vliegen." Samuel van Hoogstraten, *Inleyding tot de Hooge Schoole der Schilderkonst* (Holland, 1678; repr., Davaco, 1969), p. 195.

6. Susan Barnes, *Van Dyck: A Complete Catalogue of the Paintings* (Yale University Press, 2003), cat. III.140; Erik Larsen, *The Paintings of Anthony van Dyck* (Luca, 1988), cat. 525.

7. On Van Dyck's innovations related to costume in portraiture, particularly in his paintings of English subjects, see Emilie E. S. Gordenker, *Anthony van Dyck (1599–1641) and the Representation of Dress in Seventeenth-Century Portraiture* (Brepols, 2001).

8. Christopher Brown and Hans Vlieghe, et al., *Van Dyck, 1599–1641*, exh. cat. (Academy Publications and Antwerpen Open, 1999), cat. 53.

9. Constance Harris, *Portraiture in Prints* (McFarland, 1987), especially chapters 2 and 3, pp. 8–57.

10. Christiane L. Joost-Gaugier, "The Early Beginnings of the Notion of 'Uomini Famosi' and the 'De Viris Illustribus' in Greco-Roman Literary Tradition," *Artibus et Historiae* 3, 6 (1992), pp. 97–115.

11. *Pictorum aliquot celebrium, præcipué Germaniae Inferioris, effigies* (The Hague, 1610). For more on this series and for access to digitized editions of both the Cock and Hondius series, see *Picturing the Netherlandish Canon* (http://www .courtauld.org.uk/netherlandishcanon/index.html).

12. For a discussion of this group of related portrait prints, see Jan Piet Filedt Kok, "Artists Portrayed by Their Friends: Goltzius and His Circle," "Ten Essays for a Friend: E. de Jongh," special issue, *Simiolus: Netherlands Quarterly for the History of Art* 24, 2/3, 65 (1996), pp. 161–81.

13. See also Dorothy Limouze, "Aegidius Sadeler, Imperial Printmaker," *Philadelphia Museum of Art Bulletin* 85, 362 (Spring 1989), pp. 3–24.

14. The portrait of Müller is derived from an earlier portrait by Spranger, and the portrait of Spranger can be traced to a design by Hans von Aachen that was itself used to create a portrait print featuring Spranger alone in 1597. The conceit of combining the two likenesses—complete with the allegorical representations of the visual arts surrounding Spranger, Fame and her two trumpets in the upper left of the composition, Father Time as winged Saturn with his scythe slung over his right shoulder, a putto stretching out to hold a laurel wreath above Spranger's head, and the figures of Piety and Minerva flanking either side of Müller's tomb—remains unattributed.

15. In the original Latin: "Privataus lacrymas Bart. Sprangeri Egid. Sadeler miratus artem e amantem redamans, publicas fecit: e/ eidem promutua benevolentia dedicavit. Pragæ Anno Seculari." This is only one of the six text passages included in the print. For translations of the other texts, see Kok, "Artists Portrayed by Their Friends."

16. Goltzius used a similar device on other occasions, such as in his 1583 portrait of Hieronymous Scholiers (New Hollstein 249) and his 1592 portrait of Henry IV, King of France (New Hollstein 227).

17. Scholars have debated whether Van Dyck created fifteen, seventeen, or eighteen etchings for the *Iconography*. I accept Joaneath Spicer's reasoning for fifteen. See Spicer, "Anthony van Dyck's Iconography."

18. Arthur K. Wheelock, Jr., et al., *Jan Lievens: A Dutch Master Rediscovered*, exh. cat. (National Gallery of Art, Washington, D.C./Yale University Press, 2008), cat. 75. See also Peter Schatborn with Eva Ornstein-van Slooten, *Jan Lievens (1607–1674): Prenten & Tekeningen*, exh. cat. (Museum het Rembrandthuis, 1988), cat. 35. Stephanie Dickey has discussed Van Dyck's impact on both Rembrandt and Lievens. See Dickey, "Van Dyck in Holland: The Iconography and Its Impact on Rembrandt and Jan Lievens," in *Van Dyck 1599–1999: Conjectures and Refutations*, ed. Hans Vlieghe (Brepols, 2001) pp. 289–303.

19. Regarding Van Dyck in England, see Malcolm Rogers, "Van Dyck in England," in Brown and Vlieghe, *Van Dyck 1599–1641*, pp. 79–91; Jeremy Wood, "Van Dyck and the Earl of Northumberland: Taste and Collecting in Stuart England," in Barnes and Wheelock, *Van Dyck 350*, pp. 281–324. There is also a section on Van Dyck in England, comprising several thematic essays, in *Van Dyck 1599–1999*.

20. In the original Latin: "Fidæ Amicitiæ Monimentvm." The full printed inscription reads: "Iacobo Govtero Inter Regios Magnæ Britanniæ Orpheos Et Amphiones Lydiæ Doriæ Phrygiæ Testvdinis Fidicini Et Modvlatorvm Principi Hanc E Penicilli Svi Tabula in Æs Transscriptam Effigiem Ioannes Lævini Fidæ Amicitiæ Monimentvm. L. M. Consecravit."

21. Charles I's paintings collection has been studied extensively; on this topic, see Jonathan Brown and John Elliot, eds., *The Sale of the Century: Artistic Relations between Spain and Great Britain, 1604–55* (Yale University/Museo Nacional del Prado, 2002). Regarding Charles I's patronage of music and the humanities, see Penelope Gouk, "Horological, Mathematical and Musical Instruments: Science and Music at the Court of Charles I," in *The Late King's Goods: Collections, Possessions and Patronage of Charles I in the Light of the Commonwealth Sale Inventories*, ed. Arthur MacGregor (Alistair McAlpine/Oxford University Press, 1989), pp. 387–402.

22. The meeting and the drawing, which does not survive, are documented by Huygens, who remembered that a tree fell on his house the same day that Van Dyck drew his likeness. "28 Jany. 1632: Pingor a Van Dyckio, cum arbor in aedes lapsus esset," J. H. W. Unger, ed., *Dagboek van Constantyn Huygens* (Gebroeders Binger, 1885), p. 20; as discussed in Ger Luijten, "The *Iconography*: Van Dyck's Portraits in Print," in Depauw and Luitjen, *Anthony van Dyck as a Printmaker*, p. 73.

23. In the original Dutch: "Een boek, vol contrefijtsels soo van van Dijck, Rubens en verscheijde andere oude meesters." Walter L. Strauss and Marjon van der Meulen, with the assistance of S. A. C. Dudok van Heel and P. J. M. De Baar, *The Rembrandt Documents* (Abaris, 1979), 1656/12, no. 228, p. 371.

24. The most thorough discussion of Rembrandt's portrait prints is Stephanie Dickey, *Rembrandt: Portraits in Print*, Oculi: Studies in the Arts of the Low Countries 9 (John Benjamins, 2004).

25. New Hollstein 293 (text vol. II, pp. 261–63).

26. Lutma the Younger created at least four prints in this style; two other examples are included in this exhibition (cats. 98 and 99) and depict leading Dutch literary

figures. Lutma, therefore, quite explicitly placed both visual and literary creators on equal footing, in the tradition of reverence for intellectual figures and statesmen from antiquity.

27. New Hollstein 264 (text vol. II, pp. 201–04). Rembrandt's thoughtful use of progressive state changes also recalls Van Dyck's substantive alteration of De Wael's portrait among others in the series. Because the sitter appears older than twenty-six, the age De Jonghe would have been when the print was created, some have disputed the identification, though as early as 1668 print publisher, dealer, and collector Pierre II Mariette identified the subject as De Jonghe on the verso of one impression. D. de Hoop Scheffer and K. G. Boon, "De inventarislijst van Clement de Jonghe en Rembrandts etsplaten," *Kroniek van het Rembrandthuis* 25 (1971), pp. 1–17; and D. de Hoop Scheffer, "Nogmaals de inventarislijst van Clement de Jonghe," *Kroniek van het Rembrandthuis* 26 (1972), pp. 126–34.

28. The most recent discussion of Rembrandt's financial struggles can be found in Paul Crenshaw, *Rembrandt's Bankruptcy: The Artist, His Patrons, and the Art Market in the Seventeenth-Century Netherlands* (Cambridge University Press, 2006).

29. Historic mount preserved in the Art Institute's collection. The episode is discussed by Kennedy in the context of his decision to catalogue Whistler's etchings much in the same way Rovinski had catalogued Rembrandt's etchings. Edward G. Kennedy, *The Etched Work of Whistler* (Grolier Club, 1910), xxiii–xxv. I am grateful to Meg Hausberg for this reference.

30. At the lower margin, remnants of a composition created by another artist (before Whistler started working the plate) can also be seen. Margaret F. MacDonald, Grischka Petri, Margaret Dunwoody Hausberg, and Joanna Meacock, *James McNeill Whistler: The Etchings; A Catalogue Raisonné* (University of Glasgow, 2012), cat. 62. http://etchings.arts.gla.ac.uk.

31. In addition to the four suites of proof impressions of all the states of this print, there are at least ten more impressions in private and publicly accessible collections, including the Art Institute's. See Jeal Paul-Bouillon, with an introduction by Dominique Tonneau-Ryckelynck, *Bracquemond/Goncourt*, exh. cat. (Musée du Dessin et de l'Estampe Originale, 2004). See also Eldon N. Van Liere, "Blurred Distinctions: Carrière, de Goncourt, Rodin, and Bracquemond," *Kresge Art Museum Journal* 5 (1990), pp. 1–15.

32. In the original French: "À Alidor Delzant, souvenir amical."

33. Louis A. Zona and Jim Pernotto, *Chuck Close Editions: A Catalog Raisonné and Exhibition* (Butler Institute of American Art, Youngstown, Ohio, 1989), cat. 52.

34. The following discussion of Van Dyck's etching technique owes a great deal to Ad Stijnman. See Stijnman, "On Feathers, Candles, and Wet Rags: The Etching Technique Used by Van Dyck and His Contemporaries," in Depauw and Luitjen, *Anthony van Dyck as a Printmaker*, pp. 26–39.

35. New Hollstein 4; Depauw and Luitjen, *Anthony van Dyck as a Printmaker*, cat. 8.

36. New Hollstein 115 (text vol. I, p. 182).

37. For more on Graff, see Robert Eberbardt, ed., *Anton Graff: Porträts eines Porträtisten* (Wolff, 2013); and *Anton Graff, 1736–1813*, exh. cat. (Staaliche Museen zu Berlin, Nationalgalerie, 1963).

38. For example, Degas, *Mary Cassatt in the Paintings Gallery of the Louvre* (Reed and Shapiro 52 [1982.1568], for which the Art Institute also has a pastel touched impression [1949.515]). See also *Manet Seated, Turned to the Right* (Reed and Shapiro 18 [1958.12]).

39. Richard Brettell and Suzanne Folds McCullagh, *Degas in the Art Institute*, exh. cat. (Art Institute of Chicago, 1984), cat. 5.

40. For a general discussion of the collecting history for Van Dyck's prints, see Ger Luijtjen and Saskia Sombogaart, " . . . With the Hand: The Collecting of Van Dyck Prints," in Depauw and Luitjen, *Anthony van Dyck as a Printmaker*, pp. 9–18.

41. John Evelyn, *Sculptura: or the History and Art of Chalcography and Engraving in Copper . . .* (London: Printed by J.C. for G. Beedle, and T. Collings, and the Middle-Temple Gate, and J. Crook in St. Pauls Church-yard, 1662), p. 73.

42. In the original Latin: "In Libros Iconum Illustr. Virorum Anton: Dyckij / Vivitur ingenio: servat cum vertice dextras / Dyckius, et, sunto caetera mortis, ait." Mar. 11, 1632, first published in 1644 and reprinted as part of the collected poems of Huygens in J. A. Worp, ed., *De gedichten van Constantijn Huygens* (J. B. Wolters, 1892–99), vol. 2, p. 234. Translation and further discussion of this epigram and two others written by Huygens on the same day can be found in Ger Luijten, "The *Iconography*: Van Dyck's Portraits in Print," in Depauw and Luitjen, *Anthony van Dyck as a Printmaker*, pp. 73–74.

43. "Vandeik a dessiné les têtes & les mains dans la derniére perfection; . . . . Il savoit choisir les Attitudes convenables aux personnes, & les momens les plus avantageux des visages. Il en observoit tous les agrémens; il les conservoit dan sa mémoire, & il imitoit ainsi non seulement ce qu'il voyoit dans son Modéle; mais ce qu'il croyoit possible & capable d'en soûtenir un bon caractére, san altérer la ressemblance." English translation taken from Roger de Piles, *The Art of Painting, and the Lives of the Painters: Containing, a Compleat Treatise of Painting, Designing, and the Use of Prints* (J. Nutt, 1706), p. 305.

44. New Hollstein 10; Depauw and Luitjen, *Anthony van Dyck as a Printmaker*, cat. 15.

45. Stephanie Dickey cites different self-portraits by Rembrandt as examples of Van Dyck's influence, specifically his 1631 *Self-Portrait with Long, Bushy, Hair* (New Hollstein 81) and his *Self-Portrait with Soft Cap and Embroidered Cloak* (New Hollstein 90). See Dickey, "Van Dyck in Holland," pp. 294–95 (figs. 6 and 7). Ger Luitjen refers to an early state of the latter in his discussion of Van Dyck's self-portrait etching; see Depauw and Luitjen, *Anthony van Dyck as a Printmaker*, cat. 5.

46. For further discussion of the Netherlandish tradition of artistic representation following Van Dyck, see Hans-Joachim Raupp, *Untersuchungen zu Künstlerbildnis un Künstler-darstellung* (Olms, 1984), pp. 165–319.

47. For a discussion of some of these examples and for a more metaphorical discussion of self-portraiture in the graphic arts, see James Clifton, with contributions by Leslie Scattone and Andrew C. Weislogel, *A Portrait of the Artist, 1525–1825: Prints from the Collection of the Sarah Campbell Blaffer Foundation*, exh. cat. (Museum of Fine Arts, Houston, 2005).

48. While Dine has discussed Rembrandt as a source of inspiration for his own self-portraits, I am not familiar with a published discussion of his interest in Van Dyck. "I thought [Rembrandt] found himself infinitely as interesting as I find myself. I'm not talking about personality-wise—I mean [the face] you know, what you see in the mirror every morning . . . the many disguises that the visage has. And it's yours." See Clifford S. Ackley and Patrick Murphy, *Jim Dine, Printmaker: Leaving My Tracks* (Museum of Fine Arts, Boston, 2012), p. 64.

49. "Ritratti del medessimo Antonio Vandick in numº novanta."

50. Lepautre is well represented in Peter Fuhring, Louis Marchesano, Rémi Mathis, and Vanessa Selbach, eds., *A Kingdom of Images: French Prints in the Age of Louis XIV, 1660–1715*, exh. cat. (Getty Trust, 2015). See also Stefan Germer, "Pouvoir du texte, force de l'image: Félibien et les représentations gravées des fêtes royales de 1688 et de 1674," in Maria Teresa Caracciolo and Ségolène Le Men, *L'illustration: Essais d'iconographie; Actes du Séminaire CNRS (GDR 712), Paris, 1993–94*, Historie de l'art et iconographie 3 (Klincksieck, 1999), pp. 147–61.

51. For a discussion of Goya's few painted self-portraits, see Sarah Symmons, "The Virtuoso Self: A Study of Goya's Self-Portraits," in *Goya, Neue Forschungen: Das international Symposium 1991 in Osnabrück* (Mann, 1994), pp. 11–28.

52. As discussed above, see Turner, introduction to *The New Hollstein*, Guide to the Catalogue, pp. xxv–xlii.

53. Browne, *Religio Medici*, p. 130.

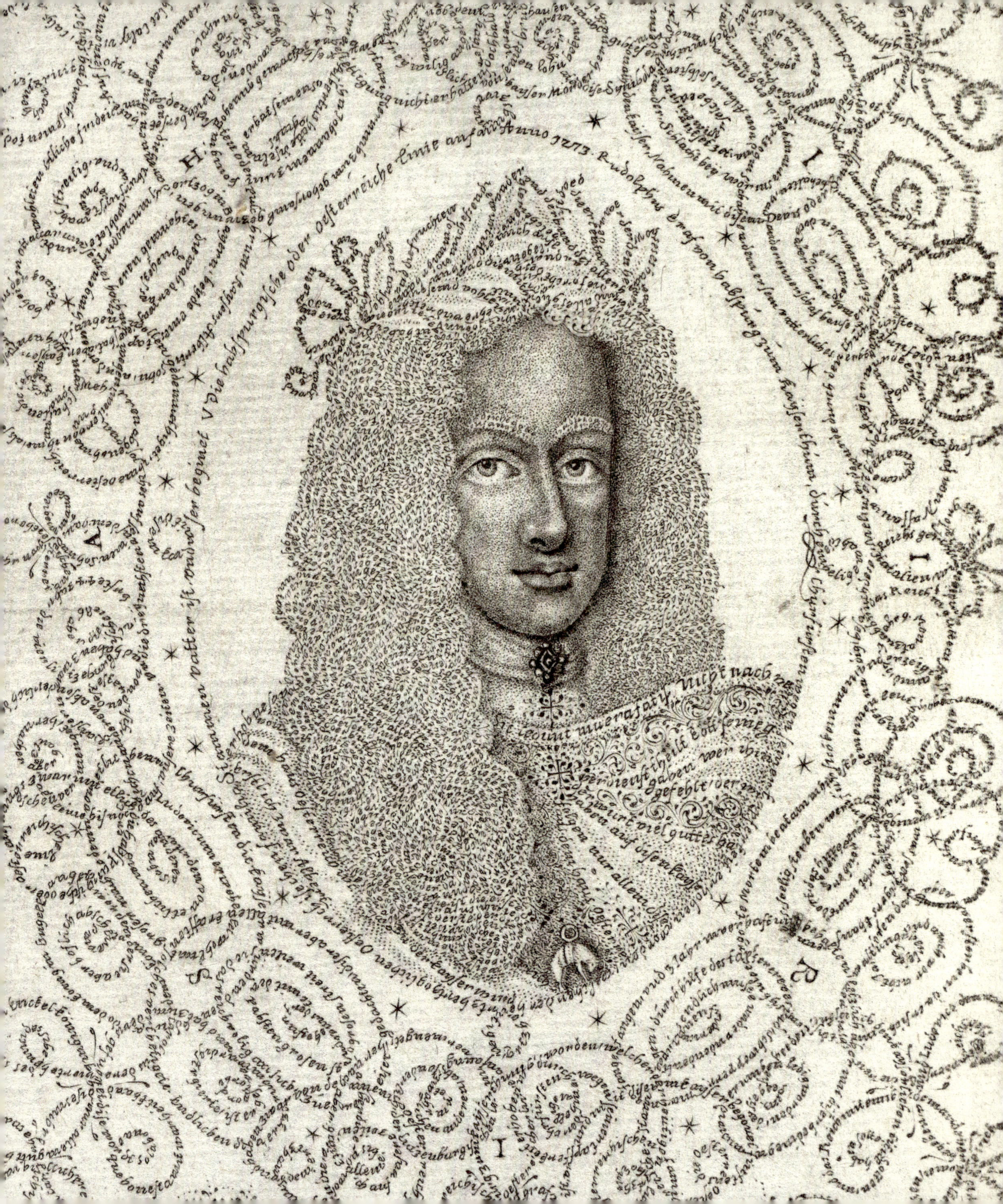

Fame's Two Trumpets

PORTRAIT PRINTS AND POLITICS
IN EARLY MODERN EUROPE

Maureen Warren

The desire to contribute to an individual's fame—or infamy—was one of the primary motivations for creating a portrait print in the early modern period. This idea was so central to Aegidius Sadeler's engraved portrait of Holy Roman Emperor Matthias (fig. 1) that the artist included two different allegorical representations of Fame in his picture. To the immediate left of the central portrait, the Roman god Mercury holds Pegasus by the mane as he prepares to take flight, an action that symbolizes Fama Chiara, or Illustrious Fame.[1] Sadeler included a more typical personification of Fame on the right: a winged woman sounding a trumpet to broadcast the good deeds of the emperor.[2] Although he depicted Fame with one trumpet, as was appropriate for his subject, typically she has two: one for fame and another for infamy. Both types of repute are well represented in portrait prints from this period, which convey the virtues and accomplishments of royalty, politicians, and heroes as well as the misdeeds of criminals, heretics, and villains. While scholars have explored the broad subject of early modern portrait prints, the subgenre of political portrait prints has yet to receive particular scrutiny. Focusing primarily on members of the House of Habsburg and English and Dutch criminals, this essay will explore depictions of famous and infamous figures by European printmakers in order to demonstrate how the medium played a crucial role in responding to and shaping political events.

FAME'S TRUMPET: HABSBURG MONARCHS

In the early fifteenth century, only a few generations after the inception of printmaking in Europe, political leaders began to use portrait prints to celebrate and enhance their power. Artists endeavored to meet the increasing demand for images of noteworthy individuals, sometimes working for themselves and at other times for a patron or publisher. While portraits of government officials and members of the nobility appeared in virtually all media, especially painting and sculpture, prints (like coins and medals) offered unique advantages in that their makers could produce hundreds of copies that could be easily transported and shared with a wide audience.[3] In addition, printed images were created in different sizes and enriched with elaborate internal frames and inscriptions. Furthermore, these portraits were printed on paper or textiles using a wide variety of inks and hand coloring.

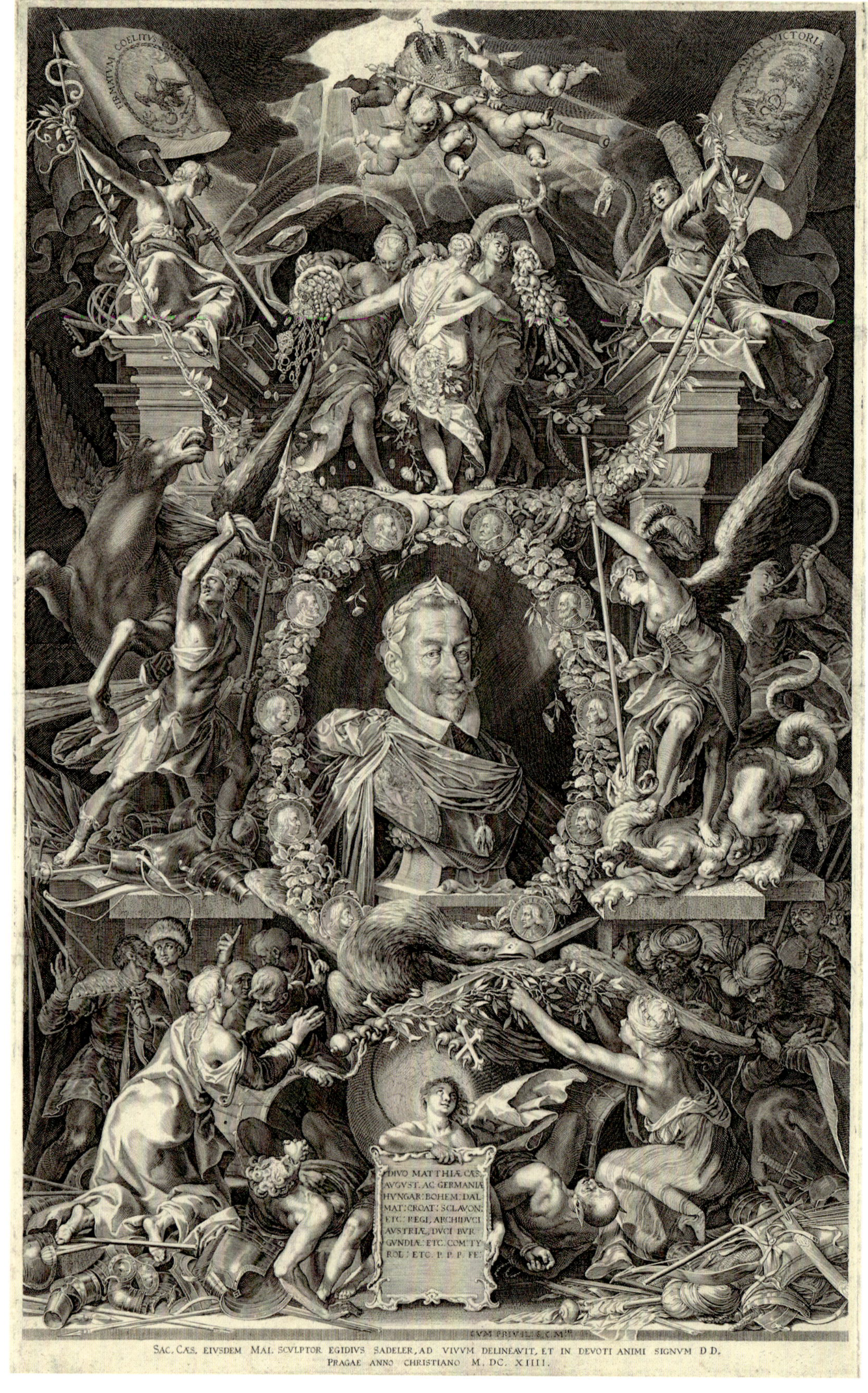

Fig. 1. Aegidius Sadeler. *Portrait of Emperor Matthias*, 1614. Cat. 24.

Some of the most ostentatious examples depict sovereign heads of state, who had the resources and connections to commission large-scale works by eminent artists. The Habsburg ruler Maximilian I was the first major European leader to commission a printed likeness, Hans Burgkmair's sumptuous portrait of 1508 (fig. 2).[4] Made the year he was crowned Holy Roman Emperor–elect, the work emphasizes Maximilian's military prowess, depicting him in full armor and holding a military leader's baton alongside the hilt of his sword. The suit, with its rounded forms, organic details, and parallel "pleated" lines, is now known as Maximilian armor and would have been worn in jousting tournaments as well as in victory parades. The equestrian pose, triumphal arch, and Latin inscription proclaiming Maximilian "Emperor Caesar Augustus" recall the long history of Roman rulers and the tradition of imperial parades. The Art Institute's impression of the print is especially luxurious and rare. An early example of chiaroscuro printing, a technique that requires multiple woodblocks (including a line block and one or more colored tone blocks), the impression might have been given to Elector Frederick the Wise of Saxony in response to his gift of prints depicting knights made by his court artist, Lucas Cranach the Elder. Whereas later chiaroscuro prints were usually executed on paper, the Art Institute's impression was printed on vellum with black and powdered gold inks, which were associated with the costly, highly esteemed medium of illuminated manuscripts.

In addition to using lavish materials, printmakers could embellish a work by incorporating an elaborate compositional frame. Sadeler's theatrical design for the portrait of Matthias, the great-great-grandson of Maximilian I, incorporates a wealth of allegorical and symbolic content. In the center, a garland with ten medallion portraits of earlier Habsburg monarchs (including Maximilian I) surrounds the sculpted bust of Matthias.[5] The inclusion of allegorical figures, Roman deities, putti, and the emperor's subjects testifies to Matthias's virtues and the prosperity of his realm. At the top, the Three Graces pour symbols of fecundity and wealth from overflowing cornucopias; at the bottom are the bound figures of Envy (eating a heart) and Ignorance (with donkey ears). The portrait allowed Matthias to glorify his leadership in a grand manner, and the work's

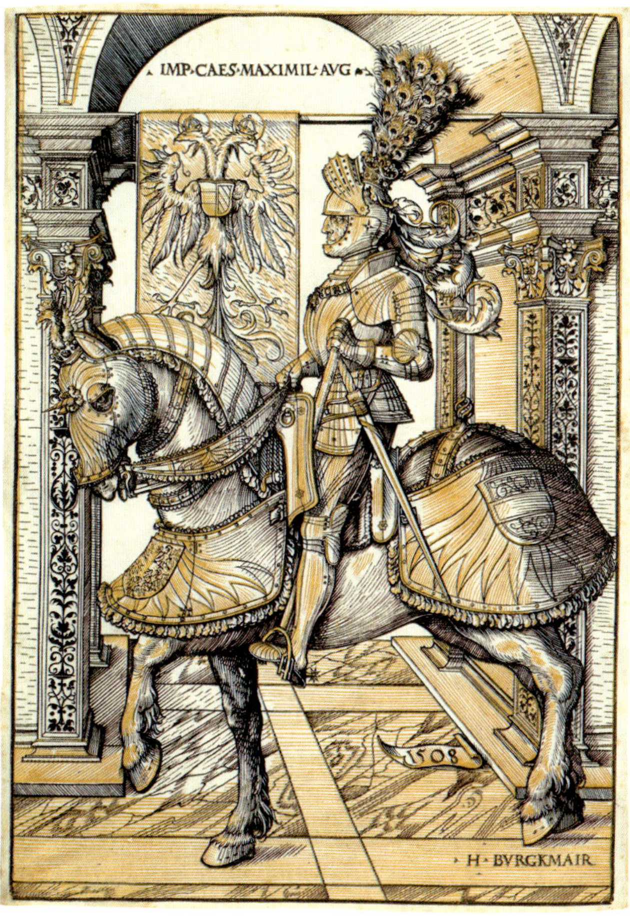

Fig. 2. Hans Burgkmair the Elder (German, 1473–1531). *Equestrian Portrait of the Emperor Maximilian I*, 1508. Woodcut from two blocks in black and gold on vellum; 318 × 225 mm (image); 323 × 235 (sheet). The Art Institute of Chicago, Clarence Buckingham Collection, 1961.3.

sophisticated visual language surely delighted the rich, erudite collectors who would have owned impressions of it.

Portrait prints did not always depict political leaders among the ornate trappings of royal power. Paulus Pontius's engraving after a 1625 painting by Peter Paul Rubens (fig. 3) portrays Isabella Clara Eugenia, the ruler of the Spanish Netherlands, dressed in a nun's habit. Isabella joined the Third Order of Saint Francis after the death of her husband, Archduke Albert (Matthias's brother) in 1621, and she was known for wearing the order's habit as a sign of mourning and religious devotion. While this image shows how Isabella sought to project her piety to her Catholic subjects, earlier in her life

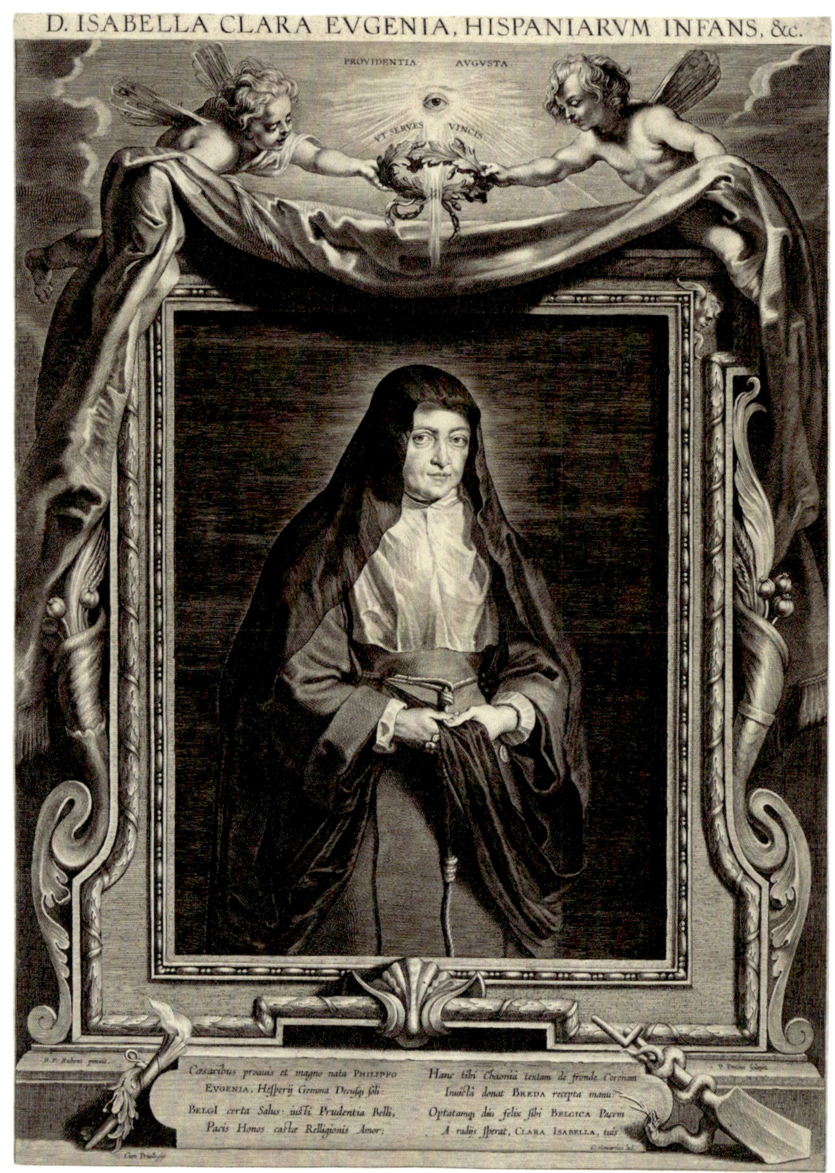

Fig. 3. Paulus Pontius. After Peter Paul Rubens. *Isabella Clara Eugenia (1566–1633)*, 1625/33. Cat. 65.

she was depicted in glittering royal attire. The occasion for Rubens's 1625 canvas was the Spanish recapture of the strategically important city of Breda from the Dutch.[6] Isabella commissioned a number of images from Rubens upon her return from visiting the city.[7] The printed version presents her as a benevolent conqueror; she is framed by two angels who crown her with an oak wreath, which the accompanying text explains was a gift from Breda. The oar at lower right is both a symbol of royal prudence and a reference to the infamous peat barge that played a role in the Dutch taking of the city in 1590.[8]

While the portraits of Matthias and Isabella are large in scale, prints that were smaller yet just as finely crafted could also convey prestige. In seventeenth- and eighteenth-century Europe, the technique of micrography—in which artists used minuscule script to realize abstract designs or figurative representations—became a popular method of making portraits.[9] One of the masters of this process, which has roots in Islamic and Judaic scribal practice, was the German printmaker Johann Michael Püchler, who created a wide variety of micrographic prints and drawings ranging from scenes of the Passion to portraits of royalty and Protestant reformers. One of his several depictions of Holy Roman Emperor Joseph I (fig. 4) incorporates the double-headed eagle, a symbol of imperial power—especially Habsburg power—into the frame. On an earlier state of the print (cat. 114), the artist included a caption clarifying his intended audience, proclaiming that the portrait was made for "noble lovers of engraving, design, and calligraphy."[10]

INFAMY'S TRUMPET: CRIMINALS AND TRAITORS

In addition to portraits of honorable monarchs and statesmen, there was also a demand for printed images of infamous men and women. One factor that contributed to the popularity of such objects was the development of media networks in Europe. While information had long circulated via letters and manuscripts, the printing press revolutionized the dissemination of knowledge and fostered an appetite for news among the broader public. Along with unillustrated reports, European publishers created single-sheet broadsides combining printed text and images. Intended to entertain as much as inform, these documents expressed a biased point of view and featured texts ranging from sensational accounts of supernatural occurrences to purportedly eyewitness descriptions of battles, royal celebrations, and public executions. Because of the topical nature of their subject matter and the fact that the images on most illustrated broadsides were crudely made, few examples have survived. The majority of those that have were made for wealthy, educated consumers and executed by the workshops of established artists and publishers.

One such publication, made by the Cologne workshop of Abraham Hogenberg (fig. 5), depicts the English criminal Thomas Percy, one of the leaders of the Gunpowder Plot, a failed attempt to blow up Parliament and kill King James I,

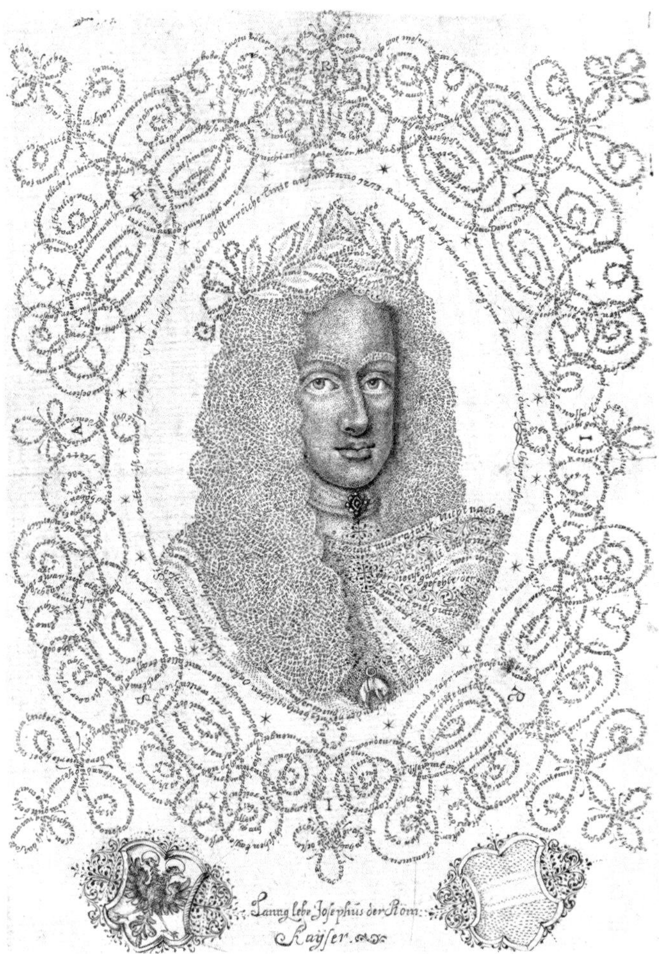

Fig. 4. Johann Michael Püchler, *Joseph I (August), Holy Roman Emperor*, c. 1705. Cat. 113. Shown at actual size.

whom its architects blamed for anti-Catholic policies.[11] The broadside depicts a portrait of a dapper-looking Percy at the top, the arrest of fellow conspirator Guy Fawkes on the left, and Percy's arrest on the right, with explanatory inscriptions in German and Latin. It was probably made when reports of the plot were first reaching Germany, as some of its information is incorrect. While Fawkes was caught red-handed and eventually executed, Percy managed to flee London before being shot and killed; in the image printed on the broadside, however, Percy is shown being taken alive, and the Latin caption at the bottom states that he was "captured and died in prison from a wound."[12] It was many months before the trials

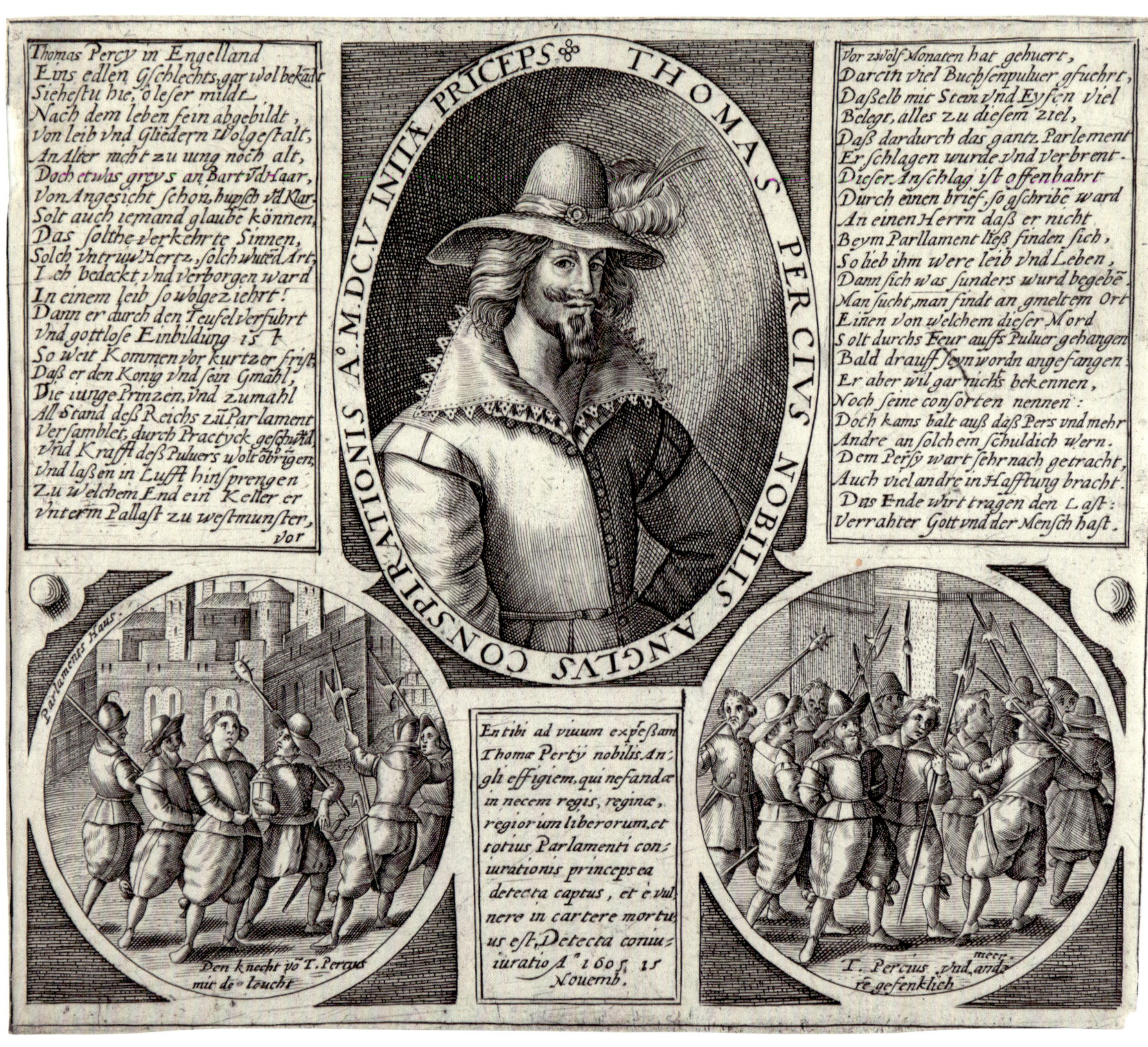

Fig. 5. Workshop of Abraham Hogenberg. *Portrait of Thomas Percy with Two Circles at Lower Left and Right Depicting the Arrest of Guy Fawkes and Percy, Respectively*, 1605/06. Cat. 25.

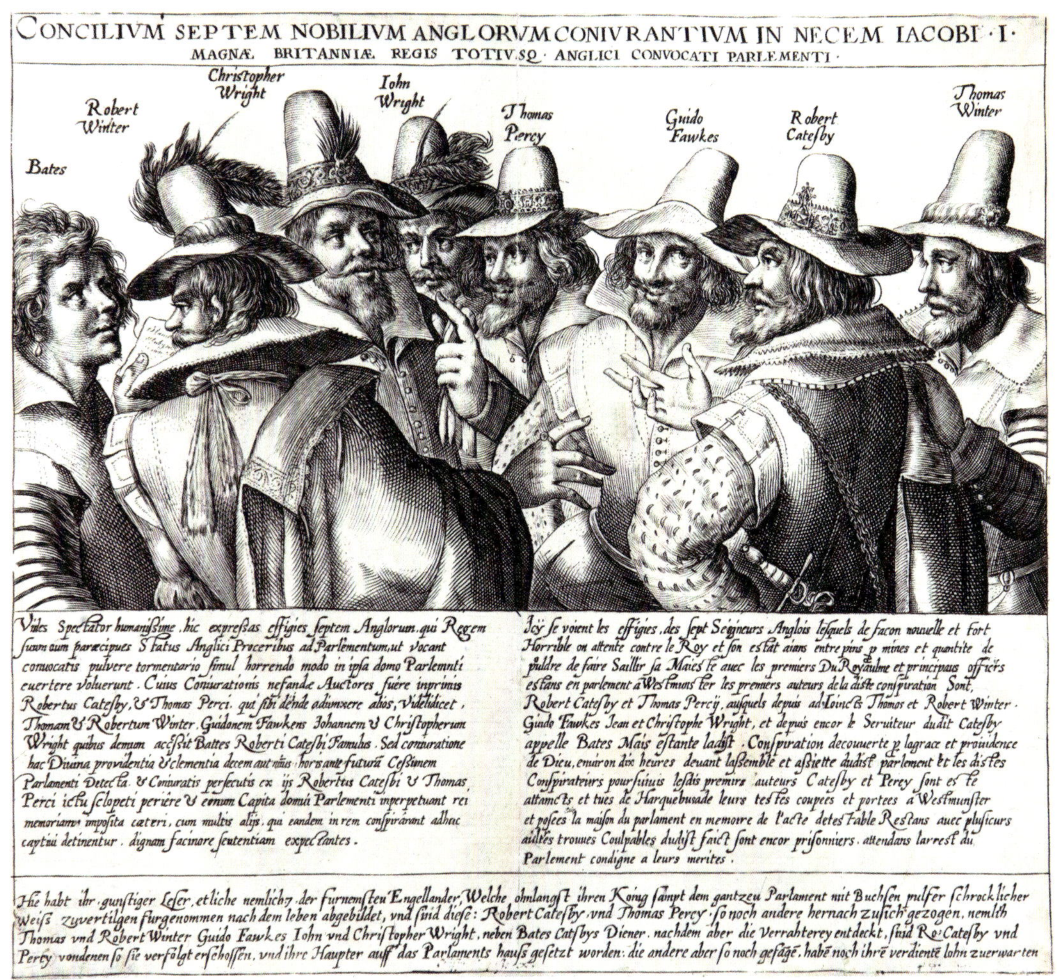

Fig. 6. Workshop of Crispijn de Passe the Elder. *The Gunpowder Plotters*, 1605/06. Cat. 18.

of the other organizers took place and all the details of the scheme were known, but the competitive, time-sensitive market for such pieces compelled most publishers to make due with early reports, which were sometimes conflicting or incorrect. Nevertheless, Hogenberg's print captured the essence of the scintillating story for an eager audience: a devious villain had attempted to orchestrate "an abominable plot" but was foiled just in time.[13]

The Gunpowder Plot was considered a major event throughout Europe, and Hogenberg was not the only publisher on the Continent to issue portraits of the would-be assassins.[14] For example, Dutch printmaker Crispijn de Passe the Elder issued a broadside that depicts eight of the conspirators huddled together (fig. 6).[15] Here, the garments and accessories worn by the men indicate their respective positions in society: the two servants (Thomas Bates and Fawkes) are dressed in simple clothing, while the six more well-to-do men wear chic hats adorned with woven or jeweled hatbands and feather panaches. The fact that noblemen had orchestrated the plan was an especially scandalous aspect of the story given that elites were assumed to be inherently more virtuous.[16] Like the multilingual legend from the Hogenberg portrait, explanatory texts in Latin, French, and German reflect the story's international appeal. De Passe's print was likely made later than Hogenberg's, as his information is more accurate and detailed. He correctly reports that two of the leaders,

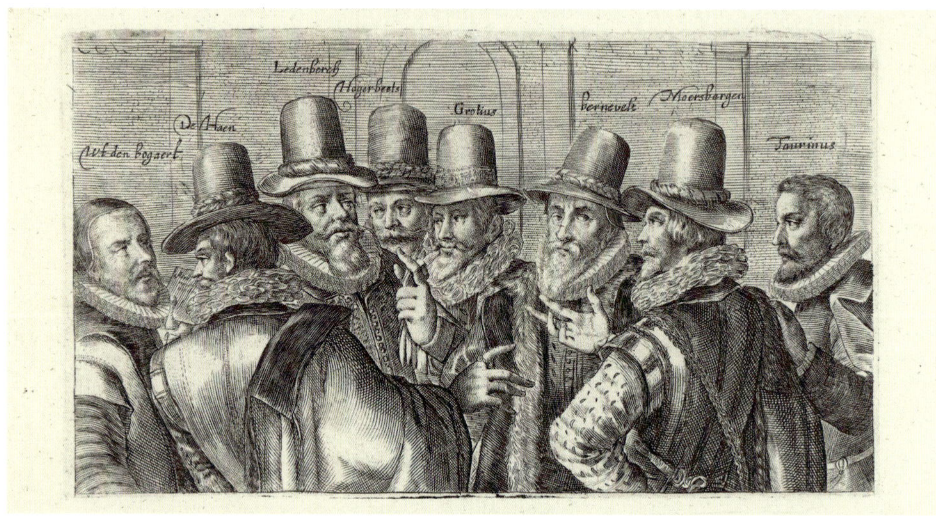

Fig. 7. Workshop of Crispijn de Passe the Elder. *Oldenbarnevelt and His Allies*, 1618. Engraving; 11 × 214 mm. Rijksmuseum RP-P-OB-15.779.

Robert Catesby and Percy, had been shot and killed, their heads transported back to London to be displayed at Parliament.[17] The captions also attribute the discovery of the plot to divine providence; the idea that God intervened in human affairs to punish criminals was widespread in seventeenth-century Europe and appeared in a wide range of inexpensive print media.[18]

When Dutch statesman Johan van Oldenbarnevelt and four of his allies were arrested and charged with conspiring to betray the Dutch Republic to its Catholic enemies in 1618, De Passe reworked the copperplate used for this image, using it to represent Oldenbarnevelt and seven political and religious leaders associated with him (fig. 7). Making minor changes to a printing matrix allowed artists to save on time and materials, but that does not seem to have been De Passe's motive in this case. Because he changed so much—cutting the bottom inscription off, reworking the faces, updating the men's clothing, and burnishing off the title—he could have more easily made a portrait from scratch. However, he probably wanted his audience to recognize this as a reworking of the previous portrait. Critics of Oldenbarnevelt, the very people most likely to buy De Passe's portrait print, would have associated him with the Catholic traitors behind the Gunpowder Plot; this would have been the case even though he was a practicing Protestant and not actually guilty of conspiring against the government of his country, but only of running afoul of Dutch authorities by advocating for greater religious tolerance and a lasting peace with Spain. Furthermore, Oldenbarnevelt was convicted of treason and publicly executed, which probably explains why he replaced Fawkes instead of one of the leaders, who were killed before they could face trial. The relatively tolerant Dutch government ultimately decided that portrait prints of Oldenbarnevelt and his allies—even ones, such as De Passe's, that vilified him—were causing continued factionalism, and in 1619 it banned them in a rare act of image censorship.[19]

While such alterations were not uncommon, printmakers did not always want their audience to know a transformation had taken place. Pierre Lombart's group of prints after the elaborate equestrian portrait of Charles I by Anthony van Dyck (fig. 8) presents an example of how numerous revisions could be made to a work due to political upheavals.[20] The most infamous print based on the painting is probably the so-called "headless horseman" print (fig. 9), mistakenly believed to have been the first state; Lombart's initial work after the painting (fig. 10) was made in 1655 and depicted not Charles I but Oliver Cromwell, who had recently led Parliamentary forces to victory in the English Civil War and overseen the execution of the English monarch. But Cromwell died in 1658, and two years later Charles II assumed the throne. After the Restoration, Lombart's portrait of Cromwell became too risky to sell, as Royalists would not have appreciated an image of Cromwell wearing the armor and riding the steed of the sovereign whose death warrant he had signed; as such, only a few impressions of this portrait survive, and on many of them Lombart's name was rubbed off the paper, probably by the artist himself.

But Lombart was not ready to cut his losses. He tried to salvage his composition by burnishing off Cromwell's head and other identifying information and replacing him with King Louis XIV of France—as George Somes Layard explained in 1922, this was the origin of the "headless horse-man" print.[21] After Lombart returned to France around 1663, printmakers in England subjected the copperplate to three more alterations over the course of the decade. First, an

unknown engraver substituted the likeness of Louis XIV with that of Cromwell. Then, another changed it to represent Charles I (fig. 11). This state, published during the reign of Charles II, seems to have been the most popular, as more impressions of it survive than any other. Ultimately, another artist altered the plate to depict Cromwell for a third and final time, presumably to cater to a Puritan clientele.

These reworkings constitute more than just a curious historical footnote; they are physical manifestations of the political transformations England underwent during the 1650s and 1660s, a turbulent period in which contentious factions battled both for immediate political power as well as for the authority to shape the public's recollection of the past. The process of selectively scraping away engraved lines, hammering the copperplate flat again, and reengraving the surface required skill and finesse on the part of Lombart and his peers. The adaptability of intaglio printmaking permitted

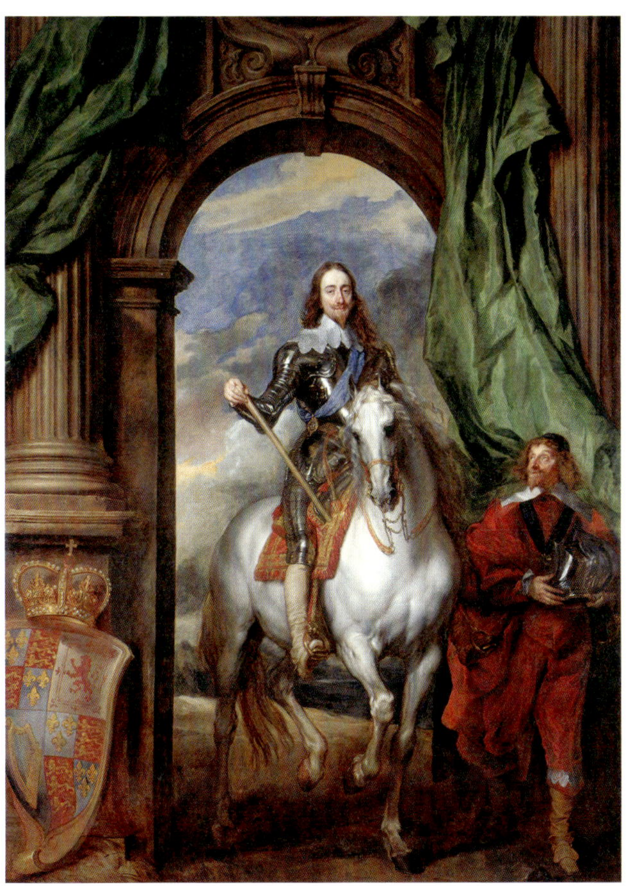

Fig. 8. Anthony van Dyck. *Charles I with M. de St Antoine*, 1633. Oil on canvas; 370 × 270 cm. Royal Collection Trust.

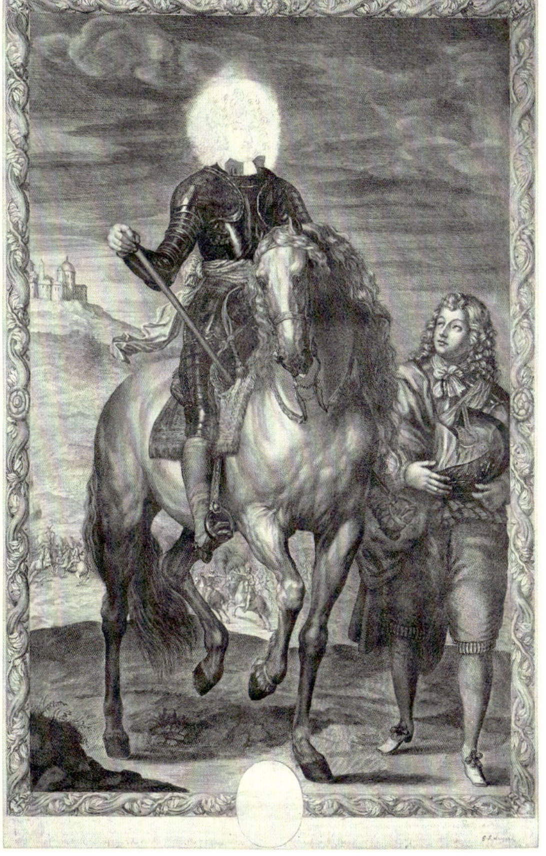

Fig. 9. Pierre Lombart. After Anthony van Dyck. *Louis XIV*, 1655/1715. Engraving on paper; 540 × 349 mm. British Museum, PD 1935-4-13-50.

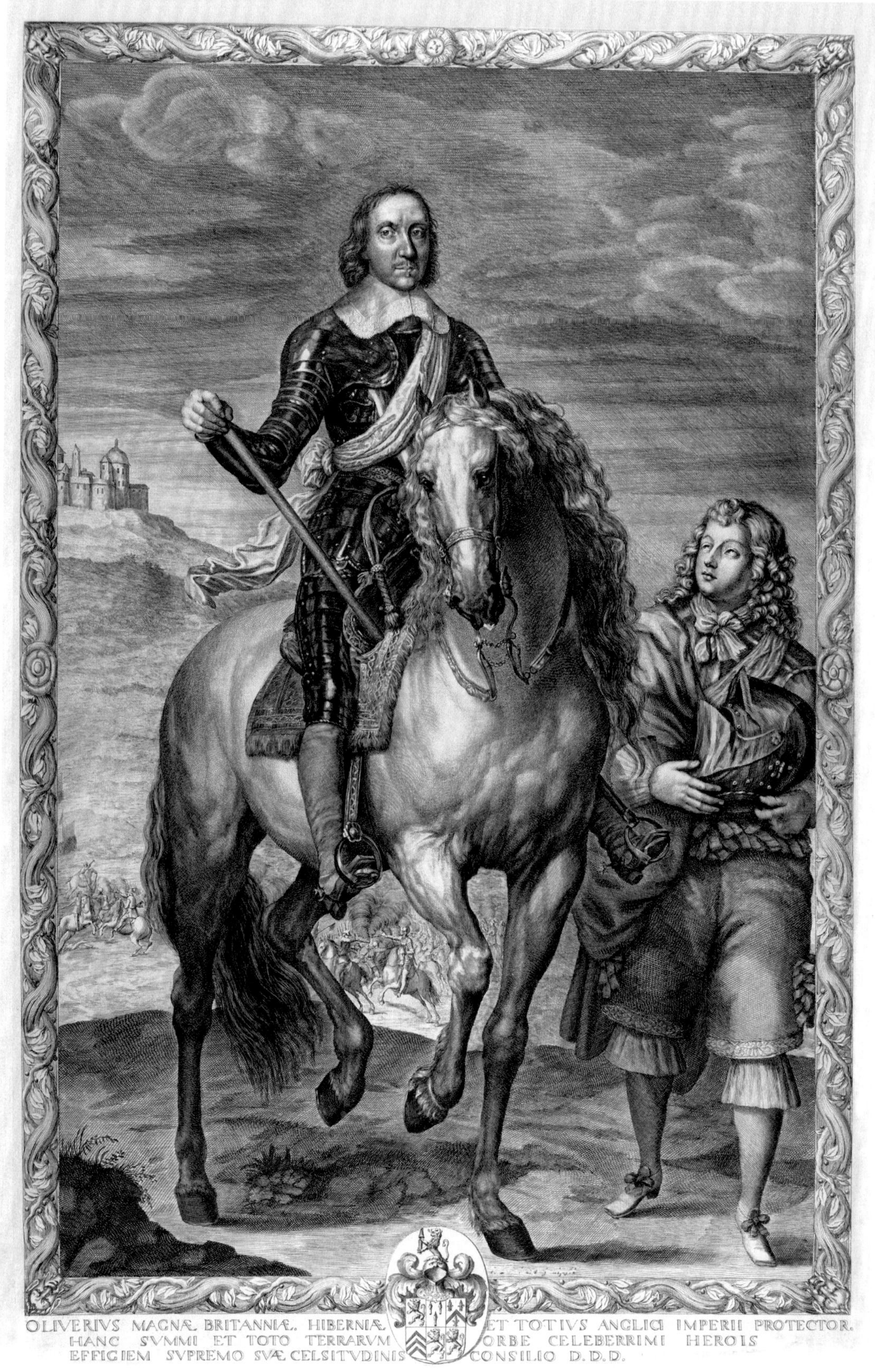

Fig. 10. Pierre Lombart. After Anthony van Dyck. *Oliver Cromwell on Horseback*, 1655. Cat. 91.

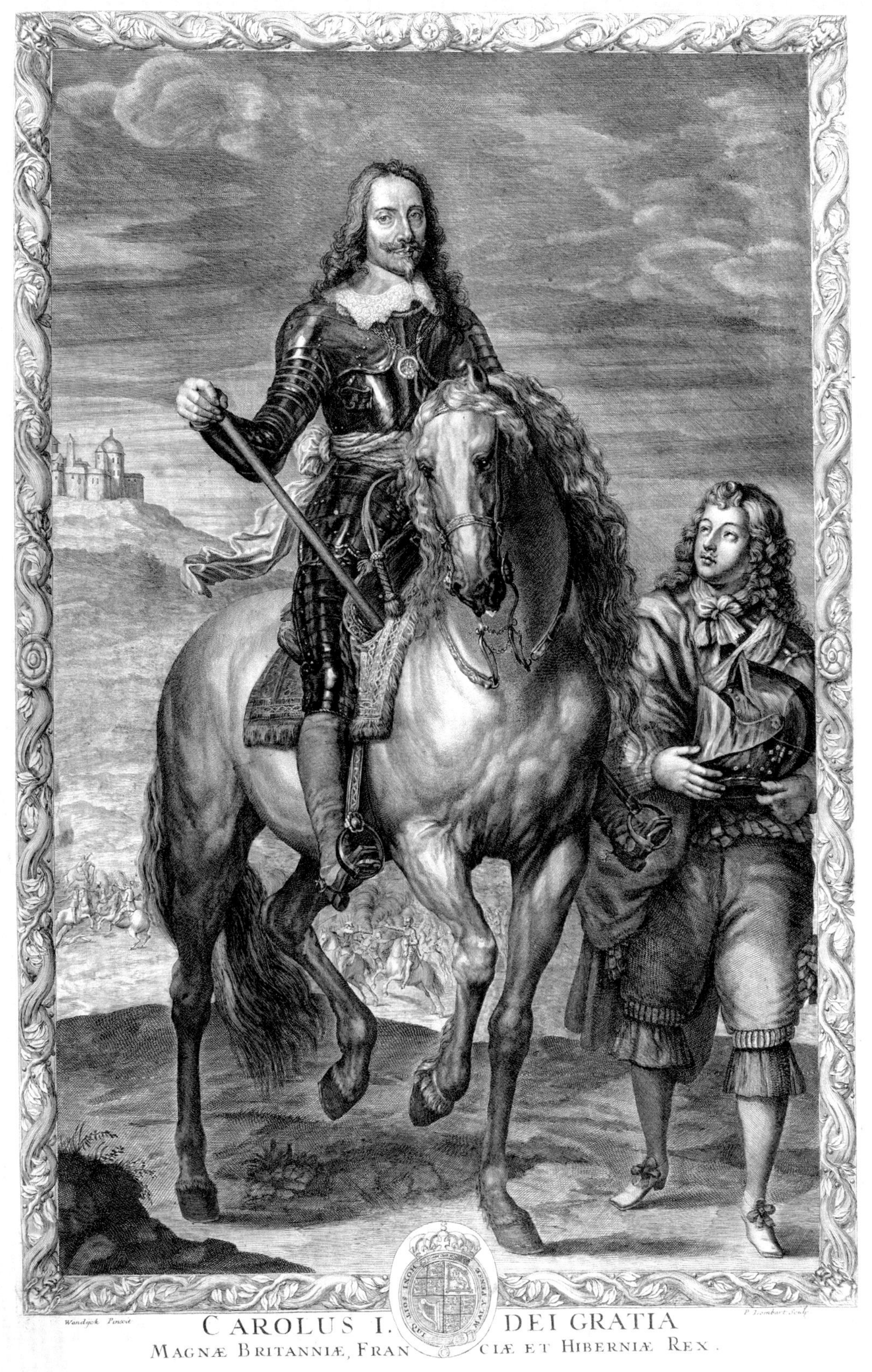

Fig. 11. Pierre Lombart. After Anthony van Dyck. Reworked by an unknown artist. *Charles I on Horseback*, 1655/67. Cat. 92.

these artists to conserve resources while also providing a fitting corollary to contemporary political upheavals in England, as heads rolled and one sovereign took the place of another.

Early modern portrait prints of both the famous and the infamous endowed their subjects with a certain immortality. Works depicting Europe's most powerful and celebrated public figures, including the above-mentioned Habsburg monarchs and their contemporaries in Van Dyck's *Iconography*, as well as the region's most notorious villains and criminals, served an edifying purpose for those who collected them. Gazing at the visage of a distinguished individual spurred the viewer to greater virtue and nobler deeds.[22] Similarly, the likeness of an enemy served as a negative example of beliefs or behavior to be avoided. These images were thus prized for what they could convey to viewers not only about notable men and women, but also about themselves.

Notes

1. *Fama Chiara* is depicted in the first illustrated edition of Cesare Ripa's *Iconologia*. Ripa, *Iconologia* (Rome: Appresso Lepido Facij, 1603), p. 144. Mercury is associated with eloquence, which is disseminated when Pegasus takes flight.

2. An illustration for this personification of Fame appears in the 1644 French edition of Ripa's *Iconologia*. Ripa, *Iconologie* (Paris: M. Guillemot, 1644), p. 80.

3. For more on prints, coins, and medals and the genre of portraiture, see Adrian W. B. Randolph, "Introduction: The Authority of Likeness," *Word and Image: A Journal of Verbal/Visual Enquiry* 19, 1–2 (2003), pp. 1–5; Larry Silver, "The Face Is Familiar: German Renaissance Portrait Multiples in Print and Medals," in ibid., pp. 6–21; and Alexander Dencher, "Hendrick Goltzius and Henry the Great: Netherlandish Printmakers and the Portrait of Henri IV of France," *Dutch Crossing* 39, 2 (July 2015), pp. 103–17.

4. Larry Silver, "Shining Armor: Maximilian I as Holy Roman Emperor," *Art Institute of Chicago Museum Studies* 12, 1 (Fall 1985), pp. 8–29; Harold Joachim, "Maximilian I by Burgkmair," *Art Institute of Chicago Quarterly* 55, 1 (March 1961), pp. 5–9; Suzanne Karr Schmidt, *Altered and Adorned: Using Renaissance Prints in Daily Life*, exh. cat. (Art Institute of Chicago/Yale University Press, 2011), pp. 20–23.

5. Dorothy Anne Limouze, "Aegidius Sadeler (c. 1570–1629): Drawings, Prints, and Art Theory" (PhD diss., Princeton University, 1990), pp. 271–73; Dorothy Limouze, "Aegidius Sadeler, Imperial Printmaker," *Philadelphia Museum of Art Bulletin* 85, 362 (Spring 1989), pp. 14–16; Sara Stevenson, *A Face for Any Occasion: Some Aspects of Portrait Engraving* (Trustees of the National Galleries of Scotland, 1976), pp. 46–49.

6. Hans Vlieghe, *Rubens Portraits of Identified Sitters Painted in Antwerp*, Corpus Rubenianum Ludwig Burchard, pt. 19, vol. 2 (Harvey Miller, 1987), pp. 119–22.

7. Alexandra Libby, "The Solomonic Ambitions of Isabel Clara Eugenia in Rubens's The Triumph of the Eucharist Tapestry Series," *Journal of the Historians of Netherlandish Art* 7, 2 (Summer 2015), http://www.jhna.org/index.php/vol -7-2-2015/313-alexandra-libby.

8. In 1590 seventy Dutch soldiers sneaked into Breda hidden in a peat barge and overpowered the garrison to capture the city. The barge became a symbol of the victory and was put in the city center. For the oar as a symbol of the barge, see Marianne Eekhout, "Celebrating a Trojan Horse: Memories of the Dutch Revolt in Breda," in *Memory before Modernity: Practices of Memory in Early Modern Europe*, ed. Erika Kuijpers and Judith Pollmann (Brill, 2013), pp. 129–48. For its connection to royal prudence, see Vlieghe, *Rubens Portraits*, p. 122.

9. Leila Avrin, "Micrography as Art," in *La lettre hébraïque et sa signification*, ed. Colette Sirat (Centre Régional de Publication de Paris, 1981), pp. 43–63.

10. The full caption reads, in the original German: "Fu diser figur sambt umbgeb / nen Züglein ist der glorwürdig / ste Stammen Ertzhauses Đesterr[eichs] / begriffen / gemacht und entworffen / Durch Joh[annes] Michael Püchler / der Edlen Stöch, Reiss und schreib / kunst liebhabern." (This image of most honorable descendent of the first house of Austria, together with the surrounding motifs, was conceptualized, produced, and designed by Johannes Michael Püchler for noble lovers of engraving, design, and calligraphy.)

11. Fritz Hellwig, *Geschichtsblätter* (Uhl, 1983), cat. 384.

12. The full caption reads, in the original Latin: "En tibi ad vivum expressam Thomae Perty nobilis Angli effigiem qui nefandae in necem regis, reginae, regiorium liberorum, et totius Parlamenti coniurationis princeps ea detecta captus, et e vulnere in carcere mortuus est, Detecta coniuratio A 1605 15 Novemb." (Behold the portrait of the English nobleman Thomas Percy, rendered for you from life, the leader of an abominable plot to kill the king, queen, royal children, and all of Parliament. With the plot discovered he was captured and died in prison of a wound. Plot discovered in the year 1605, 15 November.) With thanks to Melissa Vise for help with the translation.

13. In the original Latin: "nefandae . . . coniurationis."

14. Because of a preference for textual accounts and the powerful role of government censors in the country, there are no English prints about the conspiracy. Antony Griffiths, with the collaboration of Robert A. Gerard, *The Print in Stuart Britain, 1603–1689* (British Museum, 1998), p. 144.

15. De Passe's portrait closely resembles a print by Nuremberg printmaker Heinrich Ulrich, *Concilum septem nobilium Anglorum coniurantium in necem Iacobi magnae Britanniae regis totiusq Anglici convocati Parlementi* (c. 1606; British Museum).

16. Other than the textual explanation, there is nothing about the representation of these men to mark them as infamous. Seventeenth-century artists employed symbols, allegories, or humorous attributes to ridicule infamous people; the exaggerated facial features associated with caricature did not come into vogue until the eighteenth century.

17. In the original French: "Decouvert p[ar] la grace et proindence de Dieu . . . lesdis premirs auteurs Catesby et Perey sont este attamcts et tues de Harque-busade leurs testes coupees et portees a Westminster et posees sur la maison du parlament." (Discovered by the grace and Providence of God. . . the said principal authors Catesby and Percy authors were attacked and killed by harquebusade, their heads cut off and carried to Westminster and placed on the House of Parliament.)

18. Alexandra Walsham, "'The Theatre of Gods Judgements': Sudden Deaths and Providential Punishments," in *Providence in Early Modern England* (Oxford University Press, 2001), 65–115.

19. J. D. Smit, *Resolutiën Staten-Generaal Oude en Nieuwe Reeks 1576–1625*, vol. 4, *1619–1620* (Martinus Nijhoff, 1981), p. 296.

20. George Somes Layard, *The Headless Horseman: Pierre Lombart's Engraving, Charles or Cromwell?* (Philip Allan, 1922); Griffiths, *The Print in Stuart Britain*, pp. 180–81.

21. Layard, *The Headless Horseman*.

22. The idea that depictions of famous individuals have an edifying function goes back to antiquity. Christiane L. Joost-Gaugier, "The Early Beginnings of the Notion of 'Uomini Famois' and the 'De Viris Illustribus' in Greco-Roman Literary Tradition," *Artibus et Historiae* 3, 6 (1982), pp. 97–115; Christiane L. Joost-Gaugier, "Poggio and Visual Tradition: 'Uomini Famosi' in Classical Literary Description," *Artibus et Historiae* 6, 12 (1985), pp. 57–74. In his 1516 *Education of a Christian Prince,* Dutch humanist Desiderius Erasmus instructed Charles V of Spain to surround himself with images of good kings as well as tyrants in order to learn from their example. Erasmus advised that their portraits "should be carved in rings, painted on pictures, and written on genealogical trees. . . . Noble minds are forcefully enkindled by examples of famous men." Otto Herding, *Institutio Principis Christiani* (North-Holland, 1974), cited in Kurt Johannesson, "The Portrait of the Prince as Rhetorical Genre" in *Iconography, Propaganda, and Legitimation* (Claren-don/Oxford University Press, 1998), p. 17.

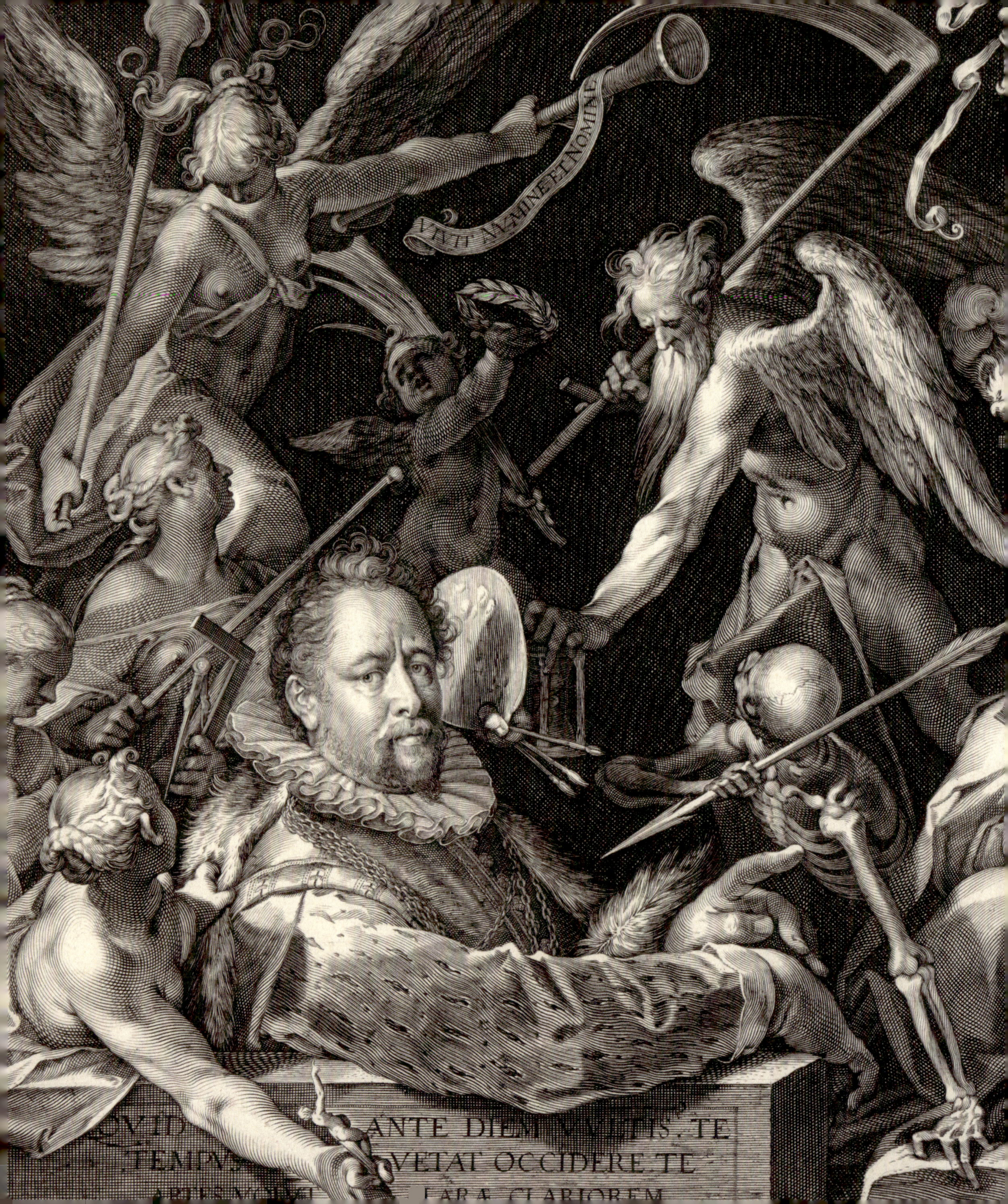
VIVIT AVMINE ET NOMINE
QVID ANTE DIEM ...IS. TE
...TEMPVS VETAT OCCIDERE TE
ARTIS NOVI... FARÆ CLARIOREM

Checklist of the Exhibition

Compiled by Victoria Sancho Lobis with additional research by Kylie Escudero, Maureen Warren, and Emily Vokt Ziemba.

Objects are listed in chronological order according to the birth dates of the artists, when known. Unattributed works are placed according to the estimated dates of their production. Measurements are given height before width; for prints, plate mark dimensions are given when known.

The following conventions for dating a work are used:

1625 — Executed in 1625
1625 (?) — Possibly executed in 1625
c. 1625 — Executed sometime around 1625
1625–30 — Begun in 1625 and completed in 1630
1625/30 — Executed sometime within or around the period 1625 to 1630

Watermark and catalogue raisonné references are shortened according to the name of the author or authors, with the following exceptions:

Butler Institute
Zona, Louis A., and Jim Pernotto. *Chuck Close Editions: A Catalog Raisonné and Exhibition.* Exh. cat. Butler Institute of American Art, Youngstown, Ohio, 1989.

Fonds Français
Laran, Jean. *Inventaire du fonds français après 1800.* Bibliothèque Nationale, 1930–. Weigert, Roger-Armand, and Maxime Préaud. *Inventaire du fonds français, graveurs du XVIIe siècle.* Bibliothèque Nationale, 1939–.

Glasgow
MacDonald, Margaret F., Grischka Petri, Margaret Dunwoody Hausberg, and Joanna Meacock. *James McNeill Whistler: The Etchings, a Catalogue Raisonné.* University of Glasgow, 2011–. http://etchings.arts.gla.ac.uk.

New Hollstein
Hollstein, F. W. H. *The New Hollstein Dutch and Flemish Etchings, Engravings and Woodcuts, 1450–1700.* Sound and Vision, 1995–.
——. *The New Hollstein German Engravings, Etchings and Woodcuts, 1400–1700.* Sound and Vision, 1995–.

Full citations to all references are listed in the selected bibliography.

Printed inscriptions are withheld; only manuscript inscriptions unique to these objects are provided. Annotations related to the Art Institute's internal cataloguing procedures are also withheld.

The locations of inscriptions are abbreviated as follows:

u.l.: — upper left
u.c.: — upper center
u.r.: — upper right
c.l.: — center left
c.: — center
c.r.: — center right
l.l.: — lower left
l.c.: — lower center
l.r.: — lower right

Provenance information is given in chronological sequence, as completely as possible, with indication of transfer of ownership when available. For additional information related to provenance, please consult the Index of Print Collectors (pp. 100–03). Unless otherwise noted, all works are from the collection of the Art Institute of Chicago.

Albrecht Dürer (German, 1471–1528)

1
Philip Melanchthon, 1526
Engraving in black on ivory laid paper; 173 × 128 mm (plate mark); 176 × 131 mm (sheet)
Bequest of Mrs. Potter Palmer, Jr., 1956.956
REFERENCES: Bartsch 105; Meder 104 b/f; Schoch/Mende/Scherbaum 101
WATERMARK: Jug (Meder 158)
INSCRIPTIONS: verso, l.c., in graphite: *c. 15715.* and *3/-*; l.c., in graphite: *B105*; l.r., in graphite: *C 2199–650*

2
Erasmus of Rotterdam, 1526
Engraving in black on ivory laid paper; 251 × 193 mm (plate mark); 258 × 197 mm (sheet)
Bequest of Mrs. Potter Palmer, Jr., 1956.957
REFERENCES: Bartsch 107; Meder 105 b–d/i; Schoch/Mende/Scherbaum 102
INSCRIPTION: recto, l.c., in graphite: *B – 107*

3
Ulrich Varnbüler, 1522
Printed c. 1620 by Willem Jansz. Blaeu (Dutch, 1571–1638)
Woodcut in black on ivory laid paper with added brown and sepia tone blocks; 430 × 327 mm (trimmed within plate mark)
Clarence Buckingham Collection, 1939.2080
REFERENCES: Bartsch 155; Meder 256 IIIa/IIIb; Schoch/Mende/Scherbaum 256 III/III
WATERMARK: Circle (Meder 258; related to IIIa/IIIb)
INSCRIPTION: verso, l.c., in pen and brown ink: *porcansi* (?)
PROVENANCE: Albertina Collection, Vienna (Lugt 5d).

Albrecht Altdorfer (German, c. 1480–1538)
After Lucas Cranach (German, c. 1472–1553)

4
Martin Luther, c. 1525
Engraving with stippling in black on cream laid
paper; 60 × 40 mm (plate mark); 61 × 42 mm (sheet)
The Charles Deering Collection, 1939.2078
REFERENCES: Bartsch 61; New Hollstein e.80
INSCRIPTIONS: verso, u.c., in graphite: *Martin
Luther / B 61*; l.c., in brown ink: (illegible initials)
PROVENANCE: Kupferstichkabinett der Staatlichen
Museen, Berlin (Lugt 234 and Lugt 1609).
Unidentified collector (Lugt 1474a). Unidentified
stamp in black ink, *PP* (not in Lugt).

Unidentified European artist

5
Pendant, 16th century
Gold and stone; 2.6 × 2.1 cm (1¹⁄₁₆ × ⅞ in.)
Gift of Marilynn B. Alsdorf, 1992.546
PROVENANCE: Minneapolis Institute of Art. Melvin
Gutman, New York, by 1961; his sale, New York,
Parke-Bernet, Dec. 6, 1969, lot 5; Marilynn B.
Alsdorf, Chicago; given to the Art Institute, 1992.

Jacob Binck (German, c. 1500–1569)

6
Portrait of Reinneir, 1525
Engraving and etching in black on buff laid paper;
diam. 67 mm (trimmed within plate mark)
William McCallin McKee Memorial Endowment,
1947.541
REFERENCES: Bartsch 94; Aumüller 141
INSCRIPTION: verso, l.c., in graphite: *10810*

Melchior Lorck (Danish, 1526/27–after 1588)

7
*Ismael, the Persian Ambassador of Tahmasp,
King of Persia*, 1569
Engraving in black on cream laid paper;
395 × 265 mm (plate mark); 410 × 310 mm (sheet)
Through prior acquisition of John H. Wrenn
Memorial Collection, 1991.127
REFERENCES: Bartsch 16; Hollstein 29 II/III
WATERMARK: Horn (cf. Heawood 2628)
INSCRIPTION: recto, l.r., in orange pencil: *31*.

Unidentified Flemish artist

8
Portrait of a Man, c. 1575
Oil on panel; 46.8 × 33.9 cm (18⁷⁄₁₆ × 13⅜ in.)
Samuel P. Avery Fund, 1951.224
PROVENANCE: Probably Charles Jennens (d. 1773),
Gopsall, Leicestershire, by 1767; by descent to
Richard George Penn Curzon, 4th Earl Howe,
Gopsall, until 1918; sold to Agnew's, London, 1918;
sold to W. L. Peacock and Co., London, 1921.
Mrs. Helen Hilston Cowie (d. 1947), Ravensleigh,
Dowanhill, Glasgow; by descent to her husband
Thomas Rennie Cowie (d. 1950); sold by his heirs
at Christie's, London, May 18, 1951, lot 62, to
P. and D. Colnaghi and Co., London, 1951; sold
to the Art Institute, 1951.

**Unidentified German artist,
active in Nuremberg**

9
Portrait of Bartholomeus Lother, 1584
Wax on glass; diam. 7 cm (2¾ in.)
Gift of Mrs. Alfred Ernest Hamill, 1959.498
INSCRIPTION: recto: *BARTHOLOME. LOTHER.
AETATIS LIIII 1584*
PROVENANCE: Fréderic Spitzer (1815–1890).

10
Portrait of Ursula Lother, 1584
Wax on glass; diam. 7 cm (2¾ in.)
Gift of Mrs. Alfred Ernest Hamill, 1959.497
INSCRIPTION: recto: *VRSVLA LOEHERIN.
AETATIS XLVI AO 1584*
PROVENANCE: Fréderic Spitzer (1815–1890).

Hieronymus Wierix (Flemish, 1553–1619)

11
Philip II, King of Spain, 1586
Engraving in black on ivory laid paper;
355 × 249 mm (trimmed within plate mark)
Gift of Mr. and Mrs. D. T. Bergen, 1967.20
REFERENCES: Hollstein 2134 I/II; Mauquoy-
Hendrickx 1892
WATERMARK: Basel crosier (Laurentius 267) with
unidentified countermark circle with initials *AV*
INSCRIPTIONS: verso, l.l., in graphite: *Lbj*; l.l.,
in graphite: *6089/unn/nop*; l.l., in graphite: *P24553*
PROVENANCE: Henri Beraldi (Lugt 230). Carl Otto
Schniewind (Lugt 641a).

Hendrick Goltzius (Dutch, 1558–1617)

12
*Philips Galle (1537–1612), Pupil of Coornhert
from Haarlem, Engraver and Publisher in
Antwerp from 1570; The Baptism of the Eunuch
in Background Left*, 1582
Engraving, with stippling, in black on off-white laid
paper; 216 × 136 mm (trimmed within plate mark)
Gift of Mrs. Morris Woolf, 1941.431
REFERENCES: Strauss 156 II/III; New Hollstein 223 II/III
INSCRIPTIONS: verso, u.c., in brown ink: *£ 18*; l.l.,
in graphite: *a 32343*; l.c., in graphite: *Philip Galle*
PROVENANCE: Emanuel Levy (Lugt 876).

13
*Robert Dudley, Earl of Leicester (1532–1588),
English Nobleman, Governor-General of the
United Provinces in 1585–87*, 1586
Engraving in black on ivory laid paper; 61 × 52 mm
(trimmed within plate mark)
Gift of Mrs. Morris Woolf, 1941.432
REFERENCES: Strauss 226 I/I; New Hollstein 213 I/I
WATERMARK: Coat of arms (fragment)
INSCRIPTION: verso, l.r., in graphite: *n. fol*
PROVENANCE: Friedrich Kalle (Lugt 1021). Emanuel
Levy (Lugt 876).

14
Gillis van Breen, 1588/92
Chiaroscuro woodcut in black, ocher, and brown
on cream laid paper; 211 × 144 mm (trimmed
within plate mark)
Gift of Alfred E. Hamill, 1951.53
REFERENCES: Strauss 404 III/III; Bialler 23 II/II; New
Hollstein 305 IIb/IIb
INSCRIPTIONS: verso, c., in graphite: *23g*; l.l., in
graphite: *36/£*; l.l., in graphite: *H. 375*

15
*Dirck Volckertsz. Coornhert (1522–1590),
Author, Secretary of the City of Haarlem,
Printmaker, Goltzius's Teacher*, 1591
Engraving in black on ivory laid paper;
425 × 324 mm (trimmed within plate mark)
Gift from Harold Joachim, 1961.878
REFERENCES: Strauss 287 III/III; New Hollstein
211 III/III
WATERMARK: Coat of arms with a bear
(cf. Briquet 1052)
INSCRIPTIONS: verso, u.c., in pen and brown ink:
Henry Goltzius 1558/1617; c., in graphite: *p/s*; l.l.,
in pen and brown ink: *B 164*; l.c., in pen and
brown ink: *601—*; l.r., in graphite: *No. 105*
PROVENANCE: Pierre II Mariette (Lugt 1787).
Thomas Graf (Lugt 1092b). E. Fabricius
(Lugt 847a and 919ter).

Attributed to Isaac Oliver
(English, born France, 1558/68–1617)

16
Portrait of a Man, late 16th/early 17th century
Opaque watercolor on parchment; 4.8 × 3.8 cm
(1⅞ × 1½ in.)
The Colonel Alexander F. and Jeannie C.
Stevenson Memorial Collection, gift of Mary
Louise Stevenson, 1958.84

Crispijn de Passe the Elder (Dutch, 1564–1637)
After Isaac Oliver (English, born France, 1558/68–1617)

17
Queen Elizabeth I, 1603/04
Engraving in black on laid paper; 347 × 225 mm
(plate mark); 361 × 240 mm (sheet)
Collection of Nicholas Stogdon
REFERENCES: Hind I, p. 282, 1; Hollstein 712 III/III
WATERMARK: Cockatrice (or baselisk) with house
and Basel crosier above (cf. Tschudin 291–92
and Heawood 842 or 844)
PROVENANCE: E. Heckett; sale, London, Sotheby's,
July 11, 1983 (*The English Renaissance*), lot 49.
R. A. Hobson (not in Lugt).

Workshop of Crispijn de Passe the Elder
(Dutch, 1564–1637)

18
The Gunpowder Plotters, 1605/06
Engraving in black on laid paper; 190 × 210 mm
(trimmed to plate mark)
Collection of Nicholas Stogdon
REFERENCE: Hind II, pp. 391–92, 64.
WATERMARK: Single-headed eagle breasting an
indistinct charge, pendant shield with scrolled top
(cf. Heawood 1241 and 1243)
PROVENANCE: R. A. Hobson (not in Lugt).

Jacques de Gheyn II (Dutch, 1565–1629)

19
Carolus Clusius, 1601
Engraving, with stippling, in black on cream
laid paper; 219 × 183 mm (plate mark);
222 × 186 mm (sheet)
The Wallace L. DeWolf and Joseph Brooks Fair
Collections, 1920.2184
REFERENCE: New Hollstein 241 I/I
INSCRIPTIONS: verso, l.c., in graphite: *Page 1/*
with his face very bookish (?); l.l., in graphite:
1402bg½
PROVENANCE: Paul Davidsohn (Lugt 654).

Jacques de Fornazeris (French, active 1590–1622)

20
Marie de Médicis, 1601
Etching and engraving in red ink with brush and
red ink on laid paper; 477 × 349 mm (plate mark);
480 × 354 mm (sheet)
Collection of Nicholas Stogdon
REFERENCES: Robert-Dumesnil 51; Fonds
Français IV, 12
WATERMARK: Bunch of grapes, countermark with
initials including a *G* (cf. Briquet 13207 to 13214)
PROVENANCE: George Burns (not in Lugt).

Aegidius Sadeler (Flemish, c. 1570–1629)

21
Portrait of Bartolomeus Spranger with an Allegory
of the Death of His Wife, Christina
Müller, 1600
Engraving with etching in black on ivory laid paper;
293 × 416 mm (trimmed within plate mark)
Bernard F. Rogers Collection, 1935.432
REFERENCE: Hollstein 332 I/II
WATERMARK: Capital *R* in a circle (Briquet 8975)
INSCRIPTIONS: recto, l.l., in graphite: *44*; verso, u.l.,
in pen and brown ink: *c 14 71*; u.l., in graphite, with
light brown ink: *14*
PROVENANCE: Pierre II Mariette (Lugt 1789 and 2096).

22
Georg III Thurzo of Bethlendorf, 1607
Pen and black ink, over black chalk, with red chalk
and touches of white chalk, on paper prepared
with an opaque gray ground; 168 × 122 mm
Gift of Mrs. Benjamin F. Stein, 1959.534a
INSCRIPTIONS: secondary support, verso, u.l., in
graphite: *572*; u.c., in graphite: *No. 1279*; c., in
graphite: *31*; l.c. in graphite: *16*
PROVENANCE: August Grahl (Lugt 1199).

23
Georg III Thurzo of Bethlendorf, 1607
Engraving and etching in black on cream
paper; 205 × 148 mm (trimmed within plate mark)
Gift of Mrs. Benjamin F. Stein in memory of
her husband, 1959.534b
REFERENCE: Hollstein 337 I/I
WATERMARK: Tower (fragment; Heawood 3941)
INSCRIPTIONS: verso, c., in graphite: (illegible initial);
l.c., in graphite: *16*.

24
Portrait of Emperor Matthias, 1614
Engraving in black on ivory laid paper; 682 ×
426 mm (plate mark); 683 × 467 mm (sheet)
Amanda S. Johnson and Marion J. Livingston
Fund, 2014.14
REFERENCE: Hollstein 310 II/III

Workshop of Abraham Hogenberg
(Flemish, active in Germany, active 1605–after 1653)

25
Portrait of Thomas Percy with Two Circles at Lower
Left and Right Depicting the Arrest of Guy Fawkes
and Percy, Respectively, 1605/06
Engraving in black on laid paper; 170 × 194 mm
(trimmed to plate mark)
Collection of Nicholas Stogdon
WATERMARK: Eagle with shield below
PROVENANCE: R. A. Hobson (not in Lugt).

Unidentifed Dutch artist

26
Allegory on the Futility of Peace Talks with
Spain, 1608
Engraving in black on cream laid paper;
303 × 213 mm (trimmed within plate mark)
Collection of Meg and Mark Hausberg
INSCRIPTION: verso, c., in pen and black ink: *W*

Jan Harmensz. Muller (Dutch, 1571–1628)
After Hendrick Goltzius (Dutch, 1558–1617)

27
Portrait of Hendrick Goltzius, c. 1617
Engraving in black on buff laid paper; 580 ×
429 mm (plate mark); 600 × 440 mm (sheet)
Joseph Brooks Fair Fund, 1926.1924
REFERENCES: New Hollstein 92 III/III; New Hollstein
(Goltzius) 752 III/III
INSCRIPTIONS: verso, u.r., in pen and black ink:
(illegible); l.l., in graphite: *18463 MK*; l.r.,
in graphite: *1 of* (?)

William Jacobsz. Delff (Dutch, 1580–1638)
After Michiel Jansz. van Mierevelt
(Dutch, 1567–1641)

28
Johan van Oldenbarnevelt, Grand Pensionary
of Holland, 1617
Engraving in black on buff laid paper; 279 ×
190 mm (plate mark); 279 × 190 mm (sheet)
Private collection
REFERENCE: Hollstein 54 II/II
WATERMARK: Fleur-de-lis with initials (fragment;
cf. Heawood 1480)
INSCRIPTION: verso, l.r., in graphite: *fm 3961 B*

29
Sophia Hedwichia, Countess of Nassau-Dietz, 1631
Engraving in black on ivory laid paper; 425 ×
310 mm (plate mark); 450 × 334 mm (sheet)
Elizabeth Hammond Stickney Collection, 1887.294
REFERENCE: Hollstein 15 I/II
WATERMARK: Fleur-de-lis (cf. Laurentius 419; from
the Strasbourg area)
INSCRIPTIONS: recto, l.l., in graphite: *Gräfin Ernesti
Casimir zur Nassau - dietz*; l.c., in graphite:
Countess Nassau; l.r., in graphite: *Delff oc-*; verso,
l.l., in graphite: *i.ne*

William Jacobsz. Delff (Dutch, 1580–1638)
After Daniel Mytens
(Dutch, active in England, c. 1590–before 1648)

30
Portrait of Charles I, King of England, 1628/30
Engraving in black on silk; 420 × 289 mm
(measured within frame)
Collection of Nicholas Stogdon
REFERENCE: Hollstein 2 I/I
PROVENANCE: Richard Bull (Lugt 314).

31
Hendrik, Count van de Bergh, 1634
Engraving in black on cream laid paper; 422 ×
299 mm (plate mark); 450 × 323 mm (sheet)
The Wallace L. DeWolf and Joseph Brooks Fair
Collections, 1922.5706
REFERENCE: Hollstein 6 I/I
WATERMARK: Coat of arms of Burgundy-Austria
(cf. Laurentius 153)
INSCRIPTIONS: verso, l.l., in graphite: *Siegen;*
l.l., in graphite: *15902 G*; l.c., in graphite: *F6*
PROVENANCE: Paul Davidsohn (Lugt 654).

Schelte Adamsz. Bolswert (Flemish, c. 1586–1659)
After Anthony van Dyck (Flemish, 1599–1641)

32
Sebastiaan Vrancx, 1630/45
Engraving in black on ivory laid paper;
242 × 166 mm (trimmed within lower plate mark)
Gift of John E. Irwin, 1887.714
REFERENCES: Mauquoy-Hendrickx (Van Dyck) 25 V/V;
New Hollstein (Van Dyck) 101 V/V
WATERMARK: Foolscap (cf. Mauquoy-Hendrickx 139)
INSCRIPTION: verso, l.r., in graphite: *21-*

Claes Jansz. Visscher (Dutch, 1587–1652)

33
*Portrait and Execution of
Gilles van Ledenberg, 1619*
Contained within volume of forty prints, portraits,
and pamphlets, bound in cream vellum;
203 × 160 × 40 mm (closed)
Amanda S. Johnson and Marion J. Livingston
Fund, 2015.296
REFERENCE: Hollstein 32 I/I

34
Execution of Arminians in Leiden, 1623
Hand-colored etching with engraving and
letterpress in black on cream laid paper;
311 × 250 mm (trimmed within plate mark)
Amanda S. Johnson and Marion J. Livingtson
Fund, 2015.297
REFERENCE: Hollstein 49 I/I
INSCRIPTION: verso, c., in graphite: *3752296*

Jean Morin (French, c. 1590–1650)
After Philippe de Champaigne
(French, 1602–1674)

35
Antoine Vitré, 1640/50
Etching with stippling in black on ivory laid paper;
312 × 213 mm (trimmed within plate mark)
Gift in memory of Tom and Ann Tice from their
daughters, 2000.444
REFERENCES: Robert-Dumesnil 88 II/III; Hornibrook
and Petitjean 49 III/IV; Mazel 094 II/III

Lucas Emil Vorsterman (Flemish, 1595–1675)
After Anthony van Dyck (Flemish, 1599–1641)

36
Antoon Cornelissen, 1630/45
Etching and engraving in black on ivory laid paper;
236 × 136 mm (plate mark); 249 × 169 mm (sheet)
Clarence Buckingham Collection, 1928.154
REFERENCES: Mauquoy-Hendrickx 3 III/X;
New Hollstein 55 III/IX
WATERMARKS: Fleur-de-lis with crown above
(Mauquoy-Hendrickx 146; Wibiral 6a);
countermark *LM*
INSCRIPTIONS: recto, l.l., in graphite (erased):
Vorsterman; verso, l.l., in graphite: *K.7201;*
l.l., in graphite: *5*; l.l., in brown ink: *gs* (in an oval);
l.r., in graphite: *c. 16771*; l.r., in graphite: *16*
PROVENANCE: Alfred Morrison (Lugt 151). Clarence
Buckingham (Lugt 497).

37
Jan Lievens, 1630/45
Etching in black on cream laid paper; 246 × 168 mm
Gift of John E. Irwin, 1887.713
REFERENCES: Mauquoy-Hendrickx 85 IV or VI/VI;
New Hollstein 72 IV or VI/VI
WATERMARK: Foolscap (fragment)

Lucas Emil Vorsterman (Flemish, 1595–1675) and
Paulus Pontius (Flemish, 1603–1658)
After Anthony van Dyck (Flemish, 1599–1641)

38
Jan van den Wouwer, 1630/45
Etching in black on ivory laid paper; 235 × 155 mm
(plate mark); 247 × 173 mm (sheet)
Clarence Buckingham Collection, 1928.153
REFERENCES: Mauquoy-Hendrickx 18 (Van Dyck) IV/IX;
New Hollstein (Van Dyck) 47 IV/IX
WATERMARK: Fleur-de-lis with crown above
(Mauquoy-Hendrickx 159); countermark with *SI*
INSCRIPTIONS: recto, l.r., in graphite: *33*; verso,
l.l., in graphite: *k.7207*; l.r., in graphite: *c16777*
PROVENANCE: William Hookham Carpenter (Lugt
2626). Alfred Morrison (Lugt 151). Marseille
Holloway (Lugt 1875). Clarence Buckingham
(Lugt 497).

Christoffel Jegher (Flemish, 1596–1652/53)
After Peter Paul Rubens (Flemish, 1577–1640)

39
Portrait of Doge Giovanni Cornaro, 1632/36
Chiaroscuro woodcut in beige, ocher, and two tones
of brown on cream laid paper; 305 × 233 mm
Everett D. Graff Fund, 1967.493
REFERENCES: Hollstein 20 II; Schneevoogt 188.286
INSCRIPTIONS: verso, l.l., in graphite: *3965;*
l.r., in graphite: *13x16 – 412*
PROVENANCE: Alfred Morrison (Lugt 151).

Robert van Voerst (Flemish, 1597–1636/37)
After Anthony van Dyck (Flemish, 1599–1641)

40
Inigo Jones, 1630/36
Printed c. 1800
Engraving in black on wove paper; 243 × 177 mm
(plate mark); 252 × 185 mm (sheet)
Gift of John E. Irwin, 1887.710
REFERENCES: Mauquoy-Hendrickx (Van Dyck) 72 V
or VII/VII; New Hollstein (Van Dyck) 70 V or VII/VII

41
Simon Vouet, 1630/36
Engraving in black on cream laid paper;
243 × 177 mm (trimmed to plate mark)
Gift of John E. Irwin, 1887.716
REFERENCES: Mauquoy-Hendrickx (Van Dyck) 74 V/VII;
New Hollstein (Van Dyck) 100 V/VII
WATERMARK: Foolscap
INSCRIPTION: recto, l.l., in graphite: *1 / 504*

42
Robert van Voerst, 1630/36
Engraving in black on cream laid paper; 239 ×
170 mm (plate mark); 362 × 275 mm (sheet)
The Wallace L. DeWolf and Joseph Brooks Fair
Collections, 1920.2463
REFERENCES: Mauquoy-Hendrickx (Van Dyck) 73 IV/VI;
New Hollstein (Van Dyck) 97 IV/VI
WATERMARK: Foolscap (cf. Mauquoy-Henricks 20
and Wibiral 3b)
PROVENANCE: Paul Davidsohn (Lugt 654).

Anthony van Dyck (Flemish, 1599–1641)

43
Self-Portrait, 1630/33
Etching in black on ivory laid paper; 246 × 157 mm
(plate mark); 257 × 169 mm (sheet)
Clarence Buckingham Collection, 1927.391
REFERENCES: Mauquoy-Hendrickx 4 I/VII;
New Hollstein 1 I/VII
WATERMARK: Crowned interlaced *C*s with Cross
of Lorraine (cf. Mauquoy-Hendrickx 1)
INSCRIPTION: verso, l.l., in graphite (partially
erased): *150 c.2 / TFx* (?)
PROVENANCE: Clarence Buckingham (Lugt 497).

44
Jan Brueghel the Elder, 1630/33
Etching and engraving in black on ivory laid paper;
243 × 151 mm (trimmed within plate mark)
Clarence Buckingham Collection, 1938.1479
REFERENCES: Mauquoy-Hendrickx 1 II/VII;
New Hollstein 2 II/VII
WATERMARK: Phoenix in a laurel wreath (Wibiral 11c
and Mauquoy-Hendrickx 252)
INSCRIPTIONS: verso, l.l., in brown ink: *pix*;
l.c., in graphite: *W.1*; l.c., in graphite: *A69777*;
l.r., in graphite: *N.1*
PROVENANCE: Henry Studdy Theobald (Lugt 1375).
Clarence Buckingham (Lugt 497).

45
Pieter Brueghel the Younger, 1630/33
Etching in black on ivory laid paper; 243 × 156 mm
(trimmed within plate mark)
Clarence Buckingham Collection, 1938.1480
REFERENCES: Mauquoy-Hendrickx 2 I/VI;
New Hollstein 3 I/VI
WATERMARK: Phoenix in a laurel wreath
(Mauquoy-Hendrickx 254)
INSCRIPTION: recto, l.c., in brown ink: *PETRUS
BREUGEL / ANTWERPIAE PICTOR RURALIUM
ACTIONUM*
PROVENANCE: Clarence Buckingham (Lugt 497).

46
After Hans Holbein the Younger (German, 1497–1543)
Desiderius Erasmus, 1630/33
Etching in black on ivory laid paper; 243 × 152 mm
(trimmed within plate mark)
Clarence Buckingham Collection, 1928.155
REFERENCES: Mauquoy-Hendrickx 5 I/V;
New Hollstein 4 I/V
WATERMARK: Phoenix in a laurel wreath (Wibiral 11c
and Mauquoy-Hendrickx 252)
INSCRIPTIONS: verso, c., in graphite: *c 16336*;
c., in graphite: *Dutuit 4 1*; l.c., in graphite: *k6904*
PROVENANCE: Pierre II Mariette (Lugt 1787).
Clarence Buckingham (Lugt 497).

47
Frans Francken, 1630/33
Etching and engraving in black on ivory laid paper;
247 × 159 mm (plate mark); 253 × 168 mm (sheet)
Clarence Buckingham Collection, 1928.199
REFERENCES: Mauquoy-Hendrickx 6 II/VII;
New Hollstein 5 II/VII
WATERMARK: Phoenix in a laurel wreath (Wibiral 11c
and Mauquoy-Hendrickx 252)
INSCRIPTIONS: recto, u.r., in brown ink: *148*
(trimmed); verso, u.c., in graphite: *X*; l.l., in
graphite: *2533*; l.l., in graphite: *c 27748*; l.l., in
graphite: *MK 28374*; l.l., in graphite: *P*
PROVENANCE: Clarence Buckingham (Lugt 497).

48
Joos de Momper, 1630/33
Etching in black on ivory laid paper; 243 × 156 mm
(trimmed within plate mark)
Clarence Buckingham Collection, 1938.1481
REFERENCES: Mauquoy-Hendrickx 7 I/V;
New Hollstein 6 I/V
WATERMARK: Crowned interlaced *C*s with Cross
of Lorraine (cf. Mauquoy-Hendrickx 1)
INSCRIPTIONS: verso, l.l., in graphite: *R. 5760*;
l.l., in graphite: *w 71*
PROVENANCE: Bernard du Bus de Gisignies
(Lugt 732). Henry Studdy Theobald (Lugt 1375).
Clarence Buckingham (Lugt 497).

49
Adam van Noort, 1630/33
Etching and engraving in black on ivory laid paper;
239 × 154 mm (trimmed within plate mark)
Clarence Buckingham Collection, 1928.156
REFERENCES: Mauquoy-Hendrickx 8 II/VII;
New Hollstein 7 II/VII
WATERMARK: Fleur-de-lis with crown above
(Mauquoy-Hendrickx 158 or 159)
INSCRIPTIONS: verso, c., in graphite: *c.16340*;
c., in graphite: *Dutuit 8 III*; l.l., in graphite: *K6908*
PROVENANCE: Clarence Buckingham (Lugt 497).

50
Paulus Pontius, 1630/33
Etching and engraving in black on ivory laid paper;
230 × 182 mm (plate mark); 255 × 190 mm (sheet)
Clarence Buckingham Collection, 1927.392
REFERENCES: Mauquoy-Hendrickx 9 II/IX;
New Hollstein 8 II/VIII
WATERMARK: Crowned interlaced *C*s with Cross of
Lorraine (cf. Mauquoy-Hendrickx 1)
INSCRIPTIONS: recto, l.c., in brown ink: *Paulus
Pontius. / Geb:1603.*; verso, u.c., in graphite: *No
113.*; l.c., in graphite: (illegible); l.r., in graphite:
c9314; l.r., in graphite: *mk23831*; l.r., in graphite:
D. 9 II; l.r., in graphite: ~~*c 5121 MK*~~
PROVENANCE: British Museum, London (Lugt 300
and 305). Clarence Buckingham (Lugt 497).

51
Jan Snellinx, 1630/33
Etching in black on ivory laid paper; 245 × 155 mm
(plate mark); 374 × 245 mm (sheet)
Clarence Buckingham Collection, 1926.418
REFERENCES: Mauquoy-Hendrickx 10 II/VIII;
New Hollstein 9 II/VII
WATERMARK: Phoenix in a laurel wreath
(Mauquoy-Hendrickx 254)
INSCRIPTIONS: recto, l.c., in brown ink: *Joannes
Snellinx Pictor. Humanarum figurarum / in Aulais
et tapetibus Antuerpiae. / Ant. van Dyck. fecit aqua
forti.*; verso, l.l., in graphite: *2568*; l.l., in graphite:
K4999 / c5297; l.c., in graphite: *W. 10 I / D. 10 I*; l.c.,
in graphite: *c. 13337*; l.c., in graphite: *P*
PROVENANCE: Clarence Buckingham (Lugt 497).

52
Jan Snellinx, 1630/45
Etching in black on laid paper; 246 × 155 mm
(plate mark); 374 × 246 mm (sheet)
Amanda S. Johnson and Marion J. Livingston
Fund, 2014.1134
REFERENCE: New Hollstein 9 VI or VII/VII
WATERMARK: Fleur-de-lis with crown
INSCRIPTION: recto, l.r., in graphite: *MH 10 viii*
PROVENANCE: Sold by Craddock and Barnard to
Anne-Marie Logan, 1986; acquired by the Art
Institute, 2014.

53
Frans Snyders, 1630/33
Etching in black on ivory laid paper; 243 × 155 mm
(plate mark); 258 × 169 mm (sheet)
Clarence Buckingham Collection, 1927.394
REFERENCES: Mauquoy-Hendrickx 11 I/VII;
New Hollstein 10 I/VII
WATERMARK: Foolscap (Mauquoy-Hendrickx 20;
Wibiral 3b)
INSCRIPTIONS: verso, c., in graphite: *W 11 / D 11*; c.,
in graphite: *c. 13320*; l.l., in graphite: *K 5000 / C
5298*; l.c., in graphite: *P*; l.r., in graphite: *5*
PROVENANCE: Clarence Buckingham (Lugt 497).

54
Justus Sustermans, 1630/33
Etching in black on ivory laid paper; 250 × 167 mm
(trimmed within plate mark)
Clarence Buckingham Collection, 1938.1482
REFERENCES: Mauquoy-Hendrickx 12 I/V;
New Hollstein 11 I/V
WATERMARK: Double-headed eagle (Mauquoy-
Hendrickx 243; Wibiral 11a; Heawood 1300)
INSCRIPTIONS: recto, l.c., in brown ink: *Justus
Suttermans*; l.l., in graphite: *15*
PROVENANCE: Unknown eighteenth-century English
collector (Lugt 1414). Clarence Buckingham
(Lugt 497).

55
Lucas Vorsterman, 1630/33
Etching in black on ivory laid paper; 218 × 151 mm
(trimmed within plate mark)
Clarence Buckingham Collection, 1928.157
REFERENCES: Mauquoy-Hendrickx 14 I/VII;
New Hollstein 12 I/VII
INSCRIPTIONS: verso, l.c., in graphite: *Dutuit 13 I*;
l.c., in graphite: *c. 16346*; l.c., in graphite: *K6914*
PROVENANCE: Clarence Buckingham (Lugt 497).

56
Lucas Vorsterman, 1630/33
Etching in black on cream laid paper; 241 × 156 mm
(plate mark); 292 × 216 mm (sheet)
Clarence Buckingham Collection, 1944.607
REFERENCES: Mauquoy-Hendricks 14 I/VII; New
Hollstein 12 I/VII
WATERMARK: Crowned interlaced *C*s with Cross of
Lorraine (cf. Heawood 2896)
PROVENANCE: Harris Whittemore (Lugt 1384a).

57
Lucas Vorsterman, 1630/45
Etching in black on cream laid paper; 245 ×
156 mm (plate mark); 247 × 159 mm (sheet)
Gift of Mrs. Morris Woolf, 1941.419
REFERENCES: Mauquoy-Hendrickx 14; New Hollstein
12 VI or VII/VII
INSCRIPTIONS: verso, l.l., in graphite: *M 157374*;
l.l., in graphite: [?] / *DS.-*
PROVENANCE: William Sharp (Lugt 2650). Emanuel
Levy (Lugt 876).

58
Paul de Vos, 1630/33
Etching in black on ivory laid paper; 242 × 150 mm
(trimmed within plate mark)
Clarence Buckingham Collection, 1927.827
REFERENCES: Mauquoy-Hendrickx 16 I/X;
New Hollstein 13 I/X
INSCRIPTIONS: recto, l.c., in brown ink: *16*; bottom
edge, in brown ink: *Paulus de Vos*; verso, l.l., in
graphite: *K5004 / C5302*; l.r., in graphite: *2*; l.r.,
in graphite: *c. 13321 / W. 16 I / D. 15 I*
PROVENANCE: Pierre II Mariette (Lugt 1787);
Clarence Buckingham (Lugt 497).

59
Willem de Vos, 1630/33
Etching and engraving in black on ivory laid paper;
242 × 155 mm (plate mark); 403 × 272 mm (sheet)
Clarence Buckingham Collection, 1928.198
REFERENCES: Mauquoy-Hendrickx 15 II/VII;
New Hollstein 14 II/VII
WATERMARK: Fragment, similar to crowned
interlaced *C*s with Cross of Lorraine (cf. Mauquoy-
Hendrickx 1)
INSCRIPTIONS: recto, u.r., in brown ink: *126*; l.l., in
graphite: *Willem de Vos*; l.c., in graphite: *Rg 136*
PROVENANCE: Clarence Buckingham (Lugt 497).

60
Jan de Wael, 1630/33
Etching and engraving in black on ivory laid paper;
250 × 178 mm (plate mark); 258 × 185 mm (sheet)
Clarence Buckingham Collection, 1927.828
REFERENCES: Mauquoy-Hendrickx 17 II/VI;
New Hollstein 15 II/VI
WATERMARK: Crowned interlaced *C*s with Cross of
Lorraine (cf. Mauquoy-Hendrickx 1)
INSCRIPTIONS: verso, c., in graphite: *W. 17 I / D. 16 I
(now II)*; c., in graphite: *C.13335*; l.l., in graphite:
2596; l.l., in graphite: *K 5005 / C 5303*; l.c., in
graphite: *P*
PROVENANCE: Clarence Buckingham (Lugt 497).

61
Jan de Wael, 1630/33
Etching and engraving in black on ivory laid paper;
245 × 170 mm (trimmed within plate mark)
Elizabeth Hammond Stickney Collection, 1887.465
REFERENCES: Mauquoy-Hendrickx 17 V/VI;
New Hollstein 15 V/VI
WATERMARK: Foolscap, partially visible

62
Philippe Le Roy, 1630/40
Etching in black on ivory laid paper; 241 × 155 mm
(plate mark); 256 × 169 mm (sheet)
Clarence Buckingham Collection, 1927.393
REFERENCES: Mauquoy-Hendrickx C I/IX;
New Hollstein 470 I/IX
WATERMARK: Fleur-de-lis with crown above (cf.
Mauquoy-Hendrickx 184)
INSCRIPTIONS: verso, c., in graphite: *w . P . 69 . c / D.
6 II*; c., in graphite: *c. 13333*; l.l., in graphite: *2541*;
l.l., in graphite: *K4997 / c 5295*; l.c., in graphite: *P*
PROVENANCE: Clarence Buckingham (Lugt 497).

Unknown artist (Italian, 17th century)
After Anthony van Dyck (Flemish, 1599–1641)

63
Title Page from the "Iconography," late
seventeenth century
Pen and iron-gall ink on cream laid paper;
299 × 190 mm
Gift of Monroe Warshaw in honor of Seymour
Slive, 2015.291
INSCRIPTIONS: recto, l.c., in pen and iron-gall ink:
*Ritratti del medesimo Antonio / Vandick in num(ero)
novanta.*; l.r., in pen and iron-gall ink: *2*; verso, u.l.,
in pen and black ink: *papier . . . marque flamand*
(illegible); u.l., in graphite: *no. / 26*; l.l., in graphite:
950ter; l.r., in graphite: *25017* (?)
PROVENANCE: Unidentified stamp in black ink (not
in Lugt). Sold by Paul Zappert (d. 2007), New York,
to Monroe Warshaw, New York, 2005; given to
the Art Institute, 2015.

Various artists
After Anthony van Dyck (Flemish, 1599–1641)

64

*Album of Seventeenth-Century Portrait Prints,
Most after Van Dyck*
52 intaglio prints (etchings and engravings) in
leather binding with gold tooling; album boards
possibly dating to the late seventeenth century, with
evidence of later restoration; 433 × 291 mm (closed)
Ryerson and Burnham Libraries, the Art Institute
of Chicago, gift of William O. Goodman, 1918.

Paulus Pontius (Flemish, 1603–1658)
After Peter Paul Rubens (Flemish, 1577–1640)

65

Isabella Clara Eugenia (1566–1633), 1625/33
Engraving in black on cream laid paper; 590 ×
432 mm (trimmed within plate mark)
Amanda S. Johnson and Marion J. Livingston
Fund, 2014.1137
REFERENCE: Hollstein 91 I/I
INSCRIPTIONS: verso, c., in graphite: *Schn. IX,206*;
l.r., in graphite: *40– / R. 970*
PROVENANCE: Pierre II Mariette (Lugt 1788). Ludwig
Burchard (not in Lugt). Sold by Paul McCarron to
Anne-Marie Logan, January 3, 2000; acquired by
the Art Institute, 2014.

Paulus Pontius (Flemish, 1603–1658)
After Anthony van Dyck (Flemish, 1599–1641)

66

Hendrick van Balen, 1630/45
Engraving in black on ivory laid paper; 246 ×
156 mm (plate mark); 298 × 203 (sheet)
Gift of Mr. and Mrs. Henrik Rosenmeier, 1959.34
REFERENCES: Mauquoy-Hendrickx (Van Dyck) 42 II/VI;
New Hollstein (Van Dyck) 48 III/VII
WATERMARK: Fleur-de-lis with crown above (Wibiral
6a and Mauquoy-Hendrickx 146)
INSCRIPTIONS: recto, l.l., in graphite: *K9157*;
l.l., in graphite: *36410 MK*; verso, c., in graphite:
27; l.c., in graphite: *Holl. 554*; l.l., in graphite:
JC 20760; l.l., in graphite: *Dutuit 48 II/ V*
PROVENANCE: Peter Lely (Lugt 2092).

67

Daniel Mytens, 1630/45
Engraving in black on cream laid paper; 249 ×
185 mm (plate mark); 313 × 243 mm (sheet)
Gift of John E. Irwin, 1887.708
REFERENCES: Mauquoy-Hendrickx (Van Dyck) 56 IX/IX;
New Hollstein (Van Dyck) 77 IX/IX
WATERMARK: Crowned interlaced *C*s, possibly with
Cross of Lorraine (cf. Mauquoy-Hendrickx 13)

68

Peter Paul Rubens, 1630/45
Etching and engraving in black on cream laid paper;
234 × 156 mm (plate mark); 244 × 166 mm (sheet)
Bequest of Mary Morley Sellers, 1940.1339
REFERENCES: Mauquoy-Hendrickx (Van Dyck) VI/VIII;
New Hollstein (Van Dyck) 85 V or VII/VII
INSCRIPTIONS: verso, l.l., in graphite: *flet* (?); l.c., in
graphite: *25 mars 1811*; l.r., in graphite: (illegible)
PROVENANCE: Arthur Friedrich Theodor
Bohnenberger (Lugt 68).

Rembrandt van Rijn (Dutch, 1606–1669)

69

*Sheet of Studies: Head of the Artist,
a Beggar Couple, Heads of an Old Man
and Old Woman, Etc., 1632*
Etching in black on buff laid paper; 99 × 102 mm
(plate mark); 105 × 107 mm (sheet)
The Charles Deering Collection, 1927.5185
REFERENCES: White and Boon 363 II/II;
New Hollstein 115 II/II
WATERMARK: Unidentified fragment
INSCRIPTIONS: recto, l.l., in graphite: *wa*(?);
verso, u.l., in graphite: *O.W.O. / 45*
PROVENANCE: Charles Deering (Lugt 516).

70

*Self-Portrait in a Cap and Scarf with
the Face Dark: Bust, 1633*
Etching in black on ivory laid paper; 133 × 104 mm
(plate mark); 136 × 107 mm (sheet)
Clarence Buckingham Collection, 1938.1793
REFERENCES: White and Boon 17 II/II;
New Hollstein 120 II/V
INSCRIPTIONS: verso, l.l., in graphite: *Nº22*; l.l., in
graphite: *17*
PROVENANCE: A. C. de Poggi (Lugt 617). Maxime
Dethomas? (Lugt 669a). Albert Rouiller (Lugt 170).
Clarence Buckingham (Lugt 497).

71

*Jan Uytenbogaert, Preacher of
the Remonstrants, 1635*
Etching and drypoint in black on buff laid paper;
225 × 187 mm (plate mark); 239 × 197 mm (sheet)
Clarence Buckingham Collection, 1938.1814
REFERENCES: White and Boon 279 IV/VI; New
Hollstein 153 IV/IX
WATERMARK: Double-headed eagle (Heawood 1302)
INSCRIPTIONS: recto, l.r., in brown ink: *m bd*(?);
verso, u.l., in red chalk: *OI*; u.c., in graphite: *259*;
u.c., in graphite: *221*(?); l.l., in graphite: *Earliest
finished state*; l.c., in graphite: *Duke of
Buckingham's / Harding's / Garford's*; l.c., in
graphite: *before the retouch, in which the waistcoat
/ is darker, the plate still angular in which / state
there is an impression in the British Museum*;
l.r., in graphite: *281*
PROVENANCE: Maxime Dethomas? (Lugt 669a).
Albert Rouiller (Lugt 170). Clarence Buckingham
(Lugt 497).

72

Cornelis Claesz. Anslo, Preacher, 1641
Etching and drypoint in black on cream laid paper;
187 × 157 mm (trimmed within plate mark)
Clarence Buckingham Collection, 1938.1739
REFERENCES: White and Boon 271 II/II;
New Hollstein 197 II/V
INSCRIPTIONS: verso, l.l., in graphite: *21711 / a*(?)(?);
l.l., in graphite: *.Epreuve. belle.*; l.l., in graphite:
a20845; l.l., in graphite: *I 1*; l.c., in graphite: *W. S.
C.*; l.c., in graphite: *B. 271*; l.c., in graphite: *X; D254*
PROVENANCE: Gustav Ritter von Franck (Lugt 1152).
Johann Wilhelm Nahl (Lugt 1954). Edward G.
Kennedy (Lugt 857). Walter Steuben Carter,
graphite initials (not in Lugt); sale, New York,
American Art Galleries, Feb. 23-25, 1905, lot 332.
Felix Joubert, graphite inscription (not in Lugt).
Clarence Buckingham (Lugt 497).

73

Jan Cornelius Sylvius, Preacher, 1646
Etching, engraving, and drypoint in black on
ivory laid paper; 280 × 188 mm (plate mark);
283 × 192 mm (sheet)
Clarence Buckingham Collection, 1938.1808
REFERENCES: White and Boon 280 II/II;
New Hollstein 235 II/II
INSCRIPTIONS: verso, u.l., in graphite: *27*; l.c., in
graphite: *3*
WATERMARK: Strasbourg Bend (Ash and Fletcher A.a.)
PROVENANCE: Alfred Hubert (Lugt 130). Clarence
Buckingham (Lugt 497).

74

Ephraim Bonus, Jewish Physician, 1647
Etching and drypoint in black on ivory laid paper;
240 × 171 mm (plate mark); 242 × 180 mm (sheet)
Clarence Buckingham Collection, 1938.1743
REFERENCES: White and Boon 278 II/II;
New Hollstein 237 II/II
INSCRIPTIONS: verso, l.l., in graphite: *280*; l.l., in
brown ink: *a a*; l.l., in graphite: *8140*(?); l.r., in
graphite: *2*
PROVENANCE: Alfred Seymour (Lugt 176). Clarence
Buckingham (Lugt 497).

75

Self-Portrait Etching at a Window, 1648
Etching, drypoint, and burin in black on ivory
laid paper; 156 × 130 mm (plate mark);
165 × 136 mm (sheet)
Amanda S. Johnson and Marion J. Livingston
Endowment and Clarence Buckingham
Collection, 2004.88
REFERENCES: White and Boon 22 II/V;
New Hollstein 240 II/IX
PROVENANCE: Pierre II Mariette (Lugt 1789).
Comte Moritz von Fries, based on
the signature of his curator, Franz Rechberger
(Lugt 2133). Dukes of Arenberg (Lugt 567). Sold
April 29/30, 1930, Hollstein and Puppel, Berlin, lot
691. Felix Somary (Lugt 4384). August Laube II
(not in Lugt); private collector; sold through
Daniela Laube, New York, to the Art Institute.

76

Clement de Jonghe, Printseller, 1651
Etching in black on buff laid paper; 207 × 161 mm
(plate mark); 253 × 200 mm (sheet)
Clarence Buckingham Collection, 1938.1752
REFERENCES: White and Boon 272 I/VI;
New Hollstein 264 I/X
INSCRIPTIONS: verso, u.c., in graphite: *No. 272:1 ère
épreuve*; l.l., in graphite: *a66155*; l.c., in graphite:
D263; l.c., in graphite: *887*; l.r., in graphite: *887*
PROVENANCE: Pierre II Mariette (Lugt 1790). Francis
Seymour Haden (Lugt 1227). Robert Hoe III
(not in Lugt). Clarence Buckingham (Lugt 497).

77

Clement de Jonghe, Printseller, 1651
Etching and drypoint in black on buff laid paper;
208 × 161 mm (plate mark); 212 × 165 mm (sheet)
Clarence Buckingham Collection, 1934.122.1
REFERENCES: White and Boon 272 III/VI;
New Hollstein 264 III/X
WATERMARK: Paschal lamb on a shield (Ash and
Fletcher B.a.)
INSCRIPTIONS: on historic mount, in graphite:
*Without flaw! – Beautiful / as a greek marble – or a
canvas / by Tintoret. / A masterpiece in all its /
elements – beyond which / there is nothing – /*
(butterfly device of James McNeill Whistler);
verso, l.l., in graphite: *a 35005*; l.l., in graphite: *274*
PROVENANCE: John Webster (Lugt 1554). Edward G.
Kennedy (Lugt 857). Julius Rosenberg (Lugt 1519).
John H. Wrenn (Lugt 1475). Clarence Buckingham
(Lugt 497).

78

Jan Lutma, Goldsmith, 1656
Etching and drypoint in black on buff laid paper;
197 × 149 mm (plate mark); 205 × 153 mm (sheet)
John H. Wrenn Memorial Collection, 1924.626
REFERENCES: White and Boon 276 I/III;
New Hollstein 293 I/V
INSCRIPTIONS: verso, c., in graphite: *Bt off Claussin /
n. Prf.*; l.l., in brown ink: *CA*; l.l., in light brown ink:
25 Fr; l.l., in graphite: *214/f10*; l.c., in graphite:
2517
PROVENANCE: Robert Dighton (Lugt 727 and 2198).
John H. Wrenn (Lugt 1475).

79

*Lieven Willemsz. van Coppenol, Writing Master:
The Smaller Plate*, c. 1658
Etching, drypoint, and burin in black on buff
laid paper; 233 × 191 mm (plate mark);
235 × 193 mm (sheet)
The Charles Deering Collection, 1927.5172
REFERENCES: White and Boon 282 IV/VI;
New Hollstein 305 IV/VII
INSCRIPTIONS: verso, l.l., in graphite: *C&O 154*;
l.c., in graphite: *330*; l.r., in graphite: *9*
PROVENANCE: Heneage Finch, 5th Earl of Aylesford
(Lugt 58). Ambroise Firmin-Didot (Lugt 119).
Charles Deering (Lugt 516).

Pieter de Jode II (Flemish, 1606–c. 1674)
After Anthony van Dyck (Flemish, 1599–1641)

80

Antoon Triest, 1630/45
Etching and engraving in black on ivory laid paper;
237 × 173 mm (plate mark); 249 × 185 mm (sheet)
Clarence Buckingham Collection, 1928.152
REFERENCES: Mauquoy-Hendrickx (Van Dyck) 13 III/X;
New Hollstein (Van Dyck) 45 III/X
WATERMARK: Fleur-de-lis with crown above
(Wibiral 7 and Mauquoy-Hendrickx 158 or 159)
INSCRIPTIONS: verso, l.c., in graphite: *16*;
l.c., in graphite: *K.7205*; l.r., in graphite: *c.16775*;
l.r., in graphite: *MH 13 II von VI*
PROVENANCE: Clarence Buckingham (Lugt 497).

81

Theodore van Tulden, 1630/45
Engraving with etching in black on ivory laid
paper; 274 × 175 mm (trimmed to plate mark)
Amanda S. Johnson and Marion J. Livingston
Fund, 2014.1135
REFERENCES: Mauquoy-Hendrickx (Van Dyck) 38 IV/VII;
New Hollstein (Van Dyck) 46 IV/VII
WATERMARK: Fleur-de-lis with crown above
(Mauquoy-Hendrickx 167 and Wibiral 7a)
INSCRIPTIONS: verso, l.r., in graphite: *W 38 2 state*;
l.l., in graphite: *22906*; u.l., in graphite:
watermark 7a 1640-60
PROVENANCE: Peter Lely (Lugt 2092). George Ambrose
Cardew (Lugt 1134). Sold by R. E. Lewis, Larkspur
Landing, Calif., to Anne-Marie Logan, December
17, 1990; acquired by the Art Institute, 2014.

82

Cornelis van Poelenburch, 1630/45
Engraving in black on ivory laid paper; 230 ×
164 mm (plate mark); 336 × 258 mm (sheet)
The Wallace L. DeWolf and Joseph Brooks Fair
Collections, 1920.2460
REFERENCES: Mauquoy-Hendrickx (Van Dyck) 35
VII/VIII; New Hollstein (Van Dyck) 81 VII/VIII
WATERMARK: Crowned interlaced *C*s, partially visible
(cf. Mauquoy-Hendrickx 7 and Wibiral 2)
INSCRIPTION: verso, l.c., in graphite: *17 818 / 28*(?) */
DZ* and *W* (?) *IV / W* (?) *V*

Jan Lievens (Dutch, 1607–1674)

83
Joost van den Vondel, 1644/50
Etching and engraving in black on ivory laid paper;
323 × 233 mm (plate mark); 328 × 243 mm (sheet)
Everett D. Graff Fund Income, 1972.991
REFERENCES: Hollstein 21 IV/VI; Wheelock 85
WATERMARK: Foolscap five-pointed collar
(Laurentius 520)
INSCRIPTIONS: recto, l.r., in graphite: *26*; verso, u.l.,
in graphite: *AxA 15/52*; l.l., in black chalk: *B-57*;
l.r., in black chalk: *1ʳᵉ Epr.*; l.r., in graphite: *Rov. 57*
PROVENANCE: Fritz Rumpf (Lugt 2161). Dmitry
Alexandrovich Rovinski (Lugt 783).

84
Portrait of Jacques Gaultier, 1632/35
Etching, engraving, and possibly drypoint in
black on laid paper; 265 × 209 mm (trimmed to
plate mark)
Collection of Nicholas Stogdon
REFERENCES: Hollstein 23 III/V; Wheelock 75
WATERMARK: Narrow Strasbourg lily with
pendant initials
PROVENANCE: François Xavier Lousbergs (Lugt
1694). Jan Frederik Bianchi (Lugt 3761).

Wenceslaus Hollar (Czech, 1607–1677)

85
Self-Portrait, 1647
Etching in black on ivory laid paper; 135 × 97 mm
(trimmed within plate mark)
Restricted gift of Mr. and Mrs. E. W. Eisendrath,
1965.804
REFERENCES: Pennington 1420 III; New Hollstein
985 III/VIII
INSCRIPTIONS: verso, l.c., in graphite: *P. 1420f*;
l.c., in graphite: *41455*

Attributed to Jean Warin
(French, c. 1607–1672)

86
*Portrait Medallion: Anne of Austria and Her Son,
the Future King Louis XIV*, 1638/48
Bronze, cast, chased, and patinated; diam. without
hanging finial 9.4 cm (3¹¹/₁₆ in.)
Restricted gift of Dr. Maxwell Reed Mowry and
Mr. and Mrs. George O. Klotter; the Russell Tyson
Fund, 1977.494

Follower of Alessandro Algardi
(Italian, 1598–1654)

87
Posthumous Bust of Pope Pius V, c. 1650
Terracotta; h. 60.3 cm (23¾ in.)
Gift of Max Epstein, 1935.78
PROVENANCE: Max Epstein, Chicago, before 1928;
loaned to the Art Institute, 1928 (1088.28);
given to the Art Institute, June 1935.

Samuel Cooper (English, 1608–1672)

88
Portrait of a Gentleman, 1658
Watercolor on ivory, 7 × 5.6 cm (2¾ × 2³/₁₆ in.)
The Colonel Alexander F. and Jeannie C.
Stevenson Memorial Collection, gift of
Mary Louise Stevenson, 1961.416
INSCRIPTION: monogrammed: *SC* (in monogram) /
1658.

Jacob Neeffs (Flemish, 1610–c. 1660)
After Anthony van Dyck (Flemish, 1599–1641)

89
Title Page from the "Iconography," 1645
Etching and engraving in black on ivory laid paper;
245 × 157 mm (plate mark); 425 × 279 mm (sheet)
Prints and Drawings Purchase Account, 1965.803
REFERENCES: Mauquoy-Hendrickx 4 V/VII;
New Hollstein 1 V/VII
WATERMARK: Three crescents (Wibiral 22 and
Mauquoy-Hendrickx 314)
INSCRIPTIONS: recto, l.l., in graphite: *3e état*; verso,
l.l., in graphite: *8*
PROVENANCE: Dukes of Arenberg (Lugt 567).
Unknown collector (Lugt 2769).

Jonas Suyderhoef (Dutch, c. 1613–1686)
After Pieter Soutman (Dutch, c. 1580–1657)
Published by Pieter Soutman
(Dutch, c. 1580–1657)

90
Portrait of Hendrick Goltzius, c. 1649
Etching and engraving in black on ivory laid paper;
402 × 267 mm (trimmed within plate mark)
Charles Greene Fund, 1960.339
REFERENCES: Hollstein 78.1; New Hollstein
(Goltzius) 752 (copy c. I)
WATERMARK: Fleur-de-lis in a coat of arms
(cf. Heawood 1851)
INSCRIPTION: verso, l.l., in graphite: *3400*
PROVENANCE: Ambroise Firmin-Didot (Lugt 119).
Louis Galichon (Lugt 1060).

Pierre Lombart (French, c. 1613–1681)
After Anthony van Dyck (Flemish, 1599–1641)

91
Oliver Cromwell on Horseback, 1655
Engraving in black on laid paper; 550 × 350 mm
(measured within frame)
Collection of Nicholas Stogdon
REFERENCE: New Hollstein (Van Dyck) 392 I/VII

Pierre Lombart (French, c. 1613–1682)
After Anthony van Dyck (Flemish, 1599–1641)
Reworked by an unknown artist (17th century)

92
Charles I on Horseback, 1655/67
Engraving in black on laid paper; 550 × 350 mm
Collection of Nicholas Stogdon
REFERENCE: New Hollstein (Van Dyck) 392 VI/VII

Richard Gibson (English, c. 1615–1690)

93
*Portrait of Frances Theresa, Duchess of Richmond
(1648–1702)*, c. 1675
Watercolor on paper; 9.4 × 7.5 cm (3¹¹/₁₆ × 2¹⁵/₁₆ in.)
The Colonel Alexander F. and Jeannie C.
Stevenson Memorial Collection, gift of Mary
Louise Stevenson, 1958.30

Jean Lepautre (French, 1618–1682)

94
Self-Portrait, after 1674
Etching and engraving in black on off-white
laid paper; 215 × 300 mm (plate mark);
245 × 325 mm (sheet)
Prints and Drawings Purchase Fund, 1955.1037
REFERENCE: Fonds Français 296 III/III
WATERMARK: Grapes (perhaps Laurentius v. 1
573a or 574a)

Paul Prieur (Swiss, c. 1620–after 1683)

95
*Portrait of Elizabeth Cromwell, Daughter of
Oliver Cromwell*, c. 1650
Enamel on gold; 4.1 × 3.3 cm (1⁵/₈ × 1⁵/₁₆ in.)
Mary Louise Stevenson for addition to the Colonel
Alexander F. and Jeannie C. Stevenson Memorial
Collection, 1963.216

Wallerant Vaillant (Flemish, 1623–1677)
After Anthony van Dyck (Flemish, 1599–1641)

96

*A Standing Woman, Parting a Curtain
between Two Columns,* 1660/69
Mezzotint in black on parchment; 329 × 278 mm
(trimmed)
Collection of Nicholas Stogdon
REFERENCES: Hollstein 214 I/II; New Hollstein (Van
Dyck) 511 I/II
PROVENANCE: Christopher Lennox-Boyd (not in Lugt).

Jan Lutma II (Dutch, 1624–1689)

97

Father Lutma, 1669/81
Punched engraving with etching in black, with
plate tone and traces of brush and black wash,
on cream laid paper; 285 × 202 mm (trimmed
within plate mark)
The Wallace L. DeWolf and Joseph Brooks Fair
Collections, 1920.2319
REFERENCE: Hollstein 6 II/II
INSCRIPTION: verso, l.l., in graphite: *N. Grim* (?)
PROVENANCE: Franz Baumgartner (Lugt 223).

98

Portrait of Pieter Cornelisz. Hooft, 1669/81
Punched engraving with etching in black on
cream laid paper; 285 × 212 mm (plate mark);
304 × 217 mm (sheet)
Restricted gift of Anne Searle Bent, 2015.295
REFERENCE: Hollstein 7 I/I
INSCRIPTION: verso, c., in graphite: *P.C. Hooft
historieur Hollandais gr. par Jean Lutma orfèuve et
graveur natif d'Amsterdam (1609-1689) / Cette
estampe est rare et (?) Lutma l'a gravée au ci zelet
(?) au lieu du (?). Il a gravé ainsi trois autres
estampes. Savoir comme la Poëte Vondel, de Jean
Lutma son Pere et le sien propre. Toutes les 4 sont
tres estimées.*
PROVENANCE: George Usslaub (Lugt 1221).
Henri Ledoux (Lugt 4052).

99

J. Vondelius, 1669/81
Punched engraving with etching in black on
cream laid paper; 270 × 214 mm (trimmed to plate
mark)
Elizabeth Hammond Stickney Collection, 1887.314
REFERENCES: Hollstein 8 II/II
WATERMARK: Strasbourg lily with crown or crown
countermark (cf. Heawood 401 and 412)
INSCRIPTIONS: verso, l.l., in graphite: *P*; l.c., in
graphite: *by John Lutma / Goldsmith*; l.r., in
graphite: *y-*; l.r., in graphite: *Poce / oyx*

Jan de Bray (Dutch, c. 1627–1697)

100 and 101

Pendant Portraits of a Man and a Woman, 1650
Black and red chalk on ivory laid paper;
165 × 129 mm (male subject); 164 × 128 mm
(female subject)
Margaret Day Blake Fund, 2015.208, 2015.209
INSCRIPTIONS: male subject: verso, u.c., in graphite:
44; l.c., in graphite: *53/4 dBray f*; female subject:
recto, c.r., in black chalk: *AETAT: 56/Ao 1650*;
verso, u.c. in graphite: *45*; l.c., in graphite:
54/4 dBray f
PROVENANCE: Jeronimus Tonneman (1688–1750),
Amsterdam; sold, Amsterdam, Oct. 21, 1754,
Kbk. N no. 28, to De Leth. C. Cornelis Ploos van
Amstel (1726–1778), Amsterdam; sold, Amsterdam,
Mar. 3, 1800, to Vinkeles. B. de Bosch; sale,
Amsterdam, Mar. 10, 1817, to Hulswit. H. Willink;
sold, Amsterdam, Dec. 6, 1819, to Brondgeest. H.
Croockewit; sold, Amsterdam, Dec. 16, 1874, to De
Visser; sold, Amsterdam, May 16–18, 1881, to
Geller for Von Lanna; sold, Stuttgart, Gutekunst,
May 6, 1910, to Cornelis Hofstede de Groot (b. 1863),
The Hague (Lugt 561). I. Q. van Regteren Altena
(Lugt 4618), his heirs by descent until 2014.

Cornelis Visscher (Netherlandish, 1628/29–1658)

102

Self-Portrait, 1649
Etching and engraving in black on ivory laid paper;
139 × 93 mm (plate mark); 145 × 100 mm (sheet)
Gift of Horace S. Oakley, 1923.996
REFERENCES: Hollstein 162 II/II; Smith 84
INSCRIPTIONS: recto, l.r., in brown ink: *pc n.*; verso,
l.l., in graphite: *cu*; l.c., in graphite: *22*; *AE*;
R906K; l.r., in graphite: *a 19746*

Cornelis Visscher (Netherlandish, 1628/29–1658)
After Gerrit van Honthorst (Dutch, 1592–1656)

103

Adriaen Pauw, Lord of Heemstede, 1652
Engraving in black on cream laid paper;
357 × 244 mm (trimmed within plate mark)
Gift of Horace S. Oakley, 1923.1043
REFERENCE: Hollstein 157 III/III
WATERMARK: *IHS* (cf. Heawood 2959)
INSCRIPTIONS: verso, u.r., in graphite: *2*; l.l., in
graphite: *d I / M00*; l.l., in graphite: *a64984*;
l.l., in graphite: *S. 113 - - C. Visscher*; l.c.,
in graphite: *Ambassador to / England*;
l.c., in graphite: *HST*; l.r., in graphite: *40*
PROVENANCE: Alfred Morrison (Lugt 151).
Possibly Henry Studdy Theobald (Lugt 1375).

Bernardo Fioriti (Bernardino or Focoso)
(Italian, active 1643–74)

104

Bust of Giovanni Battista de Luca, 1650/74
Marble; h. 74.9 cm (29½ in.)
Elizabeth R. Vaughan Endowment, 1967.187
INSCRIPTION: on back: *B.S.* (Bernardino sculpsit)
PROVENANCE: Palazzo Cardinalizio di Ponziano,
Rome. Private collection, Rome. Heim Gallery,
London, by 1966; sold to the Art Institute, 1967.

Herman Hendrik Quiter (German, 1628–1708)
After Peter Lely (Dutch, active in England, 1618–1680)

105

*Portrait of Nell Gwyn as a Shepherdess
Garlanding a Lamb,* c. 1678
Mezzotint in black on blue laid paper; 345 ×
244 mm (trimmed within plate mark)
Restricted gift of Anne Searle Bent, 2015.294
INSCRIPTIONS: verso, c., in graphite: *P 108 . . .*;
l.l., in brown ink: *N. 190301*; l.r., in brown ink: *J / 4*;
l.r., in brown ink: *3 / 2*
PROVENANCE: Joseph Gulston (Lugt 1113).

Richard Gaywood (English, c. 1630–1680)

106

*Portrait of Edward Cocker, Writing-Master
and Engraver*, 1657
Etching in black on laid paper; 137 × 163 mm
(plate mark); 144 × 169 mm (sheet)
Collection of Nicholas Stogdon
WATERMARK: Name of Jesus (*IHS*)
INSCRIPTION: verso, in ink: *MMS. 1810 £ 4.4 - Ext rare*
PROVENANCE: Mark Masterman Sykes (Lugt 1896);
William Henry Miller (Christie-Miller) (not in
Lugt).

Thomas Flatman (English, 1635–1688)

107

*Portrait of James Butler, 1st Duke of Ormond
(1610–1688)*, 17th century
Watercolor on ivory; 6 × 4.9 cm (2⅜ × 1¹⁵⁄₁₆ in.)
Gift of Mary Louise Stevenson, to be added to
the Colonel Alexander F. and Jeannie C.
Stevenson Memorial Collection, 1960.101
INSCRIPTION: recto, l.l., in medium: *F*

Antoine Masson (French, 1636–1700)

108

*Denis Marin de la Châtaigneraye, Secretary to the
King*, 1672
Engraving in black on cream laid paper; 473 ×
355 mm (plate mark); 487 × 368 mm (sheet)
Print and Drawing Club Fund, 1963.70
REFERENCE: Robert-Dumesnil 50 I/II
WATERMARKS: Name of Jesus (*IHS*) within a circle;
unidentified (scrollwork?)
INSCRIPTIONS: verso, l.l., in graphite: *39*; l.c., in
graphite: *R. D. 50*; l.c., in graphite: *Marin gest
v. Masson*
PROVENANCE: Fritz Rumpf (Lugt 2161).

Caspar Netscher (Dutch, 1639–1684)

109

Portrait of a Gentleman, 1680
Oil on canvas; 48 × 39.3 cm (18½ × 15 in.)
Mr. and Mrs. Martin A. Ryerson Collection,
1933.1087
INSCRIPTION: recto, signed and dated, l.r.:
CNetscher 1680 (*CN* in monogram)

Abraham Blooteling (Dutch, 1640–1690)
After Peter Lely (Dutch, active in England, 1618–1680)

110

Portrait of James Scott, Duke of Monmouth,
1673/80
Mezzotint in black on laid paper,
646 × 494 mm (trimmed within plate mark)
Collection of Nicholas Stogdon
REFERENCE: Hollstein 186 II/II
WATERMARK: Strasbourg lily with pendant *WR*,
countermark Name of Jesus (*IHS*) with pendant *AI*
PROVENANCE: Martin Foster (not in Lugt). Christopher
Lennox-Boyd (not in Lugt).

Godfried Schalcken (Dutch, 1643–1706)

111

Portrait of Gerard Dou, the Painter, 1660/80
Etching in black on ivory laid paper; 163 × 123 mm
(plate mark); 169 × 127 mm (sheet)
John H. Wrenn Memorial Collection, 1947.572
REFERENCES: Hollstein II/IV; Beherman G4 II/IV
INSCRIPTIONS: verso, l.l., in graphite: *£35 each*;
l.c., in graphite: *A5 IXO 10986*

Attributed to Nicholas Dixon (English, active
c. 1660–65, died after 1707)

112

Portrait of Mary of Modena, c. 1673
Watercolor on vellum; 23.2 × 18.9 cm (9⅛ ×
7⁷⁄₁₆ in.)
Mary Louise Stevenson for addition to the
Colonel Alexander F. and Jeannie C. Stevenson
Memorial Collection, 1962.1063

Johann Michael Püchler (German, active 1679–1709)

113

Joseph I (August), Holy Roman Emperor, c. 1705
Engraving in black on ivory laid paper;
125 × 90 mm (trimmed within plate mark)
John H. Wrenn Endowment, 1947.568
REFERENCE: Hollstein 12 I/III

114

Joseph I (August), Holy Roman Emperor, c. 1705
Engraving in black on ivory laid paper;
132 × 90 mm (plate mark); 152 × 115 mm (sheet)
John H. Wrenn Endowment, 1947.567
REFERENCE: Hollstein 12 II/III
INSCRIPTION: verso, l.l., in graphite: *â No*

Augustin de Saint-Aubin (French, 1736–1807)

115

Adrienne-Sophie, Marquise of ——, 1779
Etching and engraving in black on ivory laid paper;
284 × 205 mm (plate mark); 300 × 218 mm (sheet)
Gift of the Print and Drawing Club, 1926.990
REFERENCE: Bocher 173 III/IV
INSCRIPTIONS: verso, u.r., in graphite: *No 12*;
u.r., in graphite: *160*; l.l., in graphite: *2173-25*;
l.r., in graphite: *m*

116

Louise Émilie, Baroness of ——, 1779
Etching and engraving in black on ivory laid paper;
280 × 202 mm (plate mark); 306 × 220 mm (sheet)
Gift of the Print and Drawing Club, 1926.993
REFERENCE: Bocher 7 IV/V
INSCRIPTIONS: verso, l.l., in graphite: *2176-25*; l.r.,
in graphite: *R.B*; l.r., in graphite: *Saint-Aubin*

Anton Graff (German, born Switzerland, 1736–1813)

117

Self-Portrait before an Easel, c. 1787
Etching in black on cream laid paper; 182 ×
127 mm (plate mark); 248 × 199 mm (sheet)
Restricted gift of the Searle Family Trust and
Anne Searle Meers (Bent), 1989.26
REFERENCE: Muther 110 I/III
INSCRIPTION: verso, l.l., in graphite: *U 1/21*

Unknown English artist
After Anthony van Dyck (Flemish, 1599–1641)

118

Inigo Jones, c. 1790
Black chalk, with brush and pale brown wash,
on ivory wove paper; 202 × 160 mm
The Leonora Hall Gurley Memorial Collection,
1922.1962R
INSCRIPTIONS: recto, l.r., in charcoal: *Jenkin Jones
praefectus Archurae / Magnae Britaniae Regis etc.-*;
verso, u.l., in graphite: *After van Dyck*; l.l., in
graphite: *8 × 6¼*; l.c., in graphite: *After Anthonis van
Dyck - 1599 - 1641*; l.r., in graphite (inverted): *180*
PROVENANCE: *BOUGHT AUG. 6-7, 1914 / PUTTICK &
SIMPSON* (stamp in purple ink); William F. E.
Gurley (1854–1943), Chicago; given to the Art
Institute of Chicago as part of the Leonora Hall
Gurley Memorial Collection (Lugt 1230b), 1922.

Jean-Jacques de Boissieu (French, 1736–1810)

119
Self-Portrait, 1796
Etching and drypoint in black on ivory laid paper;
379 × 293 mm (plate mark); 409 × 296 mm (sheet)
William McCallin McKee Memorial Endowment,
1992.749
REFERENCES: Boissieu 102 III/VI; Perez III/VIII
WATERMARK: *G V* (cf. Heawood 68, 2773)
INSCRIPTIONS: recto, l.l., in graphite: *R I*; verso,
l.l., in graphite: *00. / 2 210.*

Jean-Pierre Norblin de la Gourdaine
(French, 1745–1830)

120
Self-Portrait, c. 1778
Etching, drypoint, and engraving in black on
ivory wove paper; 137 × 149 mm (plate mark);
146 × 158 mm (sheet)
John H. Wrenn Memorial Endowment, 2005.5
REFERENCE: Hillemacher 1 between II and III/III
PROVENANCE: Friedrich August II, King of Saxony
(Lugt 971).

Francisco José de Goya y Lucientes
(Spanish, 1746–1828)

121
Francisco Goya y Lucientes, Painter, plate one
from *Los Caprichos*, 1797/99
Etching, aquatint, drypoint, and burin in black
on ivory laid paper; 217 × 152 mm (plate mark);
301 × 207 mm (sheet)
Clarence Buckingham Collection, 1948.110.1
REFERENCE: Harris 36 II.1/III
PROVENANCE: Marcel Mirault (Lugt 1892a).

Dominique-Vivant Denon (French, 1747–1825)
After Anthony van Dyck (Flemish, 1599–1641)

122
Two Portraits of a Man in Half-Length, 1784/1815
Etching in black on ivory laid paper; 275 × 200 mm
(plate mark); 285 × 211 mm (sheet)
Jean M. Massengale Memorial and Howard
Simpson Funds, 2015.292
REFERENCES: Fonds Français 243; Bartsch 330
INSCRIPTIONS: recto, l.r., in graphite: *45*; verso,
l.c., in graphite: *TIB 330 243/224*

Johann Anton Alban Ramboux
(German, 1790–1866)

123
*Portrait of the Brothers Konrad and Franz
Eberhard*, c. 1822
Lithograph in black on ivory wove paper;
370 × 446 mm
The Charles Deering Collection, 1927.5507
REFERENCE: Dussler 1
INSCRIPTION: recto, l.r. in graphite: *Ramboux 1813*
PROVENANCE: Charles Deering (Lugt 516).

Camille Pissarro (French, 1830–1903)

124
Camille Pissarro, a Self-Portrait, c. 1890
Etching with drypoint in black on cream
laid paper; 186 × 177 mm (plate mark);
365 × 262 mm (sheet)
Gift of Marjorie Blum-Kovler Collection and the
Harry and Maribel G. Blum Foundation, 1986.106
REFERENCE: Delteil 90 II/II
WATERMARK: *MBM* (with a *PORTFOLIO* countermark)
INSCRIPTIONS: recto, signed, l.r., in graphite: *C.
Pissarro*; l.l., in graphite: *1er Etat No 21 / Portrait
- de C.P*; l.l., in graphite: *7*

Félix Bracquemond (French, 1833–1914)

125
Portrait of Edmond de Goncourt, 1882
Etching in black on cream laid paper; 505 ×
335 mm (plate mark); 527 × 392 mm (sheet)
Gift of the Print and Drawing Club, 1926.451
REFERENCE: Beraldi 54 I/VIII
WATERMARK: Arches
INSCRIPTIONS: recto, l.r., in pen and brown ink:
*à Alidor Delzant / souvenir amical / Edmond de
Goncourt*; l.l., in graphite: *1822B*; l.l., in graphite:
MK 25969

Edgar Degas (French, 1834–1917)

126
Self-Portrait, 1857
Etching in black on ivory laid paper; 232 × 143 mm
(plate mark); 324 × 233 mm (sheet)
Joseph Brooks Fair Collection, 1932.1294
REFERENCES: Reed and Shapiro 8a III/IV; Delteil 1 III/V
WATERMARK: Unidentified monogram
INSCRIPTIONS: recto, l.l., in graphite: *Degas par lui
- (?) - 23 ans 1857*; verso, l.r., in graphite: *26812*
PROVENANCE: Alexis Hubert Rouart (Lugt 2187a).
Roger Marx (Lugt 2229) ; sold, Paris, April 26–
May 2, 1914. Sold by Marcel Guiot, Paris, to the
Art Institute, 1932.

James McNeill Whistler (American, 1834–1903)

127
J. Becquet, Sculptor, 1859
Etching and drypoint with foul biting and roulette
in black on ivory laid paper; 255 × 194 mm
(plate mark); 320 × 322 mm (sheet)
Bryan Lathrop Collection, 1934.576
REFERENCES: Kennedy 52 III/IV; Glasgow 62 V/VI
WATERMARK: Unidentified
INSCRIPTION: recto, l.l. in graphite: *N.48*

Eugène Carrière (French, 1849–1906)

128
Portrait of Paul Verlaine, 1896
Lithograph in black from two stones on China
paper, laid down on cream wove paper
(chine collé); 530 × 480 mm
Anonymous gift, 1938.1259
REFERENCE: Delteil 26 I/I
INSCRIPTIONS: recto, signed l.l., in black crayon:
Eugène Carrière; l.r., in graphite: *R*

Paul-César Helleu (French, 1859–1927)

129
Portrait of Alexis Rouart, 1897
Drypoint with etching in black on cream laid paper;
336 × 298 mm (plate mark); 575 × 415 mm (sheet)
Stanley Field and Albert H. Wolf funds, 2015.293
WATERMARK: Fin de M Iohannot
INSCRIPTIONS: recto, signed, l.l., in graphite: *Helleu*;
l.r., in graphite: *n 18*; l.r., in pen and black ink: *À
mon ami Viau / Al. Rouart / 1897*
PROVENANCE: Given by Alexis Hubert Rouart to
Georges Viau (inscription).

Edvard Munch (Norwegian, 1863–1944)

130
Self-Portrait, 1895
Lithograph in black on ivory Japanese paper;
597 × 440 mm (sheet)
Clarence Buckingham Collection, 1963.281
REFERENCES: Woll 37 II/IV; Schiefler 31 I/I
INSCRIPTIONS: recto, signed, l.l., in graphite: *Edv
Munch*; l.l., in graphite: *fol 31*; l.r., in graphite:
1115001; c., in graphite: *Selbstbildnis*; verso, l.l., in
graphite: *55.1824*; l.r., in graphite: *NEUMANN/55.1824*

Emil Nolde (German, 1867–1956)
Printed by Otto Felsing (German, 1854–1920s)

131
Self-Portrait, 1908
Etching and aquatint on buff wove paper;
306 × 238 mm (plate mark); 448 × 360 mm (sheet)
Restricted gift of Mr. and Mrs. Stanley M.
Freehling, 1969.35
REFERENCE: Schiefler-Mosel 89 II/II
INSCRIPTIONS: recto, signed, l.r., in graphite: *Emil
Nolde 08.*; l.l., in graphite: *OFesling Berlin p.r.* (?);
l.l., in graphite: *Zust . II . Drück 3. / E.N.*; verso, u.l.,
in graphite: *8*; c., in graphite: *Geboren 1774 / 2 1/2
Eiche flach altbraun gebeizt / matt*; c., in graphite: *L
40/50 / 4.75* (?) */ d. Boten zuruck*; l.l., in graphite:
Benn. A. – SOTT – 6/62.; l.l., in graphite: *K07648*

Käthe Kollwitz (German, 1867–1945)

132
Self-Portrait, 1924
Transfer lithograph in black on cream
wove paper; 540 × 382 mm
Gift of Earle Ludgin, 1963.129
REFERENCE: Klipstein 198b
INSCRIPTIONS: recto, signed and dated, l.r., in
graphite: *Käthe Kollwitz / Selbstbild 1924*; verso,
stamped, l.r., in dark blue ink: *Made in Germany*

Rockwell Kent (American, 1882–1971)

133
Self-Portrait, 1934
Lithograph in black on ivory wove paper;
413 × 305 mm
Gift of Jamee J. and Marshall Field, 1990.163.6
REFERENCE: Jones 104 I/I
INSCRIPTION: recto, signed, l.r., in graphite: *Rockwell
Kent*; l.l., in graphite: *"It's Me O Lord"*

David Alfaro Siqueiros (Mexican, 1896–1974)

134
Self-Portrait, 1936
Lithograph in black on ivory wove paper;
584 × 404 mm
Gift of Earle Ludgin, 1963.134
REFERENCE: Williams 7 I/I
WATERMARK: *BFK FRANCE*
INSCRIPTIONS: recto, l.l., in graphite: *3/25*; l.l., in
graphite: *3*; signed, l.r., in graphite: *A Siqueiros*

Jack Beal (American, 1931–2013)
Printed by Carl Reisig
(American, active 20th century)

135
Portrait of Harold Joachim, 1978
Linocut in brown and black on cream wove
paper; 168 × 128 mm (image/block); 257 ×
185 mm (sheet)
Gift of Barbara and Lawrence Spitz in honor
of Joan and Stanley Freehling, 2008.552
INSCRIPTIONS: recto, l.l., in graphite:
To Joan and Stan; l.r., in graphite: *Harold Joachim*;
along bottom edge, in graphite: *in honor of HJ
by Jack Beal / linecut in an edition of 100 printed by
Carl Reisig / E.S. for J.B.*

Jim Dine (American, born 1935)
Printed by Alan Uglow (English, 1941–2011)
and Winston Roeth (American, born 1945)

136
Self-Portrait in a Flat Cap (Winter), First State,
1974
Etching in black on ivory handmade paper; 270 ×
330 mm (plate mark); 800 × 620 mm (sheet)
Restricted gift of Barbara Neff Smith and
Solomon B. Smith; Print and Drawing Club Fund,
1975.44
REFERENCE: Krens and Castleman 180
WATERMARK: *HMP*
INSCRIPTION: recto, signed, c., in graphite: *27/30 Jim
Dine 1973*

Chuck Close (American, born 1940)

137
Arne, 1989
Spit-bite etching and aquatint in black on
ivory wove paper; 570 × 450 mm (plate mark);
792 × 608 mm (sheet)
Restricted gift of Kaye and Howard Haas, 1991.133
REFERENCE: Butler Institute 52
WATERMARK: Hahnemuhle
INSCRIPTIONS: recto, signed, l.r., in graphite: *C.
Close*; l.l., in graphite: *33/35*; l.r., in graphite: *1989*;
publisher chop mark, l.l.: *ALDO / CROMME LYNCK
/ NEW YORK*

Shelley Reed (American, born 1958)

138
Men (after Van Dyck), 1993
Seven drawings; pen and black ink with graphite
on opaque white ground on white wove paper; each
approximately 224 × 220 mm
Courtesy of the artist and Danese/Corey Gallery

Index of Print Collectors

Victoria Sancho Lobis and Frances Blair

Princes and Dukes of Arenberg (sixteenth century to World War I), Brussels (Lugt 567)
Duke Louis-Englebert of Arenberg (1750–1820) was among the most active collectors of this aristocratic dynasty. In 1902 a sale of some forty thousand prints was held at Christie's; this and subsequent sales have revealed highlights of the collection to have included prints by Lucas Cranach, Albrecht Dürer, Israhel van Meckenem, Martin Schongauer, Rembrandt van Rijn, and proof impressions of Anthony van Dyck's portrait etchings. Cats. 75 and 89.

Friedrich August II, King of Saxony (1797–1854), Dresden (Lugt 971)
Nephew of Duke Albert of Saxony, founder of the Albertina, Vienna, Friedrich August collected over 110,000 prints and several hundred drawings of different schools and centuries. Particular strengths of the print collection included works by Lucas van Leyden, Dürer, and Marcantonio Raimondi, and etchings of the Dutch and Flemish Schools. Cat. 120.

Heneage Finch, 5th Earl of Aylesford (1786–1859), Packington Hall, Warwickshire, England (Lugt 58)
Finch was acknowledged in his own lifetime as possessor of one of the finest print collections ever assembled; his Rembrandt prints are particularly celebrated. Cat. 79.

Franz Baumgartner (active mid-19th century), Vienna (Lugt 223, possibly also Lugt 975, 2827, and 2900)
Baumgartner was a dealer of prints and drawings; sales of his collection began in 1860. Cat. 97.

Henri Beraldi (1849–1931), Paris (Lugt 230)
An art historian who wrote extensively about printmakers, Beraldi concentrated on eighteenth- and nineteenth-century French prints as a collector, but he also acquired portrait prints from the sixteenth through nineteenth centuries as well as some drawings. Cat. 11.

Jan Frederik Bianchi (1878–1963), Amsterdam (Lugt 3761)
An accountant with a particular enthusiasm for Dutch and Flemish works on paper, Bianchi built a collection that also included Italian prints and Japanese paintings, drawings, and prints. Cat. 84.

Arthur Friederich Theodor Bohnenberger (1826–1893), Stuttgart (Lugt 68)
A friend and neighbor of print dealer H. G. Gutekunst, Bohnenberger collected prints and drawings for himself, with a special interest in the etchings of Rembrandt. His son, the painter Theodor Bohnenberger, inherited the collection and sold it piecemeal over a number of years. In 1920–21, what remained of the collection was acquired for stock by Gutekunst and Klipstein. Cat. 68.

Clarence Buckingham (1854–1913), Chicago (Lugt 497)
A businessman engaged in banking and real estate as well as a philanthropist and trustee of the Art Institute of Chicago, Buckingham was especially active as a collector of Old Master prints, Japanese woodblock prints, and the prints of James McNeill Whistler. Over five thousand objects currently in the museum's holdings can be traced to Buckingham's collection or the funds provided by his estate. Cats. 36, 38, 43–51, 53–55, 58–60, 62, 70–74, 76–77, and 80.

Richard Bull (1725–1805), Ongar, Essex, England (Lugt 314)
A print collector and previous owner of what became known as the Bute-Granger (today preserved in the Huntington Library, Art Collections, and Botanical Gardens, San Marino, California), Bull also assembled a richly extra-illustrated copy of Walpole's *Anecdotes of Painting*, which was disassembled and sold in separate lots in 1881. Cat. 30.

Ludwig Burchard (1886–1960), Mainz and London (not in Lugt)
Burchard was a scholar of Peter Paul Rubens and a tireless promoter of the effort to create a catalogue raisonné for Rubens's works, which was based on a documentary archive created by Burchard and now housed at the Rubenianum, Antwerp. Burchard collected paintings, prints, and drawings related to Rubens and his workshop. Works from his collection were sold in separate sales at Christie's in 1999. Cat. 65.

George Burns (1911–1997), North Mymms Park, Hertfordshire, England (not in Lugt)
A major general who served with distinction in World War II and retired to country life, Burns devoted great attention to breeding racehorses; his print collection was likely of decorative interest to him though it contained important and perhaps overlooked examples. Cat. 20.

Viscount Bernard du Bus de Gisignies (1808–1874) Brussels (Lugt 732)
An expert ornithologist and paleontologist, Bus de Gisignies was also a devoted collector of Flemish paintings and prints. He concentrated a good deal of his energies on the portrait prints by and after Van Dyck, many of which were sold after his death, though his son and descendants have remained active as paintings collectors. Cat. 48.

George Ambrose Cardew (1865–1942), London (Lugt 1134)
A collector of drawings and Old Master prints, Cardew was particularly interested in the portrait prints of Van Dyck as well as in the etchings of Wenceslaus Hollar. Cat. 81.

William Hookham Carpenter (1792–1866), London (Lugt 2626)
The son of a London bookseller, Carpenter eventually worked as a curator of prints and drawings at the British Museum. After his death, his personal collection was sold at Sotheby's, and it included portraits by and after Van Dyck, among many other subjects. His book on Van Dyck was published in 1844. Cat. 38.

Walter Steuben Carter (1824–1904), New York (not in Lugt)
Carter was a partner in a New York law firm, and through his professional connections, he might have become familiar with the print collection of attorney Howard Mansfield, who had a special interest in Whistler. Carter acquired etchings and developed his own collection of Whistler etchings, among other objects. Cat. 72.

Paul Davidsohn (1839–1924?), London, Vienna, and Berlin (Lugt 654)
Davidsohn was an avid print collector who favored Old Master works and attempted to construct complete representations of the printed oeuvres of artists such as Dürer, Adriaen van Ostade, and Rembrandt. The sale of his collection over the course of the early 1920s at C. G. Boerner in Leipzig is well documented. Cats. 19, 31, and 42.

Charles Deering (1852–1927), Evanston, Illinois; Sitges, Spain; and Cutler, Florida (Lugt 516)
Chair of the International Harvester Company, Deering also served as a trustee of the Art Institute of Chicago and was an avid Hispanist. In addition to his interest in Spanish art and Old Master prints and drawings, Deering championed several artists working during his lifetime, including John Singer Sargent, Anders Zorn, Augustus Saint-Gaudens, and Ramon Casas i Carbó. Cats. 69, 79, and 123.

Maxime Dethomas (1867–1928), Paris (Lugt 669a)
Dethomas was a painter and set designer in the circle of Henri de Toulouse-Lautrec. The mark attributed to Dethomas has been found on a number of Rembrandt etchings, but the connection to him remains tentative at best. Cats. 70 and 71.

Robert Dighton (1751–1814), London (Lugt 675, 727, 1547a, 1551, 2198, 2447a, 3393–94, and 4501–02).
In 1806 painter, caricaturist, and print dealer Robert Dighton stole hundreds of prints from the British Museum, the greatest concentration falling within the oeuvre of Rembrandt. Although a good number were eventually recovered by the museum, Dighton succeeded in selling some of his ill-gotten wares, in some cases aided by the falsification of collectors' marks, which he used to substantiate the provenance for his inventory. Cat. 78.

E. Fabricius (died c. 1920), Berlin (Lugt 847a, 919bis, and 919ter)
This print collector concentrated on Dutch Mannerist artists such as Hendrick Goltzius and Jan Saenredam. Cat. 15.

Ambroise Firmin-Didot (1790–1876), Paris (Lugt 119)
An author, publisher, and editor, Firmin-Didot was a passionate scholar of antiquity and collector of Old Master prints and drawings, with special interest in Dürer woodcuts, Rembrandt etchings, and eighteenth-century French prints. Cats. 79 and 90.

Gustav Ritter von Franck (1807–1860), Vienna, Leipzig, and London (Lugt 1152)
Trained as a lawyer, Franck was later active as a soldier and, and most notably, as a writer and publisher of such journals as *Wiener Zeitschrift für Kunst, Literatur und Mode* and *Wiener Bote*; his collecting habits inclined toward coins and prints. Cat. 72.

Comte Moritz von Fries (1777–1826), Vienna (Lugt 2133)
This banker and voracious collector of books, paintings, coins, and minerals possessed over one hundred thousand prints and drawings. He was inspired by his older brother Josef (1765–1788), whose interest in collecting was described by Johann Wolfgang von Goethe in his letters. Although a dry stamp is connected to Fries, the ownership of cat. 75 is based on the signature of his curator, Franz Rechberger (Lugt 2133), an artist and director of the Albertina, Vienna. Cat. 75.

Louis Galichon (1829–1893), Paris (Lugt 1060)
Brother of the editor and art critic Emile Galichon (Lugt 1058), who was also active as a collector, Louis Galichon built a collection that featured a select number of Old Master prints and drawings, which included rare states of prints with prestigious provenance. Cat. 90.

Edmond de Goncourt (1822–1896), Paris
(Lugt 1089)
Together with his brother Jules, Edmond
de Goncourt played a prominent role in late
nineteenth-century Parisian society as a tastemaker
and dealer. He hosted salons where his collection
was viewed by other art enthusiasts. In addition
to amassing a significant collection of eighteenth-
and nineteenth-century prints and drawings
(primarily French), Edmond also realized his
passion for Japanese prints through his acquisitions.
The Goncourts were active as critics and historians,
publishing extensively on the art of the eighteenth
century in particular. Owing to his friendship
with many of his artistic contemporaries, several
portraits of Edmond were created, including those
prints by Braquemond and Carrière. Cat. 125.

Thomas Graf (1878–1951), Berlin (Lugt 1092a,
1092b, and 2431a)
Graf served as an aide to Thomas Edison during
a long sojourn in the United States, after which he
returned to Berlin and worked as a bookseller.
He had a special fondness for Dutch prints of the
seventeenth century and German nineteenth-
century prints. Cat. 15.

Joseph Gulston (1745–1786), Ealing Grove,
Middlesex, England (Lugt 1113, 1461, 2986)
Gulston was a member of Parliament and a
prolific collector of books and prints, especially
those featuring British portraits and caricatures.
Cat. 105.

Francis Seymour Haden (1818–1910), London
and Alresford, Essex, England (Lugt 1227)
Haden was a surgeon, a printmaker, and a
committed advocate for the art of etching. The
founder and longtime president of the Royal
Society of Painter-Etchers, he was the author of
a monograph on the etchings of Rembrandt. In
his time as well as today, he was considered one
of the great judges of quality in a printed
impression. Cat. 76.

R. A. Hobson (twentieth century–early twenty-
first century), Hove, East Sussex, England
(not in Lugt)
Hobson worked as a specialist lens grinder and
expressed his interest in seventeenth-century
portraiture through his print collecting activities.
His collection was put up for sale in 2011 in a
regional English auction. Cats. 17–18 and 25.

Robert Hoe III (1839–1909), New York and
London (not in Lugt)
Hoe was an American businessman and producer
of printing press equipment. His interest in
printing extended beyond business, however; he
was one of the founders and the first president
of the Grolier Club in New York, which promotes
bookmaking as an art. He edited a publication
about print collecting and also acquired rare
books, manuscripts, and other art objects in great
quantities. Shortly following his death, his
collection was sold at auction, and nearly half of
the lots were purchased by Henry E. Huntington,
whose legacy established the Huntington Library,
Art Collections, and Botanical Gardens in San
Marino, California. Cat. 76.

Marseille Holloway (died c. 1910), London
(Lugt 1875 and 1876)
After the death of this print dealer and publisher,
a sale took place at Sotheby's containing only 31
lots. Cat. 38.

Alfred Hubert (died 1908), Paris (Lugt 130).
Hubert concentrated his collecting efforts on
Old Master prints, particularly those of
Raimondi, Dürer, and Rembrandt. His sale at
Danlos in Paris in May 1909 included a number
of celebrated prints, which in turn fetched
impressive prices. Cat. 73.

Felix Joubert (died 1953), London (Lugt 1502a)
Much of the collection of this decorator and
collector of armor and objets d'art was given to
the Musée des Beaux-Arts de Nice. As a collector
of prints he focused on French portrait engravers
such as Robert Nanteuil and Antoine Masson.
Cat. 72.

Friedrich Kalle (1804–1875), Cologne and Bonn
(Lugt 1021)
Kalle was an Old Master print enthusiast with a
special preference for the Dutch School. Cat. 13.

Edward G. Kennedy (1849–1932), New York
(Lugt 857)
The premier print dealer in the United States,
Kennedy worked for Hermann Wunderlich
and Company, which later became Kennedy and
Company. He was also the author of the first
catalogue raisonné of Whistler's etchings and
organized a monographic exhibition for Haden at
the Grolier Club, New York. Cats. 72 and 77.

August Laube II (1927–1988), Zurich
(not in Lugt)
Laube inherited his father's book and print dealing
business in 1973 and expanded the company's
purview to include a broader representation of
Old Master works on paper as well as modern
examples. His daughters, Daniela and Brigitta
Laube, have continued in the family profession
with independently operated firms. Cat. 75.

Henri Ledoux (20th century), Paris (Lugt 4052)
Though no single sale is associated with Ledoux,
the presence of his mark on a number of prints,
drawings, and autograph manuscripts—many
appearing at auction in the 1980s—has allowed
for a partial reconstruction of his collection, which
included French and Italian drawings of the
eighteenth and nineteenth centuries as well as
prints from the seventeenth, eighteenth, and
nineteenth centuries, particularly those with
color. Cat. 98.

Peter Lely (1618–1680), London (Lugt 2092)
Lely was a portrait painter and the successor to
Van Dyck at the English court. He was also one
of the most important early collectors of prints
and drawings, his legacy safeguarded by his
studio assistant, Roger North, who stamped each
of the ten thousand prints and drawings with a
collector's mark. A seven-day sale took place in
1688, but there appears to have been no printed
catalogue or other itemized record. Cats. 66
and 81.

Christopher Lennox-Boyd (1941–2012),
Oxford and London (not in Lugt)
Author, book- and printseller, and devoted
collector of prints—principally mezzotints—
Lennox-Boyd also collected watercolors and
English artifacts such as shoes, fans, and picture
frames. Cats. 96 and 110.

Emanuel Levy (active late 19th/early 20th
century), New York (Lugt 876)
The mark connected to Levy is associated with
three New York sales in the 1910s, and it has been
found on various Old Master prints, including
those by Lucas van Leyden, Annibale Carracci,
and Jan Muller. Cats. 12–13 and 57.

Anne-Marie Logan (born 1936), Easton,
Connecticut (not in Lugt)
An art historian with specialized knowledge of
Flemish drawings, particularly those of Rubens,
Logan has been active in acquiring modern prints
as well as the etchings, engravings, and woodcuts
produced by Rubens and his school. Cats. 52, 65,
and 81.

François Xavier Lousbergs (died 1805), Ghent
(Lugt 1026 and 1694)
This businessman formed an important collection
of prints that featured works of the Flemish
School, especially those designed by Rubens and
Van Dyck. Cat. 84.

Pierre II Mariette (1634–1716), Paris (Lugt
1787–90 and 2096)
This print dealer and collector inherited an
extremely successful family business in the trade
for prints, drawings, and printed books. Cats. 15,
21, 46, 58, 65, and 75–76.

Roger Marx (1859–1913), Paris (Lugt 1800b
and 2229)
Marx worked as a civil servant, an art critic, and a
journalist. As a collector he focused on the prints
and drawings of contemporaries such as Edgar
Degas, Georges Seurat, and Lautrec, whose work
he also championed through his writing and
editorial work. Cat. 126.

William Henry Miller (1789–1848), Edinburgh,
London, and Burnham, Buckinghamshire
(not in Lugt)
In addition to serving in Parliament during the
1830s, Miller was an avid antiquarian book
collector known for his discerning taste regarding
condition and binding. His collection passed by
descent to his cousin Samuel Cristy (1810–1889),
who adopted the name Christie-Miller. He and
his heir, nephew Wakefield Cristy (also later
Christie-Miller), added considerably to the
original collection, most of which was eventually
sold privately and through auction in the early
twentieth century. Cat. 106.

Marcel Mirault (1860–1929), Tours (Lugt 1892a)
A collector of prints and drawings, Mirault had
a special passion for Old Master prints and
eighteenth-century French watercolors and gouache
drawings. Cat. 121.

Alfred Morrison (1821–1897), London and
Fonthill Gifford, Wiltshire, England (Lugt 151)
This distinguished collector of autographs and Old
Master prints and drawings owned a remarkable
collection of portrait prints, as recorded in its
1868 catalogue. The portrait prints were sold in
1927 at C. G. Boerner; before the sale some 450
examples were allocated to the British Museum
for acquisition by combined gift and purchase.
Cats. 36, 38–39, and 103.

Johann Wilhelm Nahl (1803–1880), Kassel
(Lugt 1954)
Nahl was a painter and collector of paintings as
well as Old Master prints and drawings, the latter
totaling over ten thousand. Cat. 72.

A. C. de Poggi (active end of the 18th century/
first quarter of the 19th century–c. 1836)
London and Paris (Lugt 617)
De Poggi was a painter, engraver, and editor.
His collection featured Old Master prints as well
as Old Master and modern drawings, a portion of
which had come from the collection of Joshua
Reynolds. He sold a selection of his drawings to
Prince Nikolaus II Esterházy, Vienna, in exchange
for an annuity. Cat. 70.

Franz Rechberger (1771–1843), Vienna
(Lugt 2133)
Rechberger served as curator for the collection of
Comte Moritz von Fries and later at the Albertina,
Vienna; there is evidence that he also maintained
his own collection of prints, as demonstrated by
an inscription in an album presently in the
Kupferstichkabinett, Berlin. Cat. 75.

Julius Rosenberg (1845–1900), Copenhagen,
(Lugt 1519)
Rosenberg was a collector of Danish drawings,
Dutch Old Master prints, and Old Master
drawings; his impressions of Rembrandt prints
were among the most celebrated works in his
collection. Cat. 77.

Alexis Hubert Rouart (1839–1911), Paris
(Lugt 2187a)
Together with his brother Henri Rouart (also
a collector), he associated with Jean-Baptiste-
Camille Corot and Degas, whose work he also
collected. Additionally, he was a passionate
collector of French works on paper from the
seventeenth, eighteenth, and nineteenth
centuries. Cats. 126 and 129.

Albert Rouiller (died 1920), Chicago (Lugt 170).
This dealer of prints and drawings was a former
associate of renowned dealer Frederick Keppel.
Cats. 70–71.

Dmitry Alexandrovich Rovinski (1826–1895),
Moscow and Saint Petersburg (Lugt 783, 784,
and 2157)
Rovinski was an art historian whose special
fascination lay in Dutch prints, particularly
those of Rembrandt. Cat. 83.

Fritz Rumpf (c. 1855–1927), Potsdam (Lugt 2161)
This painter, architect, and writer built a collection
focusing on Old Master prints, many of which
were sold in successive sales at H. G. Gutekunst
beginning in 1908; in 1928 C. G. Boerner in
Düsseldorf held another sale. Cats. 83 and 108.

Carl Otto Schniewind (1900–1957), New York, Switzerland, and Chicago (Lugt 638a–b, 641a)
Before returning from Switzerland to the United States to work as a curator of prints and drawings at the Brooklyn Museum and later the Art Institute of Chicago, Schniewind developed a personal collection of works on paper largely as a source of comfort during his years of recuperation from tuberculosis. Although his collecting strength was the lithographs and drawings of Honoré-Victorin Daumier—his mother sent a new print to his sanitarium every Sunday—he also owned other nineteenth-century and Old Master prints and drawings, many of which were sold in Paris, Bern, and Berlin in the 1930s. Cat. 11.

Alfred Seymour (1824–1888), London and Trent (Lugt 176)
Seymour was a judge and member of the English Parliament who inherited a collection of Rembrandt prints from his brother, Henry Danby Seymour. Some of this collection was put up for sale in 1878, though the family arranged for forty-two prints to be bought in on their behalf. The remaining balance of the collection eventually passed to his daughter, Jane Margaret Seymour, and it was sold at Sotheby's in 1927. Cat. 74.

William Sharp (active mid-19th century), Manchester (Lugt 2650)
A collector of prints and drawings, Sharp may have drawn inspiration from the collecting activities of his friend the eminent connoisseur Mark Masterman Sykes. Sharp's collection was sold in 1878 at Sotheby's, London, and the sale included British and continental portrait prints, notably examples after Van Dyck.

Felix Somary (1881–1956), Vienna and Zurich (Lugt 4384)
This prominent banker and economist was the author of a memoir, *The Raven of Zurich*. His print collection remained a secret even within his family until the time of his death. His heirs sold works from the collection, most notably Rembrandt etchings, through C. G. Boerner and August Laube. Cat. 75.

Mark Masterman Sykes (1771–1823), York (Lugt 1897)
One of the great collectors of his time, he specialized in portrait prints. Cat. 106.

Henry Studdy Theobald (1847–1934), London (Lugt 1375)
An author of legal texts, Theobald collected prints and drawings since his university days. After becoming blind in 1909, he sold his collection at Christie's and H. G. Gutekunst over the course of the following year. Cats. 44, 48, and 103.

George Usslaub (1845–1929), Marseille (Lugt 1221)
The holdings of this passionate and lifelong collector of graphic artists totaled more than ten thousand sheets. His impressions of Van Dyck's *Iconography* are especially noted. Cat. 98.

Georges Viau (1855–1940), Paris (not in Lugt)
This physican was a personal friend of the Rouart family as well as a number of artists from whom he purchased paintings directly. His print collection included works by Mary Cassatt, Lautrec, and Félix Vallotton. Sales in 1907 and 1909 document the range of his collecting practice. Cat. 129.

John Webster (1810–1891), Aberdeen (Lugt 1554 and 1555)
The collection of this lawyer and politician included historic manuscripts, autographs, and prints by Rembrandt and George Cruikshank. Cat. 77.

Harris Whittemore (1864–1927), Naugatuck, Connecticut (Lugt 1384a)
An iron manufacturing magnate, Whittemore assembled an important collection of Impressionist paintings and works on paper. He also bought Howard Mansfield's collection of Whistler prints, much of which is now held by the Art Institute as the Mansfield-Whittemore-Crown collection. In addition to Whittemore's interest in nineteenth-century paintings and works on paper, he also collected, though rather more sparingly, in the Old Master field. Cat. 56.

John H. Wrenn (1841–1911), Chicago (Lugt 1475)
An operator of the Chicago Board of Trade and business partner of Clarence Buckingham, Wrenn collected rare books and prints, many of which were donated to the Art Institute. Cats. 77–78 and 111.

Selected Bibliography

Ackley, Clifford S. *Printmaking in the Age of Rembrandt*. Exh. cat. Museum of Fine Arts, Boston, 1981.

———. *Rembrandt's Journey: Painter, Draughtsman, Etcher*. In collaboration with Ronni Baer, Thomas E. Rassieur, and William W. Robinson. Exh. cat. MFA Publications, 2003.

Ash, Nancy, and Shelley Fletcher. *Watermarks in Rembrandt's Prints*. National Gallery of Art, Washington, D.C., 1998.

Aumüller, Édouard. *Les petits maîtres allemands*, vol. 2, *Jacques Binck et Alaart Class (Claaszen)*. Munich: Librairie de l'université M. Rieger, 1893.

Baker, Christopher, Caroline Elam, and Genevieve Warwick, eds. *Collecting Prints and Drawings in Europe, c. 1500–1750*. Ashgate/Burlington, 2003.

Barkley, Harold. *Likeness in Line: An Anthology of Tudor and Stuart Engraved Portraits*. Exh. cat. Victoria and Albert Museum/Her Majesty's Stationery Office, 1982.

Barnes, Susan. "The Uomini Illustri, Humanist Culture, and the Development of a Portrait Tradition in Early Seventeenth-Century Italy." In *Cultural Differentiation and Cultural Identity in the Visual Arts*, edited by Susan J. Barnes and Walter S. Melion, pp. 81–88. Center for Advanced Study in the Visual Arts 27. National Gallery of Art, Washington, D.C., 1989.

———. *Van Dyck: A Complete Catalogue of the Paintings*. Yale University Press, 2003.

Bartsch, Adam van, et al. *The Illustrated Bartsch*. Abaris, 1978–.

Beherman, Thierry. *Godfried Schalcken*. Maeght, 1988.

Beraldi, Henri. *Les graveurs du XIXe siècle, guide de l'amateur d'estampes modernes*. Paris: Conquet, 1885–92.

Bialler, Nancy Ann. *Chiaroscuro Woodcuts: Hendrick Goltzius (1558–1617) and His Time*. Rijksmuseum/Snoeck-Ducaju en Zoon, 1992.

Blasse-Hegeman, H. E., Domela Nieuwenhuis, R. E. O. Ekkart, A. de Jong, and E. J. Sluitjer, eds. *Nederlandse Portretten: Bijdragen over de Portretkunst in de Nederlanden uit de Zestiende, Zeventiende en Achttiende Eeuw*. Leids Kunsthistorisch Jaarkboek 8. SDU Uitgevers, 1990.

Bocher, Emmanuel. *Augustin de Saint-Aubin: Les gravures françaises de XVIIIe siècle*, vol. 5. Paris: Damascène Morgand et Charles Fatout, 1879.

Boissieu, Jean-Jacques de. *Catalogue des morceaux qui composent l'oeuvre à l'eau-forte de Jean-Jacques Boissieu*. Lyon: J.-L. Maillet, 1801.

Brilliant, Richard. *Portraiture*. Reaktion, 1991.

Briquet, Charles-Moïse. *Les filigranes: Dictionnaire historique des marques du papier dès leur apparition ver 1282 jusqu'en [sic] 1600*. 1907. Reprint, Martino, 1997.

Clifton, James. *A Portrait of the Artist, 1525–1825: Prints from the Collection of the Sarah Campbell Blaffer Foundation*. With contributions by Leslie Scattone and Andrew C. Weislogel. Exh. cat. Museum of Fine Arts, Houston, 2005.

Costa, Dominique. *Le portrait gravé au XVII siècle en France*. Musées Départementaux de Loire-Atlantique/Musée Dobrée, 1979.

Crenshaw, Paul. *Rembrandt's Bankruptcy: The Artist, His Patrons, and the Art Market in the Seventeenth-Century Netherlands*. Cambridge University Press, 2006.

Delteil, Loys. *Le peintre-graveur illustré*. Delteil, 1906–26.

Depauw, Carl, and Ger Luijten. *Anthony van Dyck as a Printmaker*. With contributions by Erik Duverger, Danielle Maufort, Saskia Sombogaart, and Ad Stijnman. Exh. cat. Stedelijk Prentenkabinet/Rijksmuseum, 1999.

Dickey, Stephanie. *Rembrandt: Portraits in Print*. Oculi: Studies in the Arts of the Low Countries 9. John Benjamins, 2004.

———. "Van Dyck in Holland: The Iconography and Its Impact on Rembrandt and Jan Lievens." In *Van Dyck 1599–1999: Conjectures and Refutations*, edited by Hans Vlieghe, pp. 289–303. Brepols, 2001.

Dussler, Luitpold. *Die Incunabeln der deutschen Lithographie (1796–1821)*. Heinrich Tiedemann, 1925.

Filedt Kok, Jan Piet. "Artists Portrayed by Their Friends: Goltzius and His Circle." Special issue, "Ten Essays for a Friend: E. de Jongh 65," *Simiolus: Netherlands Quarterly for the History of Art* 24, 2/3 (1996), pp. 161–81.

Freedberg, David. *The Power of Images: Studies in the History and Theory of Response*. University of Chicago Press, 1989.

Ganz, James A. *Rembrandt's Century*. Exh. cat. Fine Arts Museums of San Francisco, 2013.

Gombrich, Ernst. *Art and Illusion: A Study in the Psychology of Pictorial Representation.* Princeton University Press, 1969.

Griffiths, Antony. "Print Collecting in Rome, Paris, and London in the Early Eighteenth Century," *Harvard University Art Museums Bulletin* 2, 3 (1994), pp. 37–58.

———. *The Print in Stuart Britain, 1603–1689.* With the collaboration of Robert A. Gerard. Exh. cat. British Museum, 1998.

———, ed. *Landmarks in Print Collecting: Connoisseurs and Donors at the British Museum Since 1753.* Exh. cat. British Museum, 1996.

Harris, Constance. *Portraiture in Prints.* McFarland, 1987.

Harris, Tomás. *Goya: Engravings and Lithographs.* Cassirer, 1964.

Heawood, Edward. *Watermarks: Mainly of the 17th and 18th Centuries.* Monumenta chartae papyraceae historiam illustrantia 1. Paper Publications Society, 1950.

Hillemacher, Frédéric. *Catalogue des estampes qui composent l'oeuvre de Jean-Pierre Norblin, peintre français, graveur à l'eau-forte. Deuxième édition avec des modifications et additions receuillies sur la collection qui appartient à la Bibliothèque nationale.* 1877. Reprint, Galerie Martinez, c. 2000.

Hind, Arthur Mayger. *Engraving in England in the Sixteenth and Seventeenth Centuries: A Descriptive Catalogue with Introductions.* 3 vols. Cambridge University Press, 1952–64.

———. *Van Dyck: His Original Etchings and His Iconography.* Houghton Mifflin, 1915.

Hinterding, Erik. *The History of Rembrandt's Copperplates.* Waanders Uitgevers, 1995.

———. *Rembrandt as an Etcher: The Practice of Production and Distribution.* 3 vols. Translated by Michael Hoyle. Studies in Prints and Printmaking 6. Sound and Vision, 2006.

Hinterding, Erik, Ger Luijten, and Martin Royalton-Kisch, et al. *Rembrandt the Printmaker.* Exh. cat. British Museum Press/Rijksmuseum, 2000.

Hollstein, F. W. H. *Dutch and Flemish Etchings, Engravings and Woodcuts, ca. 1450–1700.* Hertzberger, 1949–.

———. *German Engravings, Etchings and Woodcuts, ca. 1400–1700.* Hertzberger, 1954–.

———. *The New Hollstein Dutch and Flemish Etchings, Engravings and Woodcuts, 1450–1700.* Sound and Vision, 1995–.

———. *The New Hollstein German Engravings, Etchings and Woodcuts, 1400–1700.* Sound and Vision, 1995–.

Hornibrook, Murray, and Charles Petitjean. *Catalogue of the Engraved Portraits by Jean Morin (c. 1590–1650).* Cambridge University Press, 1945.

Johannesson, Kurt. "The Portrait of the Prince as a Rhetorical Genre." In *Iconography, Propaganda, and Legitimation*, edited by Allan Ellenius, pp. 11–36. Clarendon/Oxford University Press, 1998.

Jones, Dan Burne. *The Prints of Rockwell Kent: A Catalogue Raisonné.* University of Chicago Press, 1975.

Joost-Gaugier, Christiane L. "The Early Beginnings of the Notion of 'Uomini Famosi' and the 'De Viris Illustribus' in Greco-Roman Literary Tradition." *Artibus et Historiae* 3, 6 (1982), pp. 97–115.

———. "Poggio and Visual Tradition: 'Uomini Famosi' in Classical Literary Description." *Artibus et Historiae* 6, 12 (1985), pp. 57–74.

Kennedy, Edward Guthrie. *The Etched Work of Whistler, Illustrated by Reproductions in Collotype of the Different States of the Plates.* Grolier Club, 1910.

Klipstein, August, and Alexandra von dem Knesebeck. *Käthe Kollwitz Werkverzeichnis der Graphik.* 2 vols. Translated by James Hofmaier. Kornfeld, 2002.

Krens, Thomas, and Riva Castleman. *Jim Dine Prints, 1970–1977.* Exh. cat. Williams College Artist-in-Residence Program/Thames and Hudson, 1977.

Laran, Jean. *Inventaire du fonds français après 1800.* Bibliothèque Nationale, 1930–.

Larsen, Erik. *The Paintings of Anthony van Dyck.* Luca Verlag Freren, 1988.

Laurentius, Theo, and Frans Laurentius. *Watermarks, 1600–1650, Found in the Zeeland Archives.* Hes & de Graaf, 2007.

———. *Watermarks, 1650–1700, Found in the Zeeland Archives.* Hes & de Graaf, 2008.

Layard, George Somes. *The Headless Horseman: Pierre Lombart's Engraving, Charles or Cromwell?* Philip Allan, 1922.

Le Blanc, Charles. *Manuel de l'amateur d'estampes, contenant le dictionnaire des gravures toutes les nations. . .* Paris: Émile Bouillon, 1854–88.

Limouze, Dorothy. "Aegidius Sadeler, Imperial Printmaker." *Philadelphia Museum of Art Bulletin* 85, 362 (Spring 1989), pp. 3–24.

Lugt, Frits. *Les marques de collections de dessign & d'estampes.* Fondation Custodia, 2010. http://www.marquesdecollections.fr.

MacDonald, Margaret F., Grischka Petri, Margaret Dunwoody Hausberg, and Joanna Meacock. *James McNeill Whistler: The Etchings, a Catalogue Raisonné.* University of Glasgow, 2011–. http://etchings.arts.gla.ac.uk.

Mauquoy-Hendrickx, Marie. *L'Iconographie d'Antoine van Dyck, catalogue raisonné.* Memoires, vol. 9. Academie Royale de Belgique, 1956.

Mauquoy-Hendrickx, Marie, Louis Lebeer, and Carl van de Velde. *Les estampes des Wierix conservées au cabinet des estampes de la bibliothèque royale Albert Ier, catalogue raisonné, enrichi de notes prises dans diverses autres collections.* Bibliothèque Royale Albert Ier, 1978–83.

Mazel, Jean A. *Catalogue raisonné de l'oeuvre gravé de Jean Morin (env. 1605–1650).* Éditions de la Marquise, 2004.

Meder, Joseph. *Dürer-Katalog: Ein Handbuch über Albrecht Dürers Stiche, Radierungen, Holzschnitte, deren Zustände, Ausgaben und Wasserzeichen.* Gilhofer und Ranschburg, 1932.

Merlo, Johann Jakob. *Kölnischer Künstler in alter und neuer Zeit; Johann Jacob Merlos neu bearb. underweiterte Nachrichten von dem Leben und den Werken Kölnischer Künstler, hrsg. von Eduard Firminich Richartz unter Mitwirkung von Hermann Keussen.* Gesellschaft für rheinische Geschichtskunde 9. Düsseldorf: L. Schwann, 1895.

Muther, Richard. *Anton Graff: Ein Beitrag zur Kunstgeschichte des achtzehnten Jahrhunderts.* Beiträge zur Kunstgeschichte 4. Leipzig: E. A. Seemann, 1881.

Parshall, Peter. "Art and the Theater of Knowledge: The Origins of Print Collecting in Northern Europe." *Harvard University Art Museums Bulletin* 2, 3 (Spring 1994), pp. 7–36.

——. "Portrait Prints and Codes of Identity in the Renaissance: Hendrik Goltzius, Justus Lipsius, and Michel de Montaigne," *Word and Image: A Journal of Verbal/Visual Enquiry* 19, 1–2 (2003), pp. 22–37.

Parshall, Peter, Stacey Sell, and Judith Brodie. *The Unfinished Print.* Exh. cat. National Gallery of Art, Washington, D.C./Lund Humphries, 2001.

Parthey, Gustav. *Wenzel Hollar: Beschreibendes Verzeichniss seiner Kupferstiche.* Berlin: Verlag der Nicolaischen Buchhandlung, 1853.

Pennington, Richard. *A Descriptive Catalogue of the Etched Work of Wenceslaus Hollar, 1607–1677.* Cambridge University Press, 1982.

Perez, Marie-Félicie. *L'oeuvre gravé de Jean-Jacques de Boissieu, 1736–1810.* Éditions du Tricorne, 1994.

Pope-Hennessey, John. *The Portrait in the Renaissance.* Bollingen Foundation, 1966.

Randolph, Adrian W. B. "Introduction: The Authority of Likeness." *Word and Image: A Journal of Verbal/Visual Enquiry* 19, 1–2 (2003), pp. 1–5.

Raupp, Hans-Joachim. *Untersuchungen zu Künstlerbildnis und Künstlerdarstellung in den Niederlanden im 17. Jahrhundert.* Studien zur Kunstgeschichte 25. Georg Olms Verlag, 1984.

Reed, Sue Welsh, and Barbara Stern Shapiro. *Edgar Degas: The Painter as Printmaker.* Exh. cat. Museum of Fine Arts, Boston, 1984.

Robert-Dumesnil, A. P. F. *Le peintre-graveur français, ou catalogue raisonné des estampes gravées par les peintres et les dessinateurs de l'école française, ouvrage faisant suite au peintre-graveur de M. Bartsch.* Paris: Gabriel Warée, Mme Huzard, etc., 1835), vol. 10, pp. 169–97; vol. 11, pp. 105–06.

Robinson, William W. "This Passion for Prints: Collecting and Connoisseurship in Northern Europe during the Seventeenth Century." In *Printmaking in the Age of Rembrandt,* pp. xxvii–xlviii. Exh. cat. Museum of Fine Arts, Boston/Graphic Society, New York, 1981.

Rovinski, Dmitry. *L'oeuvre gravé des élèves de Rembrandt et des maîtres qui ont gravé dans son goût, 478 phototypies sans retouches avec un catalogue raisonné.* Saint Petersburg: Impremiere de l'académie impériale des sciences, 1894.

Schatborn, Peter. *Rembrandt auf Papier: Werk und Wirkung.* Exh. cat. Hirmer, 2001.

Schiefler, Gustav. *Verzeichnis des graphischen Werks Edvard Munchs bis 1906.* Cassirer, 1907.

Schiefler, Gustav, and Christel Mosel. *Emil Nolde: Das graphische Werk . . . neu bearbeitet, ergänzt und mit Abbildungen versehen.* 2 vols. Schauberg, 1966–67.

Schneevoogt, C. G. Voorhelm. *Catalogue des estampes gravées d'après P. P. Rubens, avec l'indication des collections où se trouvent les tableaux et les gravures.* Haarlem: Les Héritiers Loosjes, 1873.

Schoch, Rainer, Matthias Mende, and Anna Scherbaum. *Albrecht Dürer das druckgraphische Werk.* 3 vols. Prestel, 2001–04.

Silver, Larry. "The Face Is Familiar: German Renaissance Portrait Multiples in Print and Medals." *Word and Image: A Journal of Verbal/Visual Enquiry* 19, 1–2 (2003), pp. 6–21.

Smith, William. *A Catalogue of the Works of Cornelius Visscher.* Bungay, England: John Childs and Son, 1864.

Spicer, Joaneath A. "Anthony van Dyck's Iconography: An Overview of Its Preparation." In *Van Dyck 350,* edited by Susan J. Barnes and Arthur K. Wheelock, Jr., pp. 327–64. Studies in the History of Art 46. National Gallery of Art, Washington, D.C., 1994.

Stevenson, Sara. *A Face for Any Occasion: Some Aspects of Portrait Engraving.* Trustees of the National Galleries of Scotland, 1976.

Stogdon, Nicholas. *A Descriptive Catalogue of the Etchings by Rembrandt in a Private Collection, Switzerland.* Verona: privately printed, 2011.

Strauss, Walter L., ed. *Hendrick Goltzius, 1558–1617: The Complete Engravings and Woodcuts.* Arabis, 1977.

Strauss, Walter L., and Marjon van der Meulen. *The Rembrandt Documents.* With the assistance of S. A. C. Dudok van Heel and P. J. M. De Baar. Abaris, 1979.

Torres, Pascal. *Van Dyck graveur: L'art du portrait.* Exh. cat. Musée du Louvre, 2008.

Tschudin, Walter Friedrich. *The Ancient Paper-Mills of Basle and Their Marks.* Monumenta chartae papyraceae historiam illustrantia 7. Paper Publications Society, 1958.

Vlieghe, Hans, ed. *Van Dyck 1599–1999: Conjectures and Refutations.* Brepols, 2001.

Waals, Jan van der. *Prenten in de Gouden Eeuw: Van kunst tot kastpapier.* Exh. cat. Museum Boijmans Van Beuningen, 2006.

Weigert, Roger-Armand, and Maxime Préaud. *Inventaire du fonds français, graveurs du XVIIe siècle.* Bibliothèque Nationale, 1939–.

Wheelock, Arthur, Jr. *Jan Lievens: A Dutch Master Rediscovered.* With Stephanie Dickey, E. Melanie Gifford, Gregory Rubinstein, Jaap van der Veen, and Lloyd DeWitt. Exh. cat. National Gallery of Art, Washington, D.C./Yale University Press, 2009.

White, Christopher. *Rembrandt as an Etcher: A Study of the Artist at Work.* Zwemmer, 1969.

White, Christopher, and Karel G. Boon. *Rembrandt's Etchings: An Illustrated Critical Catalogue.* 2 vols. Van Gendt/Schram, 1969.

Wibiral, Fredrich. *L'Iconographie d'Antoine van Dyck d'après les recherches de H. Weber.* Leipzig: Danz, 1877.

Williams, Reba White, and Dave H. Williams, et al. *Mexican Prints from the Collection of Reba and Dave Williams.* Exh. cat. Reba and Dave Williams, 1998.

Woll, Gerd. *Edvard Munch: The Complete Graphic Works.* Abrams/Munch-Museet, 2001.

Zona, Louis A., and Jim Pernotto. *Chuck Close Editions: A Catalog Raisonné and Exhibition.* Exh. cat. Butler Institute of American Art, Youngstown, Ohio, 1989.

Photography Credits

Unless otherwise noted, all photographs of the works in the catalogue
were made by the Department of Imaging at the Art Institute of Chicago,
Christopher Gallagher, Director of Photography, Louis Meluso, Director of
Imaging Technology, and are copyrighted by the Art Institute of Chicago.

Unless otherwise noted, all photographs of artworks appear by permission of
the lenders mentioned in the captions. Every effort has been made to contact
and acknowledge copyright holders for all reproductions; additional rights
holders are encouraged to contact the Art Institute of Chicago. The following
credits apply to all images in this catalogue for which separate
acknowledgement is due.

P. 16: © President and Fellows of Harvard College; pp. 20, 47, 78: photography
by Adrian Arbib; p. 39: bpk, Berlin / Bayerische Staatsgemäldesammlung,
Alte Pinakothek; pp. 40, 81 (right): © The Trustees of the British Museum;
p. 61: © The Frick Collection; p. 63: © 2016 Artists Rights Society (ARS), New
York / SOMAAP, Mexico City; p. 66: © 2016 Jim Dine / Artists Rights Society
(ARS), New York; p. 81 (left): Royal Collection Trust / © Her Majesty Queen
Elizabeth II 2016.